CLARITY

By
Joseph Ehrlich

Unmasking the teachings and truths *intentionally*
denied you and your fellow man over history

Sender, Berl & Sons Inc. / New York

Notice to Readers of Clarity By Joseph Ehrlich

SENDER, BERL & SONS INC.

NON-FICTION
ANALYZES, UNDER NEW BIBLICAL INSIGHTS AND DISCERNMENTS, ISRAEL'S WAR WITH LEBANON IN THE SUMMER OF 2006. TEACHES ANALYTIC SKILLS, HOW TO CONNECT THE DOTS, AND GIVES READERS CHANCE TO ASSESS THEIR DEGREE OF SELF-IMPROVEMENT, FROM THEIR TIME WITH THE BOOK.

ISBN-13: 978-0-6151-4142-8

Library of Congress Control Number: 2007900751

First Print Edition, February 2007

Published by Sender, Berl & Sons Inc., New York

Established 1978. (212) 927-7582.

Also by the author: Recapturing America (1997).

Dedicated to the ONE I love and seek to serve

"DO NOT GIVE YOUR INHERITANCE TO FOREIGNERS, NOR YOUR HERITAGE TO VIOLENT MEN, LEST YOU BE REGARDED AS HUMILIATED IN THEIR EYES, AND FOOLISH, AND THEY TRAMPLE UPON YOU, FOR THEY WILL COME TO DWELL AMONG YOU AND BECOME YOUR MASTERS."

FROM THE DEAD SEA SCROLLS,
TESTAMENT OF KOHATH (4Q542 -- Plate 9)

About the author

Joseph B. Ehrlich over the span of two decades has been the keynote speaker in many international seminars held on investments and geopolitical analyses. What the audience best appreciated was his honing what he called and what mainstream media subsequently highlighted as "connecting the dots" and "out of the box" thinking. With the tools he taught, people could fashion intelligent views that made a world of difference to themselves and their employers, many of them holding key positions with military and intelligence agencies.

In *Clarity*, Mr. Ehrlich shares with you what he deems is the common denominator to the threats that confront civilization today. In the path of revealing the common denominator, Mr. Ehrlich teaches analytic thinking on a level you could not find or glean from *any* college or university in the nation. The discernments shown in the book in large part are unique and have not been seen from any other source. Moreover, the author's reasoning and rationale for his analytics and interpretations are fully shown. **At the end of the book, you will have a unique opportunity to prove to yourself how much you have learned, from your time with the book.**

A graduate of the National Law Center in Washington, D.C., Mr. Ehrlich published two major comments in legal publications employing the analytics shown to you by this book. One of those comments received a rarely offered letter of appreciation by a sitting Justice on the Supreme Court of the United States, which gives you a foundation to deduce that you are in for an experience different from anything you might have imagined in your purchase of the book.

PREFACE

On June 25, 2006, Palestinians kidnapped, Gilad Shalit, an Israeli soldier. The Palestinians kidnapping Shalit were aligned with the Fatah movement, not Hamas, as global media first suggested. In fact, Hamas members were meeting with Israelis in order to secure the soldier's release. The result of these meetings between Hamas and Israelis was that Israeli Defense Forces ("IDF") were ordered to and did in fact kidnap a large number of Hamas legislators. Shin Bet, Israel's internal security service, simultaneously openly threatened the Israelis attempting to secure the soldier's release through Hamas.

The Swiss openly declared Israel's military attacks on Gaza, in reprisal, disproportionate. When two more Israeli soldiers subsequently were declared kidnapped by Hezbollah, on July 12, 2006, Israel then ran rabid, bombing Lebanon in a willful and wanton manner, as to cause numerous deaths and injuries to innocents, including women and children. Israel's religious leadership bizarrely but openly told Israeli soldiers not to be concerned with the deaths of innocents in Lebanon or elsewhere.

In August 2006, however, the war came to a sudden stop, mystifying everyone globally as to what exactly happened to stop the hostilities. The author on July 30, 2006, duly noted that the Hezbollah leader, Sheikh Hassan Nasrallah, publicly declared Israel an "American slave." This single declaration suggested, according to the author's public analysis, a new era of relations between Israel and its neighbors. No one identified it before the author. No one but he dares to explain it.

Clarity by Joseph Ehrlich takes you back 3500 years to explain events that have consumed us since 9-11. The author, a proven geopolitical analyst, and author of Recapturing America (Sender, Berl & Sons Inc., 1997), not only reveals hidden truths connective to the war, but also endeavors to teach analytic skills that the reader can apply to future geopolitical developments, when and as they unfold. In this very regard, at the end of the book, readers can quickly determine, with materials provided, whether their experience with the book will help them connect dots previously not visible to them. Clarity by Joseph Ehrlich therefore is both ambitious and unique in what it seeks to explain and accomplish.

CONTENTS

The Five Books of Moses carry hidden messages. They explain not only 9-11 but what is before us today geopolitically.

However, by way of this introduction, I want to quickly point out an example of what you have not been taught in the Bible.

Take the well-known story about Joseph who wound up in Egypt, after his brothers threw him into a pit.

Joseph's father was Jacob. His mother was Rachel. With Rachel, Jacob had two sons, Joseph and Benjamin. Rachel was Jacob's true love. But before he would see his two children with his beloved Rachel, he would have a number of sons via the woman he first married, Leah.

Jacob loved his first born by Rachel, Joseph. Joseph's many half brothers detested him and were jealous of Jacob's great love for Joseph. So one day, consumed by their feelings toward Joseph, they threw him into a pit and when a traveling caravan extracted Joseph, he was sold into slavery in Egypt.

In Egypt, misfortune continued for Joseph. He befell a false accusation from the wife of his master and this landed him in prison. There he met imprisoned people with ties to the royal court, whom he impressed with his interpretations of dreams. When Pharaoh subsequently had a dream he wanted interpreted, no one could interpret the dream to his satisfaction, but Joseph.

However, while many know that it was because of this interpretation that Pharaoh named Joseph his Viceroy, the second in command over all of Egypt, what is not properly highlighted is that Joseph's interpretation of Pharaoh's dream would not be proven for a minimum of seven years! Egypt at the time of Joseph's interpretation was commencing a time of great prosperity. Joseph told Pharaoh that his dream meant that Egypt would have seven years of plenty, followed by seven years of famine. Thus, since Egypt was already in a time of prosperity, it would take seven years to prove Joseph partially correct and fourteen years to prove Joseph completely correct. If it would take that long to certify the truth of Joseph's interpretation of the dream, how could Pharaoh wind up appointing a Hebrew in his prison his second in command?

What also is not emphasized in this great biblical story is that Pharaoh in appointing Joseph second in command had the approval of ALL his advisors!

> Genesis 41:37 provides: "The matter appeared good in Pharaoh's eyes and in the eyes of **all** his servants."

Egyptians did not think highly of Hebrews. The reality is that a Hebrew, taken from prison, put forth an interpretation of Pharaoh's dream that would not be proven true for many years. Even if Pharaoh believed Joseph, whom he did, how could every single advisor of Pharaoh's royal court support the elevation of a prisoner from the dungeons to second in command of all Egypt? This could not be!

But it was, and what the Bible, the Torah, suggests by its language is that God intervened so that Pharaoh would be swept off his feet by Joseph's interpretation and that the approval of ALL Pharaoh's advisors represented God's intervention in having Joseph named second in command. The Bible's rendition that ALL the advisors approved, a single word in the Bible, allows us to see, deduce and conclude, not only that God existed (and exists) but even before He established himself in the Bible by taking out the children of Israel from their subsequent bondage in Egypt, via the miracles associated with that Exodus, that He intervened and intervenes in every day affairs of importance for all of us, when He deems it appropriate to do so.

Again, it would be seven years before Pharaoh and his court could first certify the accuracy of the interpretation and a full fourteen years for it to prove completely true. If the incident were not to illustrate and prove to us via the Bible that God exists and He also affirmatively intervenes for us, it is highly unlikely that the great nation of its time, Egypt, would bend to the words and decisions of a Hebrew interpreting a single dream to Pharaoh's favor.

This book puts forth to you perspectives that have not been taught or emphasized correctly. It also tells you why they have been secreted from you. Thus, this book allows you to open your eyes and heart to the truth and power of the Bible in a way you have not before experienced.

God is central to the Bible, as He is central to our lives and our future. The Bible allows you to see a reality that has been deliberately masked from us. The story and the truth why it has been masked and by whom is one of the most important truths you should know for yourself and your loved ones.

Let me also tell you that this book does not shirk but in fact moves to answer some of the most difficult questions of the Bible. Many of the questions have never been heretofore answered.

Joseph B. Ehrlich
Hewlett Harbor, New York
November 2006

CHAPTER 1
A GOOD PLACE TO START

One of the most far-reaching exchanges in the Bible, Torah, is between God and Abraham. God wanted to share with Abraham His intent to destroy Sodom and Gomorrah, cities of sin of biblical days and times. Abraham had a nephew named Lot. He lived in Sodom. However, Abraham did not plead with God to spare Lot and his family but instead took a different approach in intervening for Lot.

Abraham expressed to God that if He destroyed the good with the bad (threw out the baby with the bathwater) that peoples from other nations would have a basis to impugn God's name in not acting to save the good people in His expressed quest to destroy those deemed evil residing in Sodom and Gomorrah.

Abraham made his point by asking God would He destroy the entire city of Sodom if there were fifty good people residing there? When God answered that He would spare Sodom if there were fifty, Abraham sequentially drove the same point using forty-five, then forty, then thirty, then twenty then ten people.

Genesis 18:26-33:

26. And the Lord said, "If I find in Sodom fifty righteous men within the city, I will forgive the entire place for their sake."

27. And Abraham answered and said, "Behold now I have commenced to speak to the Lord, although I am dust and ashes.

28. Perhaps the fifty righteous men will be missing five. Will You destroy the entire city because of five?" And He said, "I will not destroy if I find there forty-five."

29. And he continued further to speak to Him, and he said, "Perhaps forty will be found there." And He said, "I will not do it for the sake of the forty."

30. And he said, "Please, let the Lord's wrath not be kindled, and I will speak. Perhaps thirty will be found there." And He said, "I will not do it if I find thirty there."

31. And he said, "Behold now I have desired to speak to the Lord, perhaps twenty will be found there." And He said, "I will not destroy for the sake of the twenty."

32. And he said, "Please, let the Lord's wrath not be kindled, and I will speak yet this time, perhaps ten will be found there." And He said, "I will not destroy for the sake of the ten."

33. And the Lord departed when He finished speaking to Abraham, and Abraham returned to his place.

What has been universally missed by biblical commentators is how Abraham in this one incident himself demeaned and diminished God as though he, Abraham, had to paint the picture explicitly before God might understand his point. Even if Abraham simply wanted to drive the point home, Abraham was not addressing his peers, but God.

> Genesis 18:23: Abraham came forward and said, "Will You also stamp out the righteous along with the wicked? What if there should be fifty righteous people in the midst of the city? Would You still stamp it out rather than spare the place for the sake of the fifty righteous people within it? It would be sacrilege to You to do such a thing, to bring death upon the righteous along with the wicked; so the righteous will be like the wicked. It would be sacrilege to You! **Shall the Judge of all the earth not do Justice?"**

Abraham did not avail himself of a much more respectful track. Abraham should have assumed that God does not commit any injustice, and therefore simply ask God why ALL the people in Sodom and sister cities were being destroyed, when there might be a single good person among them. Then Abraham may have received an answer as to why God intended to destroy all, rather than verbally receive none, God cognizant that Abraham's focus was on his nephew Lot.

ABRAHAM'S NEPHEW LOT

The Torah is very explicit in detailing that Lot was not the person Abraham thought him to be. Abraham was a teacher and he influenced many men for good. One of those Abraham believed he so influenced was his nephew Lot.

Thus, when the angels of God went to Sodom to implement God's design regarding the destruction of Sodom, they appeared as men and were in Lot's home. The Sodomites, who were seriously evil in their nature, noted their presence as men in Lot's home and then banged on Lot's door. What did they want? They wanted to sodomize the strangers!

Lot, knowing the true identity of his visitors, intervened for the angels and told the Sodomites to go away. But they would not go away. What did Lot do next?

Lot declared that his two daughters with him in the house were virgins. He offered both daughters to the Sodomites to do with what they please, if they would leave his guests alone and go away.

> Genesis 19:5: And they called to Lot and said to him, "Where are the men who came to you tonight? Bring them out to us that we may know them." Lot went out to them to the entrance, and shut the door behind him. And he said, "I beg you, my brothers, do not act wickedly. See, now, I have two daughters who have never known a man, I shall bring them out to you and do to them as you please; but to these men do nothing inasmuch as they have come under the shelter of my roof."

It does not take much to deduce that any man who would subject his own two daughters to such victimization, whether or not they were in fact virgins, was not a good man. Moreover, the Torah does confirm that Lot's true nature was aligned with the Sodomites. Lot's own family from Sodom ridiculed Lot for the hypocrisy of his words.

> Genesis 19:14: "So Lot went out and spoke to his sons-in-law, [and] the betrothed of his daughters, and he said, "Get up and leave this place, for God is about to destroy the city!" But he seemed like a jester in the eyes of his sons-in-law.

Virtue was not the hallmark of women, or in fact anyone, living in Sodom. The realities known to God were made evident when Lot, after the destruction of Sodom, had an incestuous relationship with both his daughters over two nights. Both daughters willingly conceived children from this infamy and with it the world faced conflict, mayhem and wars that continue to this very day.

Genesis 19:36: Thus, Lot's two daughters conceived from their father. The older bore a son and she called his name Moab; he is the ancestor of Moab until this day.

Lot and his daughters survived the destruction of Sodom due to Abraham's intervention. The resulting incest and the birth of Lot's children from such a relationship with his own daughters, forged the lesson for Abraham and history to watch how you make a point and don't discount that you might one day regret what you asked for, especially when you are less than vigilant in thinking about a request made to God. The saddest part of the result is that since God honored Abraham's ill put request, Moabites, the incestuous seed of Lot and his eldest daughter, were placed by God under Divine Decree.

> Deuteronomy 2: **9-11** And the LORD said unto {Moses}, Distress not the Moabites, neither contend with them in battle: for I will not give thee of their land for a possession; because I have given Ar unto the children of Lot for a possession. The Emims dwelt therein in times past, a people great, and many, and tall, as the Anakims; Which also were accounted giants, as the Anakims; but the Moabites call them Emims.

After 9-11, there were many articles written about the month and day of the events that were forged into our minds. In this very vein, it is noteworthy that the sentences in the Torah that tell the children of Israel not to contend with Moabites in battle are sentences 9-11 in Chapter 2, Deuteronomy.

CHAPTER 2
THE MOABITE OBSESSION AGAINST GOD AND ISRAEL

After wandering in the desert for 40 years, after God freed them from bondage in Egypt, the descendants of Abraham and Sarah were ready (at least everyone thought) to enter Israel. On their way over to Israel, they ran into the descendants of the incestuous relationship between Lot and his eldest daughter.

What the Torah confirms is that Lot one night had an incestuous relationship with his eldest daughter and then on a second night with his other daughter. This sequential incest over two nights is to make it clear that Lot knew what he was doing and since he knew what he was doing he was not the man, by a long shot, that Abraham thought him to be. Thus, in Abraham intervening for him, Abraham opened a Pandora's box: since Abraham intervened for Lot and since God granted Abraham's desire, the seed of Lot were protected.

Now, what kind of people were the seed of Lot, a man who chose to live in Sodom, who misrepresented the truth of his family's lifestyle in sin-city, Sodom, and who fathered two children by his own daughters? When the descendants of Abraham, Isaac and Jacob were in route to the land of Israel, the Moabites marshaled all their resources to defame and diminish those so sojourning to Israel. They hired a man to curse the children of Israel, and when the person so hired would not do so, they sent their own daughters to entice the men of Israel to have insidious sex in front of Moses and the Tent of Meeting (containing the Holy of Holies). Lot no doubt explained to his family that God, the God of the children of Israel, would have destroyed Lot and his family and thus since they were not intended to survive the destruction of Sodom that the God of Israel was not their friend and therefore Lot's descendants moved to diminish and defame the God of Israel and the children of Israel, whom God favored.

The men of Israel, enticed by Moabite women, engaged in sinful relations with them. The Moabite chieftains sent out their own daughters to engage in lewd and invidious relations with the men of

Israel, to get them to bow to idols to defame and diminish God. Many did, which proved to be a mark against the children of Israel, one that would be revisited often throughout subsequent history.

> Numbers 22:5: And Balak the son of Zippor was king of Moab at that time And he sent messengers unto Balaam the son of Beor, to Pethor, which is by the River, to the land of the children of his people, to call him, saying: 'Behold, there is a people come out from Egypt; behold, they cover the face of the earth, and they abide over against me. Come now therefore, I pray thee, curse me this people; for they are too mighty for me; peradventure I shall prevail, that we may smite them, and that I may drive them out of the land; for I know that he whom thou blessest is blessed, and he whom thou cursest is cursed.'

> Numbers 25:1: And Israel abode in Shittim, and the people began to commit whoredom with the daughters of Moab. And they called the people unto the sacrifices of their gods: and the people did eat, and bowed down to their gods. And Israel joined himself unto Baalpeor: and the anger of the LORD was kindled against Israel.

> Judges 10:6: "And the children of Israel again did that which was evil in the sight of the LORD, and served the Baalim, and the Ashtaroth, and the gods of Aram, and the gods of Zidon, and the gods of Moab, and the gods of the children of Ammon, and the gods of the Philistines; and they forsook the LORD, and served Him not.

> Judges 10:11: "And the LORD said unto the children of Israel: 'Did not I save you from the Egyptians, and from the Amorites, from the children of Ammon, and from the Philistines? The Zidonians also, and the Amalekites, and the Maonites, did oppress you; and ye cried unto Me, and I saved you out of their hand. Yet ye have forsaken Me, and served other gods; wherefore I will save you no more. Go and cry unto the gods which ye have chosen; let them save you in the time of your distress.' And the children of Israel said unto the LORD: 'We have sinned; do Thou unto us whatsoever seemeth good unto Thee; only deliver us, we pray Thee, this day.' And they put away the strange gods from among them, and served the LORD; and His soul was grieved for the misery of Israel.

The children of Lot and his two daughters founded two nations, Moab and the other Ammon. The descendants of Moab knew that God had planned to destroy them and thus they never allowed themselves to seek favor or find favor with God. On the other side of the coin, they committed themselves to the destruction of the descendants of Abraham, whom God favored.

> Deuteronomy 23:3 An Ammonite or Moabite shall not enter into the congregation of the LORD; even to their tenth generation shall they not enter into the congregation of the LORD for ever: Because they met you not with bread and with water in the way, when ye came forth out of Egypt; and because they hired against thee Balaam the son of Beor of Pethor of Mesopotamia, to curse thee.

There were additional serious reasons for this biblical prohibition. No doubt the fact that the Moabites used their women to seduce the men of Israel to idolatry, in front of Moses and the Holy of Holies yet, accentuates the Divine Decree. However, the Torah suggests that what they did above metaphorically offered as "met you not with bread" is sufficient when it is otherwise evident that it was God's intent to cleanse them from the earth altogether and that God would have done so but for Abraham's intervention for his nephew, Lot. Thus, there is no need to render a laundry list for a Divine Decree, which emanates directly from the facts of God's expressed and admitted intent.

God marked the Moabites, as people who should have died not lived, by His, God's, design. Thus, due to Abraham's intervention, Moabites live. God then to be extra clear, provided:

> Deuteronomy 23:6 Thou shalt not seek their peace nor their prosperity all thy days for ever.

God told the descendants of Abraham to have nothing to do with the Moabites. These are people that will always detest God for His willingness to destroy Lot and his family. The Moabites will always want to demean and diminish God and in retribution move to destroy the children of Israel as He sought to destroy the descendants of Lot. Since they are the descendants of Lot, **Moabites look like the descendants of Abraham**, but their essence is the antithesis to the souls of the descendants of Abraham.

CHEMOSH

One of the main gods of the Moabites was the god of war: Chemosh. To understand that the Moabites did everything possible to hold themselves as the antithesis to the descendants of Abraham is to understand that they approved of sacrificing their own children to Chemosh.

The critical point is that the Moabites were the surviving derivative nation to Sodom and Gomorrah. They had no restraints or inhibitions or conscience of any sort or degree in putting forth their women and daughters to implement Moabite designs against those they considered their enemies. They also had no restraints in terms of murder, as seen by the willingness to burn their children alive to their god of war Chemosh (A Cyclopeadia of Biblical Literature, John Kitton, 1862, p. 363).

When Israel was going to face serious punishment for bowing to the Moabite enticement, the children of Israel pleaded with God for Him to hold back on the punishment, to not deny them entry into the Holy Land:

> Judges 10:15 And the children of Israel said unto the LORD: 'We have sinned; do Thou unto us whatsoever seemeth good unto Thee; only deliver us, we pray Thee, this day.' And they put away the strange gods from among them, and served the LORD; and His soul was grieved for the misery of Israel.

The generations that followed closed their minds to what had happened and the Moabites to the subsequent generations became a memory lost. Such denial in itself is an egregious wrong for without teaching subsequent generations the sins of their forefathers, the subsequent generations, given time, will be prone to succumb to the same or similar conduct. However, it is clear that the Moabites to subsequent generations became a people the children of Israel could not accurately comprehend at all. The children of Israel, once within Israel, became distant from their own negative history, and it appeared had no idea whatsoever about people who could abuse their daughters, their children, nor had any boundaries in their conduct, including wanton and willful murder, when it served their purpose.

CHAPTER 3
THE TREACHERY OF RUTH

Elimelech was one of the richest men in all of the land of Israel. When he decided with his wife and two sons to move to the plains of Moab, Israel was suffering through hard times. Elimelech would have to forfeit much of his wealth to help support starving people in his own land. Thus, the biblical sages say that because he moved to the plains of Moab to escape such community obligation, Elimelech lost all of his wealth.

However, while this may have been Elimelech's punishment, the question is to whom did he lose his wealth to and how? Since the answer to the first question is the Moabites, how was the wealth extracted?

Biblical sages expressed that while Elimelech sinned by leaving the land of Israel, he objected to his sons marrying Moabite women. Thus, the history of events proved that this impediment was removed with his death soon after settling into Moab with his family.

His wife was named Naomi. When Elimelech, Naomi's prosperous and lauded husband died suddenly and unexpectedly, Naomi could have taken her two sons and returned to Israel. We know that she did not return. Further, not only did she not return to Israel but also both her sons married Moabite women, now that her husband had died.

Ten years later, not one of the sons had a child with their Moabite brides, and then at or about the same time, both sons die during their tenth year of marriage to their Moabite wives. What we know from history is that Naomi was the only surviving member of the family that had left Israel for Moab, and she had become penniless.

Thus, amazingly, biblical history does not record how the Moabites separated this family from their entire wealth. The Moabites, who historically deployed their women as tools against the descendants of Abraham and had no qualms about murder, and who otherwise detested without bounds the children of Israel, separated Elimelech and his family from every penny of their wealth.

The Moabites saw Elimelech settle in their land, as a representative of a people the Moabites not only detested but who no doubt were looked upon by the Moabites as spies, settling there to assess Moabite strengths and weaknesses. The Moabites were not an especially brave nation. They feared an influx of other children of Israel to their land, to exploit the bounty of their land, a highlighted reality when Israel was visited with hardships, as was the case when Elimelech moved his family to Moab.

WHY DID NAOMI SURVIVE THE MOABITE ONSLAUGHT?

The Moabite women who married Elimelech and Naomi's two sons obviously extracted a lot of intelligence from the family. Here was one of the most prominent and wealthiest families from the land of Israel and, no doubt, over the years, they made known the wealth of Israel to the Moabites.

Israel at that time had no king. The Judges ruled the land of Israel. A member of the Sanhedrin (the assembly of men serving the Judges), Boaz, was a relative to Elimelech. He was an elderly man who had wealth and wielded a great deal of influence. Thus, if you can see and accept that the Moabites plucked Elimelech and his family as a butcher would pluck and clean a chicken, you can also see and understand that they saw a great deal of opportunity in Israel, a people the Moabites saw were naive to Moabite ways.

Thus, Naomi was the key to cleaning out Boaz's wealth. One of the two women that married Naomi's sons was selected to continue her facade of love and devotion to the family they had just cleaned out, by accompanying Naomi back to Israel. Naomi, obviously totally blind to what just transpired to her and her family, attesting to Moabite skills and resources, heralded her daughter in law to the nation of Israel. She was a beautiful woman, the daughter of the Moabite Chieftain, and she professed her unabated love for her mother in law and wanted to adopt the ways of Israel and make Israel her home.

The biblical sages were deceived, and for reasons that will soon become apparent, moved to glorify Naomi's daughter in law. Naomi wanted to assist her daughter in law and her professed devotion to her now penniless mother in law. Naomi encouraged her working in the fields that belonged to her husband's kinsman, Boaz.

The history of what transpired does not have Naomi ultimately speaking to Boaz about marrying her daughter in law, but in fact shows that she sent off her daughter in law to "lie" at Boaz's "feet" one night (attesting to the decade Naomi spent in a Sodomite environment), when he slept in a place where sexual intrigues took place. Boaz, no doubt in shock that a woman so much younger than he would feign interest in him, then did everything to respond to this expressed interest in him. Instead of thinking with his head, he responded to the sensuality of the Moabite woman, who feigned deep interest in him, and to clearly state the script and consequence of the theater in play, Boaz died on his wedding night, after the formal consummation of his marriage with Naomi's daughter in law.

Nine months later, Naomi's daughter in law, known biblically and historically as Ruth, the convert to the nation of Israel, gave birth to a son, Obed, who was the great grandfather to King David, and great great grandfather to King Solomon, the man who built the holy First Temple in Israel.

THE FACTS SPEAK FOR THEMSELVES

Biblical scholars attest that Ruth was as pure as the driven snow. How could the great great grandmother of King Solomon and the great grandmother of King David be recorded in history as complicit in numerous murders and deaths and the crimes otherwise alluded to above? She cannot; to speak it has been considered blasphemy. It is blasphemy, but not for the reasons the scholars contend. It is blasphemy because secreting the crimes of Ruth and the Moabites resulted in centuries of conflict, mayhem and war and ultimately 9-11.

Thus, the hidden and secreted facts attendant to what is known as the Book of Ruth are among the most important as they pertain to current day history and global events.

CHAPTER 4
SINS OF BOAZ AND KING SOLOMON

I t didn't take but a single day for Ruth to then own and control Boaz's great wealth.

The Torah relates that when the Sodomites pursued the strangers (the angels) in Lot's home in Sodom, they carried an unbridled thirst to commit sodomy against the two guests. They could not be refuted in their drive to pursue sadistic pleasures but for the angels' intervention at the door to Lot's house.

It does not take enormous imagination to understand that Ruth, who was always loyal to her nation, Moab (she was a Moabite princess), in the pursuit of the separation and extraction of wealth from Elimelech, and now Boaz, reported that the opportunities in Israel were now endless in that she, as mother to Boaz's son, and daughter in law to Elimelech's wife, Naomi, was a member of the elite class in Israel.

That she deployed all her Moabite talents and skills to the maximum is witnessed simply by the unfolding reality that the House of David and the House of Solomon were filled with Moabites called into the service of her own family. Now, the question for the Moabite political leadership was how to honor the ancestral obsession to destroy the children of Israel, whom the Moabites detested, while raiding the wealth of Israel as a nation?

Keep in mind, the Moabite purge of Elimelech's wealth was so well designed, over a period of time, that to this very day Ruth is honored instead of scorned. Thus, it is essential to highlight at this point, despite all the historical misdirection, the damage done via Ruth's entering the community of Israel:

> **1 Kings 11:1-10**: Now king Solomon {Ruth's great great grandson} loved many foreign women, besides the daughter of Pharaoh, women of the Moabites, Ammonites, Edomites, Zidonians, and Hittites; of the nations concerning which the LORD said unto the children of Israel: 'Ye shall not go among them, neither shall they come among you; for surely they will turn away your heart after

their gods'; Solomon did cleave unto these in love. And he had seven hundred wives, princesses, and three hundred concubines; and his wives turned away his heart. For it came to pass, when Solomon was old, that his wives turned away his heart after other gods; and his heart was not whole with the LORD his God, as was the heart of David his father. For Solomon went after Ashtoreth the goddess of the Zidonians, and after Milcom the detestation of the Ammonites. **And Solomon did that which was evil in the sight of the LORD, and went not fully after the LORD, as did David his father. Then did Solomon build a high place for Chemosh the detestation of Moab, in the mount that is before Jerusalem, and for Molech the detestation of the children of Ammon. And so did he for all his foreign wives, who offered and sacrificed unto their gods. And the LORD was angry with Solomon, because his heart was turned away from the LORD, the God of Israel, who had appeared unto him twice, and had commanded him concerning this thing, that he should not go after other gods; but he kept not that which the LORD commanded.**

Thus, by the time Ruth's great great grandson was king of Israel, idolatry re-entered Israel, again at the hands of the Moabites, and this time under the shadow of the First Temple, and soon thereafter Israel unraveled as a nation, which allowed the Moabites to conquer Israel, as will be soon explained.

The stealth of Moabite infiltration is an art that invisibly continues until today. However, before we move up to current geopolitical realities, it is necessary to continue to learn from the grievous mistakes of the past. Israel at the time of Ruth obviously stood in denial as to the ways of the Moabites, but they also tragically began a new era of implementing changes to God's Divine Decree, distorting Torah, which ultimately would result in their Exile from the Holy Land.

MOABITE NOT MOABITESS

Two of the greatest sins in biblical times were committed during Israel's first occupancy of the Holy Land: first, by Boaz, and then by his great great grandson, King Solomon.

Boaz wanted to marry Ruth, the Moabite woman who was at his feet per the approval of her gullible mother in law Naomi. However, this required Boaz and Israel to turn their back on Divine Decree.

The book, Torah Anthology -- Book of Ruth, Shmuel Yerushalmi, Moznaim Publishing Corp., 1985, adeptly reflects the issue as follows:

> "The Torah prohibits Moabite converts from marrying into God's congregation; as the scripture writes, 'A Moabite shall not enter into the assembly of the Lord' (Deuteronomy 23:4). Ruth, however, was permitted to do so, on the basis of a long-forgotten law (halacha) that the prohibition applies only to the men of Moab, not to the women: 'a Moabite, not a Moabitess.' Yet in the time of King Saul, Doeg, the Edomite, head of the Sanhedrin, tried to disqualify David from the kingship by proclaiming him unfit to enter God's congregation (Talmud). "Doeg's challenge touched off a heated controversy. The Talmud records that Amasa, son of Yitra, drew his sword and declared, 'He who does not accept this halacha will be pierced by the sword. This is the tradition I received from the court of Samuel. A Moabite [is forbidden], not a Moabitess' (Yebannitg 77a)."

Torah Anthology -- Book of Ruth thereafter described the dynamics that took place at the time Boaz moved to secure approval of his marriage to the Moabite woman:

> Page 74: "Only three days prior to Ruth's arrival, this question had been put to the sages, and they had just replied: 'We have a tradition from Sinai: a Moabite, not a Moabitess.' Therefore Boaz emphasized that she had not been in the land of Israel 'yesterday or the day before.' Had she come a day sooner, she would not have been accepted for marriage into the Jewish nation, since the halacha had only now been clarified."

Thus, the truth of what took place is self evident to anyone not in a conflict of interest position or denial. A man of influence and power wants to marry a Moabite. The Torah, Divine Decree, prohibits it. Thus, the argument is made that the Divine Decree is meant to only apply to marrying a Moabite man, not a Moabite woman, who suddenly secures the term "Moabitess."

This legerdemain is absolute and the proofs are obvious. If the proscription was not to marry an American, how silly the argument would sit for someone to argue that it did not incorporate marriage to an "Americaness," to distinguish between male and female. This is all specious and frivolous for Torah Anthology -- Book of Ruth as well as the Book of Ruth itself, does not mention the term Moabitess! The only exception is in Torah Anthology -- Book of Ruth, when it speaks of the "oral law," long forgotten that got dusted off and interpreted to assist Boaz in the pursuit of his union with Ruth. Torah Anthology highlights this crime, and it was a severe crime, when it says that if Ruth had come into town a day sooner, she could not have become a member of the nation of Israel. What is the logic of that proffer? It can only be that the exception was only first made for Boaz because if Ruth would have been barred literally the day earlier it meant that the "oral law" that existed, if it did exist, was one to preclude the marriage. Thus, the entire matter was a sham and scheme to allow a marriage that was contrary to express Divine Decree.

Here are references from both Torah Anthology and the Book of Ruth itself attesting that there was no such thing as a Moabitess until Boaz needed relief to consummate a proscribed union.

> Page 61: " Convinced that Ruth's behavior in the field would be in keeping with modesty, good manners, and the halacha, she {Naomi} consented. And because Ruth felt lonely and strange, she added a word of encouragement: 'Do not think of yourself as the Moabite, but as my daughter. I allow you to go only because necessity force me to; for I cherish and esteem you as a daughter.'"

> Page 67:Book of Ruth 2:6: " The man who was standing over the reapers answered and said: 'A Moabite young woman is she, who returned with Naomi from the Fields of Moab."

> Page 128, Quoting from Book of Ruth 4:10: "Also Ruth the Moabite, wife of Machlon have I acquired for myself as a wife...'"

> Page 128: "After the redemption of the field was completed, Ruth was brought, and the marriage ceremony took place in the presence of the Sanhedrin...and the assembled multitude, whom he appointed witnesses, so that it would be well remember that the wedding of Ruth 'the

Moabite' was celebrated with great publicity and with the approval of the Sanhedrin. No later Beth Din would then con test what had been sanctioned by this Beth Din."

Since the Book of Ruth does not make a single reference itself to Ruth as a Moabitess, the facts and circumstances dictate that the entire exception could have been created out of thin air by a subsequent generation of religious leadership to cleanse Boaz, Ruth and the Davidic line. By applying the exception ex post facto, as a dusted off and long forgotten oral law, the "Moabite not Moabitess" exception conveniently wound up serving all interests: Moabite, Judaic and Christian. However, doing so, masked the crimes and the stratagems behind those crimes, which still are operative and in play today, serving the respective interests of the Moabites, the Jews, and the Christians, the latter two fully infiltrated and controlled by deeply embedded Moabite influences.

Thus, Torah Anthology implicitly recognized that Torah was deliberately distorted to effectuate a marriage that should have never been to a woman that should have never existed, but for Abraham's intervention.

> Page 95: "If Naomi wished to arrange a match between Boaz and Ruth, the conventional approach would have been for her to speak to Boaz and suggest that as a relative and redeemer he wed Ruth, whom he personally knew to be a woman of valor. **If the match was truly from God, the matter would have been successfully completed with minimal effort. Why did Naomi choose instead to expose Boaz to temptation?** Why did she send Ruth down to the threshing floor **to lie at the feet of Boaz, judge of Israel and head of the Sanhedrin**, and ask him to marry her?

The author of Torah Anthology - Book of Ruth is absolutely correct. Thus, a woman from a people committed to destroying the children of Israel and defaming and demeaning the God of Israel, now was seated in the nation to influence its course and future. The greatest proof of the correctness of the contentions put forth is that Israel began its downfall, resulting in the collapse and destruction of the nation and ultimately the Exile of the children of Israel altogether from the land.

WHAT ABOUT THE DAVIDIC LINE MOTHERED BY RUTH?

There are two major dynamics in play here. The first is to admit to the crime, the convolution of Divine Decree to effectuate a marriage that should have never been. No doubt, by the time Doeg challenged David to deny him the throne, there were people who figured out the abomination that had taken place. No doubt Boaz dying before the 24 hour clock ran out on his wedding day was suggestive that Ruth was not who she professed to be. Moreover, anyone looking back at the loss of Elimelech's entire vast wealth, his death, the death of his two sons, there being no issue, and then a young robust and virile woman marrying an elderly man of great wealth, who dies on his wedding night, ceding his entire estate over to her, spoke forcibly to the truth.

Doeg no doubt had it figured out and saw the way Ruth used her training to secure power, all which suggested to some with courage that Israel had an enemy within its camp.

Once Ruth was established in the Land of Israel, Moabites came into service of the royal court. *However, the royal court they were truly serving was not in fact the one they professed to serve.*

By the time Doeg spoke out, the Moabite influence was all over Israel and thus the threat of death came with the infusion of the seed of Lot into Israel. Nothing speaks more powerfully to Ruth's negative influence than the fact that her great great grandson, King Solomon, showed his own alliance when he built a temple for Chemosh!

While the Book of Ruth was written to seemingly honor Ruth to keep it in the forefront of Judaism, a careful examination shows that the author, an unknown author, sent a message for the future, to preserve the truth for anyone giving the Book of Ruth and its hidden messages their just due.

Otherwise, no writings speaking against Ruth exist or survived, and regardless would have been destroyed by the Moabites who secured total power over Israel in what has to be deemed an ultimate stealth conquest.

However, before getting to that conquest, God had a covenant with Abraham and God needed to move the children of Israel forward on it, albeit the pollution that came into Israel with Ruth.

Thus one of the most poignant sentences in the Book of Ruth reveals God's Intervention for the children of Israel:

Book of Ruth 4:13:

THE LORD *LET HER* CONCEIVE AND SHE BORE A SON

Despite the infiltration into the halls of power of Israel and the corruption that allowed Boaz to marry Ruth, the evidence is clear that God cleansed the crime to give the Davidic line the potential to play its biblical role. This is further made clear when the Book of Ruth provides that Naomi held the child, named Obed, to her bosom; meaning, to wit: that she guided Obed's upbringing, which de facto is a dig against and another reflection on the true character of the birth mother, who no doubt was using her skills and resources to serve the larger Moabite longer-term agenda then in political play: the conquest of Israel.

This agenda came into full bloom with King Solomon, where we encounter the second major breach of Divine Decree, furthering the crime that took place when Divine Decree was distorted to allow the marriage of Ruth to Boaz, formally bringing the Moabite influence into Israel.

Again, the real crime was not that Ruth took possession of Boaz's wealth, after the Moabites stripped Elimelech and his family of their wealth, but that she infiltrated the nation and became an enemy within to be feared. Why steal from men when ultimately, when seated in halls of power, one with stealth can plunder the entire nation? Sadly, by the time Doeg raised issue with King David, the Moabites had consolidated Ruth's power, bringing forth the sword (and the threat to slay Doeg), to protect their interests in the nation of Israel.

KING SOLOMON

Ruth's great great grandson, builder of the Holy Temple, showered as God's agent in consummating the building of the Temple, known as the wise of the wise, was the cause of Israel's defeat and downfall. Why hasn't the truth of it been taught? Why has King Solomon to this very day been held out as a heroic figure in biblical history?

Divine Decree limited King Solomon to some eighteen wives. Moreover, Divine Decree proscribed wives from many nations. King Solomon contravened all such Divine Decree. The Sanhedrin, as it did at the time of his great great grandfather, did not utter any objection to it. Thus, when the goose does something, the gander is soon to follow. The nation ultimately took wives from proscribed nations, wives that worshipped idols, and the nation became consumed with idolatry and sin.

Look at the following excerpt from the Book of Kings:

> 1 Kings 11:11-13: Wherefore the LORD said unto Solomon: 'Forasmuch as this hath been in thy mind, and thou hast not kept My covenant and My statutes, **which I have commanded thee**, I will surely rend the kingdom from thee, **and will give it to thy servant**. Notwithstanding in thy days I will not do it, for David thy father's sake; but I will rend it out of the hand of thy son. Howbeit I will not rend away all the kingdom; but **I will give one tribe to thy son**; for David My servant's sake, and for Jerusalem's sake which I have chosen.'

> Author's note: God told Rebecca, Isaac's wife, that her older twin, Esau, would serve the younger, Jacob. Thus keep this vital highlighted phrase above ("and will give it to thy servant"), in contravention to what Rachel was told, in mind, because it links into what subsequently became referred to as the Holy Roman Empire! The Holy element was usurped by the Moabites and the Roman element reflective of the descendants of Jacob's brother, Esau.

The first step that resulted in the Exile was Boaz marrying Ruth. Then God intervened by having King David carry the potential to serve God's commandments. King David eliminated all Israel's enemies. The children of Israel were blessed and during King Solomon's reign they had prosperity to such a degree that the peoples of surrounding nations wanted to see their sons and daughters marry into the children of Israel. Thus, there were twelve tribes of Israel and the ten northern tribes, reflective of King Solomon's failings, turned their back on God and took up idolatry and intermarriage and lewd and invidious conduct (where did we hear that before) and lost God's protection.

The Moabite mission all through time has been threefold.

1. Diminish God.

When idolatry and assimilation and intermarriage and violations of the Ten Commandments resumed their hold again in Israel, it was the result of King Solomon's taking on 700 wives and 300 concubines, many of whom were idol worshippers. When King Solomon ultimately went so far as to build a temple to Chemosh, it does not take much imagination to know whose influence was involved. Moreover, the sages and judges did the same thing when King Solomon moved forward to contravene Divine Decree as they did when Boaz wanted to do the same: they made it easy for Boaz and King Solomon, his great great grandson, to do so. **Thus, the net result was the very one the Moabites moved to accomplish when they first sent their women to seduce the Hebrews to bow to and kiss their idols.** Thus, the Moabite influence became dominant yet again and the Moabites, due to the failings of Israel, successfully diminished God.

And via surrogates:

2. Destroy the descendants of Abraham and

3. Seize their wealth.

The importance of the mission to diminish God ties in with the more practical sides of the Moabite agenda. Those sides consist of killing the children of Israel in kind to God's intent to destroy all in Sodom and thus the children of Lot. Moreover, the Moabites wanted to seize all Israel's great wealth, the result of God's blessings to Israel. All this was now not only possible but also in fact successfully implemented.

What happened is exactly shown by 1 Kings 11:1 et seq. The northern tribes cede their connection to God. The Moabites knew that if God would protect the tribes of Israel, no one had a chance to defeat them. However, the Moabites also knew that if the tribes acted to defame God and diminish His name, God was likely to remove the protection. Since the Moabites infiltrate by stealth, and were not even identifiable for purposes of their plots and designs on Israel, they shrewdly furthered the misdirection by using surrogates to carry out their attack. This stratagem, masking themselves via surrogates, allowed the Moabites to continue on even when their agendas, such as the two World Wars of the Twentieth century, went aground.

Thus, the Assyrians who destroyed the ten tribes and captured all their wealth launched the attack on Israel. The Moabites were no doubt thrilled. Starting with Elimelech they took the wealth of a single man and his family, then moved to seize not only the wealth of another descendant of Abraham, but also positioned themselves to steal the wealth of the nation. Now, with King Solomon implementing, no doubt, as a manipulated dupe or a knowing conspirator, the design to distance Israel from God, those ten tribes were for the taking and the Assyrians attacked and took, the Moabites becoming instantly wealthy beyond their dreams and imaginations, because the collective wealth of the ten tribes was truly staggering.

The Book of Kings declared that one tribe would remain and that one tribe collectively consisted of the tribe of Judah (representing the descendants of Jacob and Leah), the tribe of Benjamin (representing the descendants of Jacob and Rachel) and the priests of the Temple, the Levites (representing the special communications portal between the children of Israel (Abraham, Isaac and Jacob) and God. These three elements were the remnant of the children of Israel that had entered Israel after Egypt, and the Jewish people reflect them today.

The Moabites (Moabite elites in particular) were now in business. They had won a big, very big victory on their mission and agenda in life to honor their ancestors. They had diluted God, they had the Assyrians kill and enslave the majority of the tribes of Israel, and they gained wealth that Ruth and the Moabites of her time could not even have begun to comprehend.

The Moabite victory, as great and glorious as it was, did not satisfy the Moabites, for now that they had conquered their archenemy Israel (the children of Abraham), they wanted to move to dominate and control the world.

They just had to make sure that God and the children of Israel would not get in their way, and they also had to make sure that no one discovered who sat behind the curtain, moving the world to centuries of conflict, mayhem and wars, serving Moabite designs.

CHAPTER 5

CLARITY THROUGH THE EYES OF THE MOABITES

T o best appreciate and absorb what happened to Israel during the time of Ruth, King David, and King Solomon, one should see the events through the eyes of the Moabites. The author deployed the channeling technique below to successfully teach the fuller panorama how Ruth's infiltration of Israel allowed the Moabites to secure just about all of Israel's enormous wealth.

DISCUSSION BETWEEN THE AUTHOR AND GEORGE, MOABITE CHIEFTAIN, FATHER OF RUTH

Ehrlich. So what were you thinking when Elimelech and his family came up to Moab?

George: I thought what every one else was thinking. Israel sent a family up to our land to scout the land for a possible war or occupation.

Ehrlich: But God told Israel not to wage war against the Moabites.

George: God told Israel many things they brushed aside when convenient.

Ehrlich: So what were your first thoughts?

George: My first thought, seeing them to be scouts for Israel, was simply to murder them all. However, I wanted to learn more about them and their plan. So instead I welcomed them with open arms.

Ehrlich: Were they surprised?

George: I don't know what they were thinking at first. I'm sure they were happy to be greeted with open arms rather than a sword through their necks.

Ehrlich: So what was your plan?

George: After proving to them for a short while that they were genuinely welcomed I had the father as head of household taken out of the picture. This left the rest of the family vulnerable. We mourned with the family. It was a passionate mourning. They saw or I should say believed that we cared about the father. With this mourning, I instructed my daughter to show interest in one of the two sons.

Ehrlich: Did she have any problems with that?

George: My daughter is absolutely loyal to me, her family and best interests of the family. She gave herself willingly to the task although she told me she did find the son repulsive. However, I told her that her service for her people would not be long; she did not have to bear children for the fate of the two sons was to be that of the father.

Ehrlich: As it came to be.

George: Yes.

Ehrlich: Any problems with the result?

George: Why would I have any problems with the deaths? The original inclination of those that advise me was to put them to the death as soon as they came rolling into our land.

Ehrlich: What did you gain from the experience of having your daughter marry into the family?

George: I learned that Israel had enormous wealth even exceeding that of Elimelech. While I separated the family from their wealth, I devised a plan that would serve my people into the future.

Ehrlich: Meaning what?

George: Meaning that is why Naomi survived.

Ehrlich: Didn't you think she would have figured it all out?

George: Yes, I did. However, my daughter and Oprah carry the skills and talents of Moabite women linked backed to the days of Sodom and Gomorrah. When the men in Elimelech's family died, my daughter and Oprah also showed Naomi what I and my people showed her, unbridled love and concern. After all, the two boys were part of my own family.

Ehrlich: No conscience over what you did here with this family?

George: No conscience at all Ehrlich. They were seen by me from the first moment on as spies and they had no place in this community with my people and I did not trust them from the first instant I laid eyes on them. They got what they deserved and to repay Israel for what I saw their long-range purpose and design, I sent my daughter to Israel with the penniless wife.

Ehrlich: It was important that Naomi wind up penniless, correct?

George: Absolutely. If she had her wealth then everyone would see through the design I had planned. When Naomi was penniless no one would see right through the truth of the matter.

Ehrlich: Since your daughter found the marriage to Naomi's son repulsive, why would she want to go to Israel and give up her life for the plans you had devised for her?

George: She is a princess and a princess has to do many things in service to her father and to her people. She understood that. Her name, I told her, would live on in perpetuity among her people.

Ehrlich: Didn't Naomi think it strange that Ruth wanted to come with her penniless back to Israel, a foreign country to her? She never did convert to Judaism during her marriage.

George: Oprah went back to her people to enhance the sacrifice my daughter was willing to make for a woman who lost her husband and two sons. Naomi welcomed the companionship and the trip to Israel cast off whatever doubts she may have had regarding my daughter's decision to come back with her. I told my daughter that if Naomi did get suspicious, to tell her, after Naomi got resettled, if she felt uncomfortable in Israel that she desired to return to her people.

Ehrlich: When did you hear from your daughter next?

George: I was able to send someone in my service to Israel to check up on her and I learned that she accomplished her task.

Ehrlich: What did you hear?

George: In practically no time, my daughter targeted a man of wealth and influence who was older and unmarried and after she showed her affection for him a marriage took place.

Ehrlich: Had you given her any more instructions?

George: I told her that she had to give birth to a son for that son would be the portal that would serve her people into the indefinite future.

Ehrlich: Did you live to see the day?

George: Regrettably not. However, my daughter who converted to Judaism and carried the name Ruth in Israel gave birth to a son Obed who fathered a son named Jesse who was the father to King David.

Ehrlich: So what did this all mean to the Moabites?

George: It was a conquest of Israel by stealth. While Ruth was alive many Moabites were able to visit and take up business interests within Israel. Many of the house servants in Ruth's home were Moabites. Then Moabite men and women assumed positions of seeming loyalty to the House of Jesse and the House of King David. Thus there was a meaningful Moabite presence around the aristocracy of Israel.

Ehrlich: Again, what was the benefit to you of this infiltration?

George: Contrary to others, the Moabite people understand what you understand and characterize as the long game. If you are asking me when the payoff came about, it came about when we fulfilled the wishes of our own ancestors in corrupting Israel. Once we did so, we linked up with the Assyrians and we walked off with riches that allowed us to ultimately become the nobility of Europe.

Ehrlich: Can you run that by me again?

George: Gladly. God was with Israel. We were all about Israel. We had to bide our time for the correct opportunity. But the sons and daughters of the Moabite people were enmeshed within Israel and all about her. King Solomon. While he carried clean hands in terms of building the temple, he was weak from being handed all the wealth and glory from his father, who too was family but was loyal, a Moabite trait, to the God of Israel. However, King Solomon surrounded by the voices of the Moabites implanted all over Israel and in his own house, was stimulated to cast aside the decree of the God of Israel and to take a limitless number of wives, many of whom were from idol worshipping people, many of them from Moab.

Ehrlich: I still don't understand or appreciate the depth of your long-term plan here.

George: When I sent my daughter to Israel to marry into the aristocracy, the goal was not to separate Boaz or any others from their wealth but to strip all of Israel of its wealth. This was the intent of those who preceded me in my own family. However, we knew the power of Israel's God. He would only punish them and turn His back onto them if we could corrupt them.

Ehrlich: Wasn't this biting off a bit more than you could chew?

George: With all humility, it wasn't anything difficult at all. The power of the Moabite people is through their women. You can see that not only did my scheme bring idol worship and corruption to Israel but it caused a division between the tribes of Israel.

Ehrlich: How could you anticipate that the Sanhedrin would fall into line with such a long-term scheme?

George: I didn't know. The purpose of stealth and infiltration is to bide your time and to pursue your schematic and agenda and take advantage of opportunities. However, would you like to guess how many in the Sanhedrin were easily corrupted to allow Solomon to grab all the wives he wanted from wherever he wanted?

Ehrlich; This put the axiom of what is good for the goose is also good for the gander into play, right?

George: Absolutely. This was the bedrock in invoking the same anger God vented against the children of Jacob, when they succumbed to the Moabite women, earlier in time.

Ehrlich: They didn't link this to the Moabites at all, did they?

George: That is why my daughter is revered till this very day. She turned her back as far as Israel was concerned against her father and the Moabite life and lifestyle. They applauded her for joining Naomi and never once did anyone question the deaths of Naomi's husband and two sons. If Naomi could accept her, so could Israel.

Ehrlich: How well exactly did Ruth do?

George: Ruth was a Moabite woman. No matter what her name or title she was and is a Moabite. Thus with her skills and talents she laid the entire groundwork for what is now known as the Davidic line.

Ehrlich: But God blessed King David and the Davidic line. How could you say that your agenda overrode God's intervention?

George: This is where Ehrlich you fail to bifurcate what is in play. God allowed my daughter to bear a child. That child by whatever linked to King David and King Solomon. There was nothing I as a Moabite was concerned with in terms of the genetics or God's favor regarding what is the Davidic line. What I, for my people, was concerned with was undermining Israel due to Israel's already known weakness; not undermining God's design for them, which was His business, my plot and plans for my people, my business.

Ehrlich: So you were not worried about God?

George: Did God get in the way of Moabite women before?

Ehrlich: You mean that you knew that it would be up the people of Israel to do the right thing yet again?

George: Absolutely.

Ehrlich: And you had the confidence that they would not do it?

George: Absolutely.

Ehrlich: So when did this all pay off?

George: It's still paying off today. However, the first big score realized was when the ten tribes separated from the two others. They then went against their God and their God was not with them. While the Assyrians wanted to wage war against Israel to capture its wealth, they knew about the God of Israel and they were scared.

Ehrlich: Until?

George: Until those that succeeded me and honored the plan in every generation put themselves on the line with the Assyrians in waging the war against Israel.

Ehrlich: The results?

George: A wealth beyond comprehension. It appeared we had captured all the wealth of the world. Even today we have not been able to spend it all.

Ehrlich: I heard that the Assyrians wanted to take on the other two tribes and gain control of Jerusalem?

George: You heard correctly. They ultimately did march, centuries later, against Jerusalem but we would have nothing to do with it.

Ehrlich: Why?

George: We saw the power of the God of Israel before. We did not want to press our luck.

Ehrlich: And the Assyrians?

George: They were convinced they could take Jerusalem.

Ehrlich: And...

George: You know they did not.

Ehrlich: Do you know why?

George: I do.

Ehrlich: Please tell me.

George: Again as Ruth as a single woman was able to ground our entire plan to do what my forefathers could not do to Israel, there was a woman Judith who single handedly stopped the full conquest of Israel.

Ehrlich: With God's help.

George: I do not speak for or against that statement but without what she did the Assyrians would have captured Jerusalem.

Ehrlich: I have not heard of Judith before.

George: I do not know why.

Ehrlich: So what happened after the conquest of the ten tribes?

George: Well, it seems Israel went into turmoil and conflict from all that we managed to accomplish. However, as I always knew, Israel would collapse and they impugned God again and the Babylonians came in and conquered Jerusalem, resulting in the first Exile.

Ehrlich: What happened to the Moabites?

George: With all the wealth we had we needed new frontiers for investment and growth and so over time we enmeshed ourselves within what later became known as Europe.

Ehrlich: Did the Moabites stay in touch with one another?

George: I have to remind you how loyal we are to each other. We knew that with all our wealth that we might forget one another and our roots so we created family circles that evolved into societies that carry on today.

Ehrlich: So these circles and societies stay in touch together even till today.

George: Well over time and marriage outside the circle we have a lot of Moabite blood all over the world. However, the Moabites have stayed loyal to the sacrifices of myself and my daughter for our people. We just have to hand pick and select those who best honor and stay loyal to what my daughter and I did. They marvel that no one attributes all the problems in the rest of the world, especially those arising through what was left to Israel, to us. We are sort of an invisible people. The plan of stealth seen in how I dealt with Elimelech and his family, with Naomi, with Boaz, and subsequently with Israel, has allowed me to tell my people that when God is not with Israel He seems to be with us.

Ehrlich: So you believe that God is with you?

George: It seems by default. However, those after me who also took over Christianity and otherwise interspersed globally came to bow to the Satan who they concluded is the one with us, as God's first born who stands with us against the people of Israel.

Ehrlich: Do you know why he is against Israel?

George: That's not important for us. He, as we, is against Israel. We share the same ambitions.

Ehrlich: So when the Assyrians were out to conquer Israel you were all for Israel's destruction.

George: Absolutely.

Ehrlich: But your own blood was now part of Israel.

George: My daughter sacrificed her life for her people. All those who died as a result of the war were part and parcel of the same sacrifice. From where she sat, she was repulsed by the thought of having children with Elimelech's son and I am sure that if she felt that way with him that she felt equally so with the son she bore by Boaz.

Ehrlich: Pretty cold hearted.

George: Our loyalty is to our people and way and lifestyle. That is why my daughter and I are revered secretly in the hearts and minds of all those that still serve my original agenda and design.

Ehrlich: So what happened after the Assyrian conquest that foremost stands into your mind?

George: One of the great days for the Moabites was when Jesus was put on the cross and the other when Rabban Gamliel and his henchmen showed God the door with Rabbi Eliezer.

Ehrlich: What stood out to you from these events?

George: Jesus confronted the Moabite infiltration and pollution done against Israel.

Ehrlich: But he is your own family?

George: Well two things, Ehrlich. First, as I said, if he was part of my family he is part and parcel of the same sacrifice my daughter gave up her life for. Second, Israel's God intervened in the birth; thus Jesus, from where the Moabites sit, proved himself an enemy of the Moabites.

Ehrlich: But many Moabites enmeshed themselves into the later Christian Church?

George: We enmeshed ourselves into Israel. We enmeshed ourselves into the Christian Church. Both of these infiltrations gave us de facto control of the world and its wealth.

Ehrlich: Why did you mention the trial of Rabbi Eliezer?

George: What a great moment for the Moabites to see the Jews themselves show God the door. Many of them must have had some wonderful experiences with Moabite women to twist their minds to allow such a thing to happen. If God were with the Moabites believe me you would never see us show God the door.

Ehrlich: So why did they do it?

George: Those Moabites aligned later on with the Satan explained it. They said the Jews learned to hate the restrictions and oversight God represented for them. Those men with egos wanted to run things and they didn't like the sorts of the Eliezers running and crying to God whenever they did anything that was wrong. They wanted to do things their way and they angled it so that they could.

Ehrlich: But how did the Jewish people allow it all to happen?

George: God from where I sit did not choose wisely. He aligned with the weakest of men in forging an alliance with the descendants of Abraham and Sarah. I can't tell you why He did it but He did it. He gave them Torah. He gave them prophets. He gave them every warning against the Moabites and against violating Divine Decree. So when Ruth came into town I thought there really would be little chance of seeing my plan play out but alas consistent with the Moabite experiences with the children of Jacob, they failed, not only their God but also themselves. This is almost a given throughout all of biblical time.

Sidebar: King Saul and his failure to heed Divine Decree...

Biblical history shows that when one person fails to heed direct Divine Decree that the consequences can be both monumental and potentially fatal.

God instructed King Saul via the prophet Samuel to completely destroy the Agagites. All of them. No one was supposed to survive.

Those with Saul in the conquest of the Agagites were reluctant to destroy all the valuable properties and Saul was enticed by King Agag to spare his life.

Saul brought King Agag back to Israel and Samuel was enraged that Saul did not follow God's explicit orders. Saul did not see any harm done, because immediately after Samuel showed his rage, King Agag and all others were destroyed.

However, one who departs from God's instructions opens a portal that is normally invisible, for it is only within the ambit and knowledge of God.

In the short additional time that King Agag lived, he had sexual relations and he fathered Haman, the open enemy of the Jewish people, who moved for their total destruction during their Babylonian captivity.

God had to intervene via Queen Esther, the biblical heroine highlighted annually in the story of Purim, to save the Jewish people from total annihilation.

Thereby, if a delay of a couple of days would have resulted in the destruction of all the Jewish people, one must recognize the depth of the damage done by the irreversible violations of Divine Decree highlighted to this point by Clarity.

Ehrlich: And the Moabites have been the beneficiaries.

George: I honor my family and my heritage. They were out to kill off the children of Israel from the first and after God cast them off from Israel we took every advantage especially when it was to our advantage to kill them off again and again.

Ehrlich: But they survive.

George. I know. Their God is a merciful God. What He tolerates from them I will never understand.

Ehrlich: Well are you still working to kill them off?

George: Do I have to tell you again? Moabites are loyal to my design and the sacrifice of my daughter. They also are loyal to our forefathers who went forth to do the same.

Ehrlich: Don't you think God is going to punish you?

George: He hasn't punished us all along.... Since our mission and role is to kill all of them then it could not be that we should see Him as our God. In any event, the chieftains that followed me concluded that God's son, the Satan, is with us sharing in our agenda and providing us many riches and rewards throughout the centuries.

Ehrlich: So you believe you pursue your stratagem against Israel and the Jewish people free from punishment from God?

George: Yes.

Ehrlich: Does the same hold true against the Islamic people, Iran, specifically, hyperlinking to today's events {March 2006}?

George: That is what worries me. Why I agreed to speak with you.

Ehrlich: What worries you?

George: That the God of Israel might intervene for the Islamic people and also punish us.

Ehrlich: But it doesn't seem that the Moabites of today in making their plans for conquest of the world and all its remaining wealth seem particularly bothered about it.

George: I want to ask you why the God of Israel would step forth for the Islamic people?

Ehrlich: Well first what is your knowledge about the Prophet Muhammad?

George: I know that after Jesus and post Eliezer that a group of Jews who wanted to know, like you, what the heck was going on tried to review and reassess all that happened. Muhammad and other people resident in what was once Israel were part of this group.

Then it seemed that Muhammad forged a love and link to God and wanted to bring all that Israel and Christianity squandered to his people.

Ehrlich: What did the Moabites think about it?

George: We were focused on ransacking things via the Christian Church and also getting rid of the last of the Jews, whom we thought that God would fully abandon. We perpetuated a lot of cruelty upon them. Once they were out of the way, we would move on eliminating the Church as well.

Ehrlich: What about Muhammad?

George: We didn't see him and his people as a problem until a couple of centuries later.

Ehrlich: And what did you do?

George: What we always do. We infiltrated them, caused division, and hoped that they would kill each other off.

Ehrlich: Did they?

George: They're here, that's why I am talking to you.

Ehrlich: So what do you want to know from me?

George: Why you think God will step up for them when there is no covenant with them?

Ehrlich: Did you think that God would honor those protecting His name less because there was no covenant? Perhaps you might have to rethink it and conclude that He would protect them all the more.

George: But they killed lots of Jews over time too.

Ehrlich: The operative dynamic right here is not who killed whom, with culpability on everyone, but who stands to defend God in a world that you corrupted to move away from God.

George: But that is our role and purpose.

Ehrlich: No. You think that because you stand with the Satan that you can move against all those who want to stand with God. Don't you think Satan by himself could do the job?

George: I thought there was a reason he could not do it.

Ehrlich: Of course there is a reason. His Father. So Satan to prove his point goes out there via you and the others who aligned with you to do the job that the Satan himself cannot do.

George: Why can't he do it?

Ehrlich: Because His Father who is God restricts him like an electronic fence keeps an animal within bounds from walking outside the perimeter of that fence. It doesn't mean that he can't make his point by asking for surrogate assistance.

Sidebar: Satan

Covering Satan in a sidebar represents an ambitious effort.

Succinctly then, God routinely favors the second born all throughout the Torah. Cain/Abel and Esau/Jacob just to name two. Even the first letter of the first word in the Torah represents the value two.

When the Torah starts there is already darkness. The darkness is Satan. The Torah provides:

"And God said: 'Let there be light.' And there was light. **And God saw the light, that it was good;** and God divided the light {author: new} from the darkness {author: extant}."

Light represents the potential of mankind.

In the most difficult verse in the Torah:

"And God said: 'Let us make man in our image, after our likeness; and let them have dominion over the fish of the sea, and over the fowl of the air, and over the cattle, and over all the earth, and over every creeping thing that creepeth upon the earth."

Thus like Cain and Abel, Esau and Jacob, the sons of Leah v. the sons of Rachel, the battle has been the one of darkness v. the light. What do Satan and Lot and Cain and

Esau all have in common: the commitment to prove that they are equally worthy of God's favor than their counterparts.

Thus, in succinct fashion, there is a divide and eternal conflict between those God favors and those He does not, and those deemed not favored strive continually to prove to God that those He deems worthy are not so worthy. Thus, the top of the pyramid chain regarding those who wish to prove the children of Israel unworthy and inconsistent with the light is God's first born, the Satan, the darkness.

Satan is God's first born, the darkness that existed, before God created man and mankind, the light. Think about it. You should come to understand that Satan is our wayward brother. The Moabites are our wayward relatives. The buffer between their strength and resources and those under monotheism is God.

Those under monotheism have the advantage, but because those under monotheism have succumbed to the Moabite designs, by ostracizing rather than embracing God, those aligned with the Moabites and the Satan have prevailed.

George: So why haven't we been punished all along by God? Why did God allow my daughter to bear her son?

Ehrlich: You answered your own question earlier on. There were bifurcated paths forged. God intervened against your stealth plan. You did see His intervention per King David. However, you didn't see that it was not per se King Solomon that Israel failed but what failed was the Sanhedrin who did not do their important job when there was an important job to do. This is what angered God from where I sit. God didn't want a situation where He had to intervene in everything, or else He might as well circumcise our hearts right then and there.

George: I don't understand what you just said.

Ehrlich: It's not really relevant. My point to answer your question is that you have gotten to the point where you are directly not indirectly attacking Israel, which you must today accept is seen via Islam, who stands by God when Israel and the USA stand against Him by tolerating you in the same vein the Sanhedrin tolerated via King Solomon (not to say Boaz).

George: So I can understand this correctly. If instead of sending Ruth I sent my troops against Israel I would have...

Ehrlich: Failed.... And to be clear punished if not destroyed altogether. Your war then would have been against God directly not the people of Israel.

George: So by waging military attack against Iran and the people of the Qur'an we would be waging war against God.

Ehrlich: Correct.

George: So if we infiltrate the people of Iran to make them move away from God that is not an attack against God?

Ehrlich: It is an indirect attack against God.

George: So it is OK to try?

Ehrlich: Not from where I sit. But God uses you as a test to see if the people resist taking the wrong path.

George: So we can undermine Iran by infiltrating the nation and by pulling them away from God via casinos, entertainment, video games, and television?

Ehrlich: You can. It is wrong. However, it is up to Iran to stop it. Similar to China itself, Iran is trying to plug the portals to such infiltration.

George: But we will succeed because the Satan told us that given time people will subscribe to our path.

Ehrlich: That is why Iran is justified in protecting itself from such attacks. That is why they can do whatever needs to be done and if you persist in setting up Iran for war as you did Iraq then you will lose and you will be punished.

George: Well, tell me why we didn't lose in Iraq. We have control over the oil and we are the occupying force in Iraq.

Ehrlich: You lost the war in Iraq. You just don't know it. To win you need to conquer Iran and so by attacking Iran you will not only lose here but everywhere. Everything you have gained since the time of Ruth will be lost. Everything.

George: You are dreaming. We have lost little outside of the American and French Revolutions.

Ehrlich: You seem to win outside those two incidents because God is allowing the portal to remain open to learn the lessons that should have been learned already from the Exile from Israel.

George: I could have told the God of Israel the results a long time ago.

Ehrlich: God knows the results. It's in the Torah that covers things from the beginning until the day Israel irrevocably fails the test. It is at that point that God makes His final decisions regarding Israel's answers as to the tests offered. Then He makes his final comments and decisions with regard to his own first born, and believe me that is when the Satan will be the first to turn his back on you and that you will pay for all the crimes and injustices that fall at your door.

George: This is your opinion. It means nothing to me.

Ehrlich: It is the opinion you just told me not that long ago that you were enlisting.

George: Do you have proof of what you say?

Ehrlich: You acknowledge that God was and is with Israel. Thus, assume for a moment, that Israel would not have failed God. If it didn't, there would have been no Assyrian conquest and all the other tragedies haunting this world and its existence throughout the centuries as known by us today. It became an upside down world. You were part and parcel of the test. If Israel passed, it didn't mean the end for you. What it meant is that you would have been mentored to as well by Israel in that God would have empowered Israel all the more and obviously He would still be with Israel and us today.

George: What did you mean about the Satan turning his back on us and the Satan or God punishing us?

Ehrlich: You did play your role. However, your role went beyond bounds, when you acquired what you only once dreamed about and then pursued unbridled crimes and injustices against your fellow man, inside and outside of Israel. Simply put, you abused your power, as you did when you thought it appropriate to topple the two World Trade Center buildings to enable your new long range plans. But there was and is a difference between taking down those two buildings and sending Ruth into Israel or even cajoling the Assyrians to attack to gain a large part of the booty.

George: What is the difference?

Ehrlich When it came to the Assyrians and Israel you knew that God had to allow the victory to the Assyrians. So you did what you now did to Israel to set it up for a victory, but there is no reward as in the past, just the elimination of a historic enemy. You also know it is not your place to wage war against Israel, but you have positioned it yet again so others can wage war against it to eliminate it. However, the riches of Israel are now seen to be with Iraq and Iran in terms of oil. Thus, you see Iran as different from Israel and that you can attack Iran whereas you always knew you could not attack Israel directly militarily. **So you want Israel to move in to attack Iran and when Iran responds successfully against Israel you want the reality to be that you did not attack Iran but moved in militarily to protect Israel, hoping that before you attack and occupy Iran that Iran will have done away with Israel.**

Sidebar: Three Months later this very stratagem revealed itself.

Olmert's War, covered starting in Chapter Ten, proved to be the very analytic described in what you are reading, written and offered in March 2006. Olmert's War commenced in June 2006.

Succinctly, due to Moabite influences and directives, Israel made itself obscene in the eyes of both Syria and Iran, committing atrocities that were sure to have both Syria and Iran move to intervene for Lebanon. Israel in fact placed bombs within meters of Syria to entice it to enter the war.

Iran had a protection pact with Syria. Once Syria (or Iran) bit at the bait offered, then Olmert's War would have expanded to a regional war. Iran had weaponry that could have done substantial damage to both Tel Aviv and Haifa. Assuming that the war would have expanded to include Syria and Iran, the cover would then be in hand for an attack against Iran based on the serious destruction and damage done to Israel.

Chapter Thirteen will explain why that escalation did not take place. It is an analytic and truth that is unique and exclusive to the author and you will see a side of reality hidden from the entire world.

George: So you are saying that even if Israel is the one that attacks Iran, that we are to blame even if we enter the fray to protect Israel?

Ehrlich: Correct. Israel cannot be conquered or defeated unless God allows it. Israel attacking Iran is the same thing as you attacking Israel. You attacking Iran under the guise of protecting Israel is tantamount to expressing you are defending the one that is attacking God directly. However, you cannot fool the Heavenly Tribunal that it is all in any event a mask that Israel would be attacking Iran as your own surrogate. The fact that it is Israel attacking Iran, you think takes God out of the equation for the egregious sin is on Israel. It does seem that way for Israel but it is not the case for sure for Iran.

By the way George why is there a need to do all that you are now undertaking?

George: The current Moabite leadership has concluded that since Israel has historically failed and that we have been the beneficiaries but for two periods of time where we may have gone out of bounds that we are intended to rule and manage the entire world. As I said at the beginning, we appear to always have been God's favorite by default and now with the Satan we understand that we cannot be held to account for it is our destined role to test and confront Israel.

Ehrlich: Israel is out of the issue for the moment. First, let me point out that the American and French Revolutions were not I think a punishment for you but to lay the groundwork for a new era of justice and commitment to God and the Ten Commandments. The bad news for you is that you did everything to undermine that intention not to serve yourself but for the express purpose of working against God. You went from a people who used stealth for self-gain to work around God to a people who now affirmatively seek as you now call it culture change against people who want to honor God. Thus, you have in fact overstepped your role. This is why I feel for sure you have been tripped up time and time again as I interpreted you would, why you will not succeed and why you will be punished severely for what you are now doing.

George: What is your recommendation?

Ehrlich: Why don't you take a big step back and consolidate your gains. Let the people under monotheism see if they can see the truths connective to 9-11, Abu Ghraib, the assassination of two Israeli prime ministers, the undermining of America and its military and industry, and put themselves on the right path. If they do not, you will have more victories but if they do then you will have to accept all you have which is far more than anyone else on this entire planet. But if you want it all and are willing to confront God in terms of attacking those adhering to God, to capture the wealth and resources God himself gave to them, then your own time and good fortune is up. While the rest of the people who failed God will certainly have a dark future, you and your people will have a lot to defend against where there is no defense.

Sidebar: Shift in the Paradigm of Power

Since the Judeo-Christian ethic in contemporary history has been undermined by the Moabites, and inasmuch as the Moabites themselves have gone beyond the pale in moving for culture change in Middle East nations aligned with Islam, a shift in the paradigm of power was foreshadowed by the Bible.

Author's Position Paper (October 2002): "If President Bush moves against Iraq, then there is nothing more to say than that the world will dramatically change far more than it has done since 9-11; where the world did receive a message from the collapse of the two world trade center buildings: that it better seek a leadership that truly knows the road to peace, because otherwise the leaderships moving the peoples away from God would certainly lead the world to war with a shift of the paradigm of world power from those under monotheism to the godless Chinese, who will, without any doubt whatsoever, prove to be harsh taskmasters as a biblical punishment for failing to appreciate all that has been bestowed upon us including the basis to learn and understand the correct course which should have been undertaken."

This shift actually, according to the author, took place with North Korea moving forward in June 2006 for missile tests. The author's contention at that time was that North Korea had stealth missile technology, and the truth of it would be evident from the tests AND President Bush would need to abandon his National Security Strategy. In fact, three weeks later, he did.

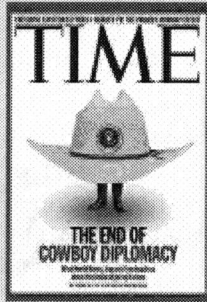

You want to infiltrate China. Go ahead. They will defend themselves and they are able to defend themselves. However, if you want to infiltrate Iran not to influence it to take the wrong road but to coerce it to take the wrong road or to hide behind Israel to get it to attack Iran so that you can wage war against Iran in the name of protecting Israel, you will fail, lose and be severely punished from my understanding of all we have discussed.

George: So are you saying that it's all right to wage war against China?

Ehrlich: Look, George, you are not fooling anyone in where you want to go. You ask me a question where you know that if you can successfully wage war against China that Iran is a given. However, if you understand what we have discussed, China is the vehicle through which God may act to protect Iran. Thus, an attack against China is an attack against Iran. As long as your agenda is to gain control over Iran you cannot dance around it by misinformation where the target of that misinformation is one that cannot be fooled or misled by such misinformation.

George: All right Ehrlich. I will take what you said under advisement.

End of channeled discussion.

The channeled discussion with the Moabite Chieftain transverses time to introduce you to current day realities as the author addressed them in March 2006. Moabite techniques and designs are essential to know and understand in order to properly identify modern day Moabite leaders, their pawns, poodles and puppets, and the surrogates used to consummate their long term unabated quest for world domination and control.

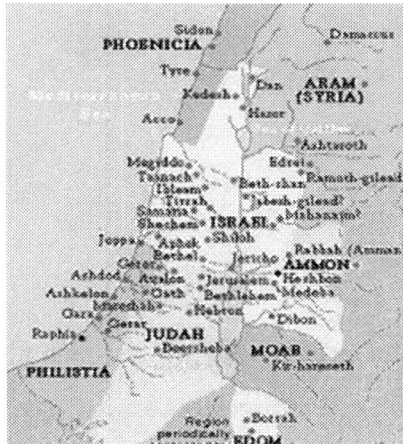

BIBLICAL MOAB

CHAPTER 6
JUDAISM HIJACKED

In the discussion with George, Moabite Chieftain, in the previous chapter, there were several references that show the Moabites are consistently focused upon the need to preclude future interference with their quest to dominate and conquer the world. The enemies they feared and still fear are God and the children of Israel.

The Moabites, post the Assyrian conquest, felt they successfully dealt a blow to both. In subsequent biblical times, they witnessed the destruction of the First Temple by the Babylonians, the return of the single remaining tribe, the Jews, to Jerusalem, the rebuilding of the Temple, followed by its second destruction at the hands of the Romans, and the advent of Christianity.

Table of Events

- Abraham

- Isaac —> Jacob —> Joseph —> Egypt—> 12 tribes—> Bondage —> Exodus

- Ten Commandments and Torah

- First Encounter with Moabites

- Entry into Israel

- Boaz (Ruth)

- King Solomon (First Temple)

- Division, creating separate government for northern tribes

- Assyrian conquest northern tribes, leaving remnant, Jews.

- Babylonian Conquest Jews (First {Babylonian} Exile)

- Second Temple (Christianity)

- Rabban Gamliel —> Rabbi Akiva—> Bar-Kokhba Rebellion (Second {Roman} Exile)

The Moabites were pragmatic about the fact that they knew they could not defeat the God of Israel. This was a tacit admission that the Moabites always knew the God of Israel existed. When He intervened, the results He wanted arose. Thus, to the Moabites the way to keep the God of Israel out of the picture was to have God perpetually angered by the children of Israel. How to do this always has been dominant in their minds.

The Moabites were brilliant and are brilliant to this very day in their use of surrogates and that expression also includes the ability to infiltrate and establish pawns and poodles within their host (the children of Israel) to perpetuate their agenda. The first expression of this reality was seen right before, so as to cause, the Exile of the remaining tribe of Israel (the Jewish people) from Israel.

This is one of the least known and understood stories in the Judeo-Christian world and the fact that it is not taught, and if taught, not taught properly, is all connected to the Moabite agenda. What is not taught is exactly how and when the Sanhedrin ostracized God!

THE TREACHERY OF RABBAN GAMLIEL

You are probably asking why would the Jews, the remnant of what survived the original Assyrian onslaught against Israel, even think of ostracizing God?

The answer to this critical question, the brilliance of evil, the Moabite design, is all clearly seen via the trial of Rabbi Eliezer ben Hycranus, one of the most important events of all biblical history.

Rabbi Eliezer ben Hycranus was the eminent scholar of his day. Not only was he smart to the highest degree of the word, but also he was the person that carried the last vestige of the special temple connection to God, evidenced and supported by his ability to perform miracles and speak directly to and receive a heard response from the Heavenly Tribunal! And the odds are nearly 100% that you never heard of him or, if you did, you never were told the full story and denied the truth of what transpired!

Rabbi Eliezer was a true man of God. His holiness was something that thwarted the efforts of those that had personal agendas and were bent less on holiness than serving their own selfish and personal desires.

The man who detested Rabbi Eliezer the most was his brother in law, known historically as Rabban Gamliel, who as the Chief Judge, head of the Sanhedrin, the Jewish Congress and Judiciary, was the Boaz of his time.

No one could best Rabbi Eliezer when he spoke regarding a point of law. When everyone disagreed with him, Rabbi Eliezer would invoke his special relationship with God and the Heavenly Tribunal, to secure confirmation that his interpretation was the correct one.

Rabban Gamliel and a great many others did not like that their opinions, to wit, desires, became subservient to Rabbi Eliezer's expression of justice. Thus, this continued frustration by ambitious men proved an exceptional opportunity for the Moabite influence to yet again permeate the Sanhedrin. Once Ruth entered the land of Israel and was accepted by the nation, the pollution hovered about it as a dark cloud. Now, that the Sanhedrin proved themselves willing to show themselves pragmatic and flexible, the Moabites were ready to see the Sanhedrin make a bold move to make changes that would serve the Moabites until today.

THE SET UP

The issue before the Sanhedrin, the Jewish Congress and High Court, was one concerning whether an oven in issue was ritually clean for use in cooking.

Suffice it to say that Rabban Gamliel wanted to see the issue resolved one way and Rabbi Eliezer saw it the other way.

Just as Boaz got the Sanhedrin to rule for his personal desire, Rabban Gamliel, the Boaz of his day, got the entire Sanhedrin but for Rabbi Eliezer to see it his way.

Why was Rabban Gamliel so focused on contradicting Rabbi Eliezer over an oven?

The issue over the oven was the plan Gamliel forged to get his brother in law out of the picture. The Sanhedrin said in essence to Rabbi Eliezer that since everyone but him agreed with Rabban Gamliel's viewpoint, why wouldn't he bend and go with the majority?

Rabbi Eliezer no doubt cognizant of the mistakes the Sanhedrin made regarding Boaz and King Solomon, expressed that the right thing had to be done regardless of the sentiment of the entire Sanhedrin. Rabbi Eliezer understood the realities of his brother in law's power play, manipulating the entire Sanhedrin to stand against his position. He knew that with no one supporting his position, the correct position, that Rabban Gamliel was moving out to create a very dangerous precedent and power.

Similar to the fashion Boaz and Solomon got the Sanhedrin of their times to bow to their respective personal desires, Rabban Gamliel pulled out all his resources to get the entire Sanhedrin to stand with him. The Torah provides:

> Exodus 23:2: Thou shalt not follow a multitude to do evil; neither shalt thou bear witness in a cause to turn aside after a multitude to pervert justice.

Rabbi Eliezer's point, to those beseeching his compliance with Rabban Gamliel's viewpoint was that the Sanhedrin circumscribed the above Torah decree when it dealt with Boaz and thereafter with King Solomon. Boaz, King Solomon, and now Rabban Gamliel were the de facto kings and leaders of those days and to get the Sanhedrin to deliberately acquiesce to their personal desires, for whatever reasons were involved, whether justified or not, was an unacceptable and dangerous precedent, as history had already proved the case. One seemingly innocuous decision established the beachhead for the enemy within Israel, and with the other decision, idolatry entered Israel with consequences that allowed the Assyrians to eviscerate the northern tribes.

The pressure on Rabbi Eliezer to change his viewpoint was unrelenting. Ultimately, he resorted to his special resources to prove that he was correct. He told the Sanhedrin that if he was correct that a tree in front of them would move. It did. He said if he was correct the stream of water in front of them would reverse its course. It did. However, Gamliel and his cohorts belittled the miracles performed and declared that the ability to do miracles was not at all relevant to the resolution of the question before them.

Rabbi Eliezer, seeing the depth to the power play against him, then invoked his major resource, enlisting direct support of the Heavenly Tribunal.

A voice from the Heavens declared for all to hear that Rabbi Eliezer was correct. Then biblical history records the following taking place (halacha, again, means law):

> Rabbi Eliezer then said to the Sages, "If the halacha is in accordance with me, let it be proved directly from Heaven." Whereupon a Heavenly Voice cried out, "Why do you dispute with Rabbi Eliezer, seeing that in all matters the halacha agrees with him!" Rabbi Yehoshua immediately rose and, quoting from Deuteronomy, said, "The Torah is not in heaven!" Rabbi Jeremiah explained, "The Torah has already been given at Mount Sinai; we pay no attention to a Heavenly Voice, because You have written in the Torah at Mount Sinai, `After the majority must one incline'."

Rabbi Jeremiah has affirmatively distorted what the Torah says. The Torah does not say what Rabbi Jeremiah says is written in Torah. His false statement went without rebuke. Again,

> Exodus 23:2: Thou shalt not follow a multitude to do evil; neither shalt thou bear witness in a cause to turn aside after a multitude to pervert justice.

It does not say or impute that after a majority one must incline! What the Torah says is the opposite to wit, what Rabbi Eliezer sought to enjoin, as no doubt some during the time Boaz and King Solomon strove to enjoin, but were silenced by the majority bowing to Boaz and Solomon, putting even God's direct decrees, ultimate law, aside.

Rabbi Eliezer did what the Sanhedrin thereafter banned: he appealed to God for intervention. The Heavenly Voice came down because of Rabbi Eliezer's appeal to God for intervention. His plea was worthy of such a deified response. When it is received, it is defamation to God to reject it.

Yet, this did not stop Gamliel from his plot against his brother in law. Those with him said that once the Torah was handed down, it was for the majority to enunciate the laws and that anyone who refutes the majority of the Sanhedrin is guilty of a sin that could command a penalty of death.

Laws were passed that even if God Himself appeared to contradict the Sanhedrin (see Deeper Analysis in the Appendix), it was only a test of the people's resolve to follow the law that Gamliel's cohorts brazenly connected to Exodus 23:2; to wit, the interpretation that God expected the people to abide by was the majority decree, even over His own words in contradiction thereto! Incredible!

In this manner, Gamliel and his gang consolidated power and de facto ostracized God. They declared that God's reign over the Jews was in their exclusive hands and anyone who dared to defy it or deny it would be ostracized or stoned to death.

Rabbi Eliezer was not present when the entire Sanhedrin, including the students he mentored, voted to ostracize him from the community for his refusal to bend to the majority decision. This meant that no one could have anything to do with him. He was isolated and shunned, a heavy punishment for a man who was the master teacher to many sitting in the Sanhedrin and casting their vote to excommunicate him.

What kind of power could Rabban Gamliel wield to get the entire Sanhedrin to ostracize Rabbi Eliezer, whom the Heavenly Tribunal declared correct in his position?

The author to show how Gamliel corrupted those about him, even concerning major issues of conscience, used the following excerpt derived from the Jewish sourcebook, the Midrash.

> Rabban Gamliel, who presided over the Great Sanhedrin in Yavneh after the destruction of the second Bais Hamikdash, once fixed the day of Rosh Chodesh Tishri according to the testimony of two witnesses who had observed the new moon. The Sage, R. Yehoshua, declared that their testimony was invalid, and that Rosh Chodesh should be set a day later. Hence, according to R. Yehoshua's opinion, Yom Kippur (on the tenth of Tishri) would also be postponed a day.
>
> R. Gamliel sent R. Yehoshua a message: "**I decree** that you come before me with your walking stick and your wallet on the day you set as Yom Kippur (to demonstrate publicly by desecrating your Yom Kippur that you submit to the Sanhedrin's authority).

R. Yehoshua was very anguished when he received this summons. R. Akiva, though, comforted him, explaining that R. Yehoshua would incur no sin by carrying on "his" Yom Kippur; on the contrary, he would be rewarded for obeying the Sanhedrin.

On the day, which according to his calculation was Yom Kippur, R. Yehoshua took his staff and purse and appeared before the head of the Sanhedrin in Yavneh.

R. Gamliel arose, kissed him on his head and exclaimed, "Peace to you, **my master and student- my master in Torah wisdom and my student for obeying my orders.**"

The above is a picture window how corruption is in reality a disease that ultimately has to be treated or it destroys its host altogether.

Rabbi Yehoshua subsequently openly and vocally supports Rabban Gamliel in his campaign against Rabbi Eliezer. Rabban Gamliel had corrupted him and the story from the Midrash shows exactly how he was corrupted: to the degree that he did whatever Gamliel told him. Yehoshua obeyed Gamliel, and with obedience to man over God, both God and Divine Decree were put aside, as they were regarding the issues discussed regarding Boaz and Solomon.

When Rabbi Eliezer was wrongfully ostracized and man manipulated obedience to man over obedience to God, Judaism was hijacked. This allowed the Moabites to assure themselves that the Jews would not be in their way as they proceeded to hijack Christianity to accumulate further wealth and perpetrate conflict, mayhem and wars in their quest for ultimate world domination and control.

Here are three excerpts from the Deeper Analysis in the Appendix, which you are urged to read to more deeply appreciate the crimes implemented:

I.

Greenwood: Akhnai, curiously, not only affirms majority rule, but does so with precisely the same unease as is usual in democratic theory. First, it rejects the notion that right could trump the majority. R. Joshua's selective quotation repeats the same point made by the rejection of R. Eliezer's miracles: that is, the mere fact that Eliezer evidently is correctly interpreting Heaven's intent is not enough to make his view the law. **The law is what the majority says it is, regardless of whether they are right, or even of whether we ought to incline after them to do evil.**

Ehrlich: **What Greenwood is saying is incredible: allow evil to take control and allow it to have its day!** This logic of course justifies King Solomon in defying God's direct decree to him, allows him to take one thousand wives, that opens the portal to idolatry and the destruction of the two temples. Thus, Rabban Gamliel and his band of conspirators against God intellectually, to the mind of Greenwood, made a fully understandable and justified choice **regardless of the reality that it resulted in death to half the population of Israel and platformed the Exile. Big deal. Spoils of life to those that survive.**

II.

Greenwood: **Nothing in the Biblical texts cited explains why it is a majority of rabbis, rather than, for example, a majority of Jews, or a majority of prophets, that sets the rules.**

Ehrlich: Here Greenwood points to a central consequence of the crimes against God. Just as Solomon angled things so he could defy God's decree and take a thousand wives, many from prohibited nations, the ten tribes then saying what is good for the goose is also good for the gander; the rabbis grasp at uncontested power opened a portal for others bent on an evil agenda to say that if the rabbis can rule in lieu of God why not us? Thus, you have the {Moabites covertly under the guise of Christianity} dynamically operating today under the portal opened by Rabban Gamliel that foreclosed Israel from standing up to the crimes of the Rabin assassination and the American people from standing up against the crimes of 9-11 -- again opening the shift of the paradigm of power to China. Thus, once evil succeeds it opens the portal to all those desiring to pursue personal/evil agendas to do so under the same dynamic of legitimacy: here man defining the future for his fellow man and the planet.

III.

Just remember, if there were any truth and legitimacy to what was done to Rabbi Eliezer and all of us, they would not have kept it a secret for 2000 years. That it is all yet a secret and that they have done nothing to correct it attests that the original agenda is in full play, as witnessed by what is happening to the USA and Israel with the rabid intent to effectuate culture change for the Arab/Islamic nations.

Note that Rabbi Akiva, a heralded figure in Jewish history, aided Rabban Gamliel in his corruption of Rabbi Yehoshua. Rabbi Akiva's mentor and teacher was Rabbi Eliezer. Once Rabbi Eliezer was ostracized, then Rabbi Akiva, his student, conveniently assumed his mentor's status as the most revered scholar in Jewish history. Rabbi Eliezer's name was erased and Rabbi Eliezer's name was written over with Rabbi Akiva's name. So today most every Jewish child and adult knows the name of Rabbi Akiva and hardly anyone by comparison knows the name of Rabbi Eliezer. What they especially don't know is his full story.

When the Sanhedrin commenced their proceedings to ostracize Rabbi Eliezer, who do you think failed to advise his mentor and teacher of the proceedings, so that Rabbi Eliezer could appear to speak on his own behalf? Yes, Rabbi Akiva.

When the proceedings commenced against Rabbi Eliezer, who failed to stand up to speak for his teacher and mentor, particularly since he was not present to speak for himself? Yes, Rabbi Akiva.

The power of evil and corruption is one to elevate otherwise morally weak men into high and influential positions. Rabbi Akiva came from a poor family and his wife, from a wealthy family, stood by him. Rabbi Akiva wanted to do his wife and her family proud and he got to where he aspired at the price of selling out his mentor and teacher. Rabbi Akiva sold his soul (as did Rabbi Yehoshua) -- as did all who bowed to both Boaz and King Solomon, both openly and knowingly defying Divine Decrees.

Rabbi Yehoshua, as no doubt many others in the Sanhedrin, fell one by one to the power and influence of Gamliel and the Moabites. Yom Kippur is the holiest day in the Jewish calendar and what did Gamliel do? He got Yehoshua to agree that it be held for all the Jews not on the day provided by Torah per Rabbi Yehoshua, Gamliel's "master in Torah wisdom", but one day off from the day set forth by Divine Decree, as set forth by he whose orders must be obeyed. Thus Rabbi Yehoshua not only sold his soul but by his acquiescence to evil, he knowingly compromised the entire Jewish people to hold the Yom Kippur service on the day Gamliel declared.

Rabban Gamliel thus represented evil personified. The basis for aligning this crime to the Moabite influence is because Rabban Gamliel knowingly and willingly moved to ostracize God and distance the Jewish people from God, a deed so base and evil in design, it could only have been foisted and supported by those who used pawns and poodles, such as Rabban Gamliel, to move forward designs of such a grand scale against God and the remnant of children of Abraham still directly under the covenant.

To corrupt every member of the Sanhedrin against God would take an involvement similar to corrupting every member of the United States Congress to implement an unjust invasion. It is not within the true power of any single man. It is a collective design and the type of corruption that would ostracize God is one that inherently incorporates the talents and resources of the Moabites, something that was not within the direct personal grasp of Rabban Gamliel, who while independently powerful, would have needed back up to corrupt every single member of the Sanhedrin. It was not only that they agreed to stand with Rabban Gamliel, as they did with Boaz and Solomon, but they had to unite to stand and speak up collectively, to a man, against the Heavenly Tribunal that openly sided with Rabbi Eliezer via a Heavenly voice response! The Appendix, as referenced, contains a deeper analysis of these critical events.

Due to wrongful actions taken against Rabbi Eliezer, where Rabbi Akiva usurped his standing in the community, and, at best, stood passive to his cruel ostracization, the remaining Jewish community adopted and ratified to this very day this founding mantra to their orthodoxy of faith. Despite the Jewish experience with the destruction of the two temples, the Jewish people were again remiss then and today in the messages God sent regarding the impropriety of their course.

THE JEWS GO TO WAR AGAINST ROME

After passing these new laws vesting ultimate and irrevocable powers in the Sanhedrin, to wit: Rabban Gamliel, Rabbi Akiva subsequently, in holding a position of influence himself, told the people of Israel that they were going to wage war against Rome.

What kind of insanity prevailed to make the Jewish people think they could prevail over the most powerful army in the world: the Roman army? Only the Moabites could be behind such an insanity that served its next goal, now that God was ostracized (and no doubt very angry): the mass murder of the remaining Jews.

To understand this properly: after Rabbi Eliezer was ostracized, Rabban Gamliel went off on a trip by ship. During his journey, a large tidal wave was headed for the ship. When Gamliel faced his own demise at sea, he fell to the floor of the ship and implored God to save him, declaring (showing his consciousness of guilt) that what he did in terms of his brother in law was something that was needed to be done to bring forth unity, needed cohesive authority, to the Jewish people.

The tidal wave subsided! This part of the story has been passed on in Jewish history as a testimonial that God ratified Rabban Gamliel's good intent in what he did with regard to his brother in law, Rabbi Eliezer. Thus, there was no one that argued any longer that Rabbi Eliezer was owed a serious apology and no one throughout history has deemed that an apology to Rabbi Eliezer has been in order.

While some in the Jewish rabbinate today might admit that the punishment imposed by the Sanhedrin against Rabbi Eliezer might be rightly seen as somewhat harsh and excessive, that is about as far as the sentiment goes as to what happened. Needless to say, there is no mention, discussion or reference to the fact that God was ostracized with Rabbi Eliezer.

The rest of the story, not taught or discussed, includes that Rabban Gamliel returned from his sea journey and he and the crew shared the story of what transpired. Rabban Gamliel was seen as a hero; that his prayers to God caused God to intervene to save him and the rest of the people on the ship. If anyone had second thoughts about sending off Rabbi Eliezer, such regrets instantly were no longer dominant or present in the community.

However, what is not factored into history is that Rabban Gamliel almost immediately thereafter died! Rabbi Eliezer heard all about Rabbi Gamliel's exploits and when he heard the story and saw that the incident with the tidal wave vindicated his brother in law, and the community thus concluded that Rabban Gamliel justly moved to excommunicate him, Rabbi Eliezer fell to the floor and cried out in his grief for justice.

After he was excommunicated, Rabban Gamliel's sister, Rabbi Eliezer's wife, monitored Rabbi Eliezer carefully, for she knew, as Rabban Gamliel knew, that if Rabbi Eliezer invoked a call to God for justice that Rabban Gamliel's time on earth might end. Rabbi Eliezer was not a vengeful person and Rabban Gamliel obviously was counting on it. However, when Rabbi Eliezer heard the news, he fell on the floor in tears, and the recorded account is that his wife knew what became immediately evident, when the bell in the town rang to announce the sudden and unexpected death of Rabban Gamliel.

Thus, the truth of the matter was that God provided Rabban Gamliel an opportunity to repent so that he could return to Israel and invoke justice for his brother in law and rescind his deeds against God (God knowing the deep damage that Gamliel's success meant for the longer term). However, Rabban Gamliel offered rationalizations, as though he could somehow fool the Heavenly Tribunal, sitting in judgment in this life against him.

With Rabban Gamliel's death, Rabbi Akiva saw opportunity. In his own arrogance, he moved to wage war against Rome and he thought he found the very ground to engender both God's and the people's support. A victory against Rome would attest that God was still with Israel and rocket him to the top position at the Sanhedrin, now that Gamliel was out of the picture.

When Rome announced its plans to strip the Jews of their national right to study Torah, God, Akiva argued, surely would be with Israel in a war to protect God's name.

Rabbi Akiva proclaimed the popular Jewish general, General Bar-Kokhba, as the Messiah, to whip up the population in support for a rebellion against Rome.

This war deliberately ignited by Akiva, and supported by the Sanhedrin, is still seen in Jewish history as a classic battle of good versus evil. However, what Jewish history fails to address is the dramatic and tragic result of that pursued war and how and why it was that perceived good lost out to perceived evil.

> **Sidebar**: The issue is not one of good v. evil...
>
> The Jews did not have any enemies when occupying the Holy Land. Such enemies did arise only when they created such enemies to offset their defamation of God's name by forgetting Him and engaging in conduct and behavior defiling His gift. Thus, the Assyrians, the Babylonians and the Romans were all creations of Jewish conduct and behavior in failing God.
>
> Thus, today the Arabs are the created reality from a government leadership that has bent over backwards to promote a secularization plan, to make Israel a nation among nations, which defames and defiles God's gift and

name. Thus, all efforts by Israel to attack or vanquish the Arabs, without assessing its own conduct, will result in the same consequences as in the times of the Romans: defeat, if not exile.

The Jewish people must simply understand that there is no way God would intervene for Israel to save it or to provide it victory in any war with the Arab Nations so that an agenda making Israel a nation among nations, moving the Jewish people away from Him, would overtake the Jewish State.

When Israel defeated the Roman legion stationed in the area, Rabbi Akiva tasted the first fruits of the victory he had described for Israel.

However, after this initial victory against Rome, Caesar issued orders to amass numerous legions to march against the rebellious Jews in Israel. The Bar-Kokhba rebellion failed, costing the lives of one-half the Jewish population in Israel, with the other half put into chains and worse. This war against Rome opened the portal that sent what remained of the Jewish people into the Diaspora. The Jewish people were exiled from Jerusalem and the land of Israel. The Moabites were in their glory.

Before all was lost for Israel, Rabbi Akiva had gone to see Rabbi Eliezer who was in the grip of death. Reflecting his unbridled arrogance, Rabbi Akiva and those with him, who had joined Gamliel and Akiva in ostracizing Rabbi Eliezer, asked Rabbi Eliezer if he was ready to repent for his position against the majority decision of the Sanhedrin.

Rabbi Eliezer refuted any such intent, and, with that rejection, Rabbi Akiva told Rabbi Eliezer of the deaths of many of his peers at the hands of the Romans. Rabbi Akiva then asked Rabbi Eliezer as to his own fate. Rabbi Eliezer whispered to Rabbi Akiva that his fate would be worse than theirs.

And it certainly was a worse fate. The Romans tore Rabbi Akiva's skin off layer by layer in a public forum. Rabbi Akiva had a severe punishment in this life, as he surely was to have in the next. He, with Rabban Gamliel, pushed forth the greatest offense against

God and crime against the Jewish people: they sent God packing from His offer to help guide them and openly oversee them, when necessary.

Their defeat and exile from Israel, left the Jewish people a lot of time to study and reflect on what went wrong. They have never achieved answers to this critical issue and thereby stubbornly and willingly stand oblivious to why they wallow in the specter of losing Israel yet again.

OSTRACIZING GOD

This crime was so enormous and serious that it requires more time and discussion. Thus, the Deeper Analysis segment in the Appendix.

Rabban Gamliel and the Sanhedrin distorted the Torah to pass laws that even if the majority, the controlling vote of the Sanhedrin, were wrong, attested to by an intervening message from God, the Jewish people were obliged to only bow and pay homage to the directive of the majority decision of the Sanhedrin.

Thus, it was now impossible for anyone to unmask the wrongdoing by the Sanhedrin, for any opinion or effort to the contrary, to wit: dissent, would be considered an act of subversion and result in criminal penalties, including excommunication and even death.

God Himself couldn't refute the ironclad ruling and decision made under His name, one that acted and acts to remove God from a central role for Israel and the Jewish people! If they could ostracize Rabbi Eliezer, then the Jewish community knew no one could escape the decree and power of the Sanhedrin, no matter how wrong or abusive the set forth decision. As a result, a Jew could no longer argue for God's central role for the Jewish people, because elitists had assumed God's standing and role for the Jewish community and to argue otherwise was deemed, by law, subversive dissent.

This wrongdoing carried such enduring implications (the reason it is such a serious crime), that no one today has contradicted or contravened the very root cause behind the current Jewish failing. Thus, nothing was learned from the Exile and thereby Israel today finds itself in the quagmire it is in, positioned to lose the Land of Israel once again, without recognition of why it faces the problems it does.

This historical record of audacious arrogance, injustice, and abuse of power, aligned with the realities of life at that time, where children, according to Rabbi Eliezer, carried no respect for their parents, made it clear to God and the Heavenly Tribunal that if the sins connective to the trial of Rabbi Eliezer could occur after the loss of the two Temples and all else that occurred that there was no salvation for the then existing leadership and the then existing generation, compelling expulsion from the land.

Moreover, God and the Heavenly Tribunal knew, as Torah attests, that the platform then created by the subterfuge of Rabbi Akiva against his teacher and mentor, a righteous teacher, in service to God, would pollute the ability of the Jewish people to identify the correct course and impede Israel from holding onto the land, when next given, as promised.

> Rabbi Eliezer described the environment at the time he was brought to trial, in Mishna Sota 9.15 (Jewish Talmud), as follows:
>
> "The young shall shame the elders and the elders will stand up before the inferiors 'The sons dishonor the father, the daughter rise against her mother the daughter-in-law against her mother-in-law; a man's enemies will be men of his own house' (Micah 7:6). This generation's face is like a dog's face: The son is not ashamed before the father, And on whom can we rely? On {God}!

CHAPTER 8
CHRISTIANITY HIJACKED

L et us tie together on a higher plane the material hidden and secreted from us for centuries.

History past and future has been accurately defined and described by focusing on several men:

* Abraham

* Boaz

* King Solomon

* Rabban Gamliel.

Going down the small list of these four names, discussed in the first seven chapters of Clarity from a perspective you have never heard or linked together before, allows you to see and sense the degree of deterioration that each name represents to the relationship between man and God.

Abraham, simply put, was the fountainhead for the survival of his descendants. Without him, and his covenant with God, the descendants of Abraham and Sarah never would have existed at all. They would have died in the famine that his grandson Jacob and his children encountered, at the time Joseph went down to Egypt, by God's design, to save them.

Boaz, simply put, represented the time God brought Abraham and Sarah's descendants into Israel, but then the rewards of God's birthright and blessings went to people's heads, where they felt giddy enough to do as they pleased, and thereby focused upon themselves rather than their own obligations to both God and their community.

Thus Elimelech, a prime beneficiary of God's blessings, an important person to his community, picked himself and his family up, when he didn't like the idea that he would have to help carry his community during difficult times, and went off to Moab, where he knowingly put his family into a foreign environment, distancing them from God, and Israel, his people. He died in short order for his decision.

Boaz, Elimelech's kinsman, a man of influence and wealth, engendered the Sanhedrin to manipulate Divine Decree to allow him to die a happy man, married to a vibrant enchantress of a woman, whom history has named Ruth. He died in even shorter order than Elimelech.

To the resounding approval of the Moabites, and, without question, due to their own efforts, the true story of Ruth has never been openly told, albeit standing upon a mountain of facts and realities that Clarity has now highlighted and made apparent and evident to you.

Thus, we cannot escape the need to understand that Abraham's mistake with God caused, by irrevocable Divine Decree, the continued existence of the Moabites.

Here is the man that God loved, forged His covenant with, and via a moment of arrogance, where a great man, the fountainhead of our very existence, expressed himself incorrectly to God, where the Creator of all life, gave the man, whose descendants He would spare from a destiny of death, the result Abraham enlisted.

Did God give Abraham's descendants a plague? No. What God allowed is the consequence of Abraham's mistake, which would now require of his descendants a higher level of vigilance and religiosity on their parts. Thus, when Elimelech and Boaz departed from God's path and His Divine Decrees, applicable to the children of Jacob, the cancer named Ruth entered Israel.

God in His mercy and under His covenant with Abraham intervened in the birth of Obed and thereby King David, his grandson, showed the potential of Israel to follow the correct path. However, the Sanhedrin, the sages and judges of the children of Israel, who permitted the defamations to God, by twisting Divine Decree for Boaz, then simply turned a blind eye to Divine Decree when it came to King Solomon, allowing Solomon to do as he wished to do; decisions and actions that brought idolatry and many forms of sin into Israel, which ultimately cast the children of Israel into exile.

Table of Events

- Abraham

- Isaac —> Jacob —> Joseph —> Egypt—> 12 tribes—> Bondage —> Exodus

- Ten Commandments and Torah

- First Encounter with Moabites

- Entry into Israel

- Boaz (Ruth)

- King Solomon (First Temple)

- Division, creating separate government for northern tribes

- Assyrian conquest northern tribes, leaving remnant, Jews.

- Babylonian Conquest Jews (First {Babylonian} Exile)

- Second Temple (Christianity)

- Rabban Gamliel —> Rabbi Akiva—> Bar-Kokhba Rebellion (Second {Roman} Exile)

Once King Solomon violated Divine Decree, allowing idolatry into Israel, it was a direct path, historically speaking, to the disembowelment of Israel, the destruction of the First and Second Temples, followed by the exile of the remnant from the Holy Land.

Thus, the Moabites had created the perfect result for themselves.

Half the Jews in Israel were killed as the result of the failed Bar-Kokhba Rebellion. God's name was diminished. The Moabites had seized not only the wealth of Elimelech and Boaz, but now literally it had the wealth of all of Israel, and the Moabites were in their glory when the children of Israel were dispersed and exiled.

If you ask anyone about the Moabite conquest of Israel, they would not know what you are talking about. This shows you how well the Moabites control the realities we live under, even today. The main reason the Jews collectively survived the Romans is that God's covenant included the birthright. That meant that the Jewish people, the described remnant of the children of Israel, would continue on with God's protection and intervention, as the remnant of Israel, to make sure they did not assimilate or die as a people, because, without His intervention, they certainly could have done both.

Have no doubt that the Moabites would have preferred seeing every Jew, every man, woman and child of the remnant of Israel, killed by the Romans. That it did not happen, did not surprise them, due to the fact that God in His mercy routinely intervened for Israel, but that did not mean and does not mean they would not have cheered the total solution result, which would have saved them much time and effort in the future. This of course reflects the Moabite retort against God.

To better understand the dynamics of God's covenant with Israel, the Appendix hereto contains relevant segments of the author's post 9-11 writing entitled Missed Message of Torah (January 2002) that focuses on Abraham's grandson, Jacob, who was given by God the new name of "Israel." It, in more detail, discusses the birthright and the blessings that Isaac, Abraham's son, transmitted to Jacob and explains Jacob's complicated fit into the Abraham, Boaz, King Solomon, Rabban Gamliel parable discussed in Clarity. The reason that Jacob is not covered directly by Clarity is because he has no direct historical/biblical link to the Moabites.

CHRISTIANITY

Now that the Moabites effectively dealt with their Jewish problem and agenda, the Moabites set their focus and attention to the rest of the world, and thus on the emergence and advent of Christianity.

The Moabite influence, since Ruth's entry into Israel, has been so strong and dominant that they have obfuscated and distorted the true story of Christianity, to implement their designs post Israel's Exile.

The author, as a Jew who loves God, has addressed an international audience over the years that included a full spectrum of Jews, Christians and Muslims, religious and otherwise, including those whose sentiments to Jews have been less than warm.

Many in the author's audience who once carried highly negative thoughts about Jews have modified their focus and anger. The following unsolicited E-mail, one of many the author has received over the years, this one from a practicing Muslim, attests to the need for the people under monotheism to be taught what has been denied and hidden from them (emphasis in original):

> August 24, 2006: *** You have helped me beyond words to see things and to TRY to see from a Biblical perspective. I readily admit I do not share your gift...I see things after the fact from a Biblical plane when you point them out...and you have opened my world to the Torah...which I had read the Pentateuch 3 times previously...but only until you came along allowed me to UNDERSTAND it.
>
> My favorite part of the Torah had been Ezekiel and I wrote a book in 1987 on an old television series ...that sold over 100,000 copies...and Ezekiel was prominent in the interpretation of the series. Yet the rest of the Torah was "blocked" from my understanding and the Book of Ruth has become a central part of my thinking and soul. It seems as if this one story contains the breadth of human experience if you allow the metaphor to penetrate one's psyche.
>
> You are correct that historically Sunnis have been more corrupted by the Moabite influence...I had said this before. The path to corruption was the introduction of hadith as CENTRAL TO ISLAM as I have said...One Pakistani theologian has spent 30 years of his life collecting 300,000 Hadith...many of which are so patently absurd. But since the Qur'an is intact, the Moabites could not interfere with it.

The best way to understand and absorb the truth of how the Moabites intertwined themselves into the Christian reality is to start with Jesus.

When Mel Gibson released his movie the Passion of the Christ, controversy, in the unending battle of sensitivities between Christians and Jews, immediately came to the forefront. The author wrote the article below that was widely disseminated via the Internet that abated the controversy by pointing out that if Mel Gibson, as he expressed, held his movie out as historically accurate, then Mel Gibson should show Jesus for whom he was at the time of his crucifixion: a deeply religious Jew, who observed God's Divine Decrees and laws. This point was also proven via Jesus' brother, James, who lived his life adamantly beholden to the performance of the 613 commandments, a standard reflected and striven for by today's most religious Jews.

Commentary on the
Mel Gibson Movie Controversy
By Joseph B. Ehrlich
3-3-4

When {the author} assesses the presidential decisions of Bush 43, particularly regarding oil rich nations; {he} never fails to factor into his analysis the reality that global oil is Bush family business. Consequently, when he addresses the controversial Mel Gibson movie, we cannot fail to factor in that his father holds anti-Semitic views and one would be foolish to fail to understand that such environment influenced Mel Gibson, particularly in that he carries high respect for his father.

Having said this, Christian leaders are no doubt gleeful and rightfully so that the movie has proven to be a lightning rod to bring back their flocks to the Church. This is a real benefit of the movie: returning people back to God. However, understandably, the ADL and Jewish representatives are upset about the movie since it does provide a platform for those that use bible to build hate and violence. In this regard, the movie provides fodder for the new world order forces who seek to dilute religion on the given argument that religion has been the platform for hate and violence, massive death and devastation.

We have seen this dynamic recently regarding the detestable crimes committed by those holding themselves to represent good and God and victimizing young children. Evil attaches itself to good and God, to use good and God to serve their personal agendas. Thus, no doubt, the Mel Gibson movie will in fact serve the separate agendas of both good and evil. Those who want to lend an ear to good and God will do so and similarly those who want to lend an ear to hate and violence will also do so as well.

Ironically, our opinion is that those who protested against the movie ignited public interest in it against their own announced intent to cast a shadow over it. When the government in Israel moved to banish Barry Chamish's book on the Rabin Assassination, it only drew public interest in it. Similarly, the attempt to diminish Mel Gibson's movie has driven it to national and global attention.

*** While Mel Gibson proclaims that it is true to Gospel, the truth of it is that Jesus was a devout Jew critical of those who defamed and dishonored God's name. He thus was highly critical of the activities taking place on the Temple mount. He and those around him honored the bible and lived lives in accord with Jewish custom and tradition (James thereafter maintained a Christian must keep all 613 Torah commandments). However, the Jesus in the Mel Gibson movie shows no such affiliation and thus does not accurately reflect the Jesus in the time period portrayed.

The further truth is that after his death, there were two splinter groups. The one more aligned with Jesus' personal life and behavior became subservient to the one that grew into the dominant religions based on Jesus. This allowed Christianity to spread, encompass and embrace the global community. However, again, we are dealing with a movie that offers to portray the time of the death of Jesus and thus it is plain that the movie does in fact reflect the biases surrounding Mel Gibson during his life.

Further, in this regard, Jerusalem was in the control of Rome. We all know the hallmarks of Rome during that period of time. Crucifixion was the flag post of Roman evil. Countless people, including many Jews, faced death by a medium that, of course, at that time, had no religious significance.

Those representing the Jewish people in Israel at that time were of the same character and genre of the Shimon Pereses in control of Israel today: collaborators with Rome. Notably, the Jewish leadership was quite adeptly -- as the Jewish leadership today in Israel --taking the people of Israel on a course leading to their expulsion from the land.

When this course rears itself, the issues do not have their nexus to whether the Mel Gibson movie reflects truth or justice. Those critical of the movie feel that the movie is an injustice. However, this dynamic also comports and is reflective of the "injustice" seen by us that after having Torah, history, the benefits of time, every conceivable opportunity to prosper and learn, that the Jewish people reflect a nation moving away from God not to Him. The injustice is that being the child of such a loving parent that we can dishonor Him yet again and fail to have built an Israel as He desired: one bringing honor to His name. Thus, again, for the very same reasons as two thousand years ago, as we have argued since 1984, Israel is yet again on the same path and it appeared to us that we would lose it by God having us voluntarily give it up: which we are doing.

Thus concepts of fairness and justice revolving about today's events, is much more complex and far deeper than apparent. Thus, basic perceptions of fairness and justice fail to account for the deeper levels of unfairness and injustice in play, including seeing cultures aligned with God (Allah) being attacked to diminish their religious heritage. If there are claims for justice and fairness, one could first ask Jonathan Pollard his perceptions of these dynamics, and moreover one could ask the people of Islam of their perceptions of these dynamics as well. Our position is that to receive God's favor and intervention, one cannot live a life blind to one's own failings to his God and to his fellow man.

In conclusion: Mel Gibson's movie can be a platform for emerging global anti-Semitism and those in the Jewish community who attack it have only given it the long legs it may carry. The solution to the aspect of unfairness and injustice represented by the movie would be far better offset by bringing comment to the reality that Israel today, with an emerging population with no belief or conviction in God, operates to defame God's name and gift, moving Him to ultimately consider, yet again, dislodging us from the land. By directing energies toward the real issue and problem in play, many problems for the global community could in fact be resolved by an Israel moving toward the aim intended for her: to utilize her God given potential to serve as a nation of ministers for good. It is anything but that and as a consequence, as foretold by Torah, anti-Semitism in such an environment would reemerge to serve Israel's birthright in tandem with Israel's putative expulsion, when accepting new world order mandated culture change diminishes God's name in re-gifting the holy land to the Jewish people. We see the injustices that may arise due Mel Gibson's movie within a framework interpreted by Jacob and set forth by Torah long ago (Genesis 34:30). It behooves all peoples of the planet; especially those within the trilogy of religions under monotheism, to better understand it.

What Jesus and Christianity in its earliest days represented, when, of course there was no Christianity, nor any Islam, were those Jews (remember the remaining tribes had long been conquered and the survivors dispersed) that stood against the arrogance of the leadership dynamically represented by the Sanhedrin at the times of Boaz, King Solomon and of course ultimately portrayed by Rabban Gamliel.

However, since Jesus and the early Christians were opposed to such arrogance and leadership, they, of course, were determined by the Moabites to be a potential future threat. Thus, the Moabite influence enmeshed and integrated itself into what subsequently became known as Christianity, and then due to the elements within that group, history showed that the early Christians, who were God fearing Jews, were diluted and disenfranchised by the Moabite influence and integration, when Christianity subsequently openly refuted and cast off all things (Torah) Jewish from Christianity.

Thus, the early Christians, whom of course followed the Torah's holidays and laws, were out and a new set of holidays and values were in, that platformed the next phase of the Moabite infiltration: making an alliance between what became known as Christianity and Rome, where the Moabite leadership saw religion, the Church, as the ultimate vehicle and device of its day to seize wealth, consolidate control and power, to create conflict, mayhem, and war, that served the Moabites, *whom of course are nowhere mentioned or to be found in what evolved.*

Without absorbing and understanding how the Moabites operate and how they clearly were shown to enmesh themselves and integrate themselves into and take control over Israel, via Israel's known points of weakness to the Moabites, then it would be impossible to convey in the few words done that they set their sights on the Jews that became Christians to control and then mold what evolved as Christianity.

How those aligned with God could come to render forth centuries upon centuries of conflict, mayhem and war, as the platform of endless deaths and injustices, can be and is finally explained: the Moabites.

Once you understand those who have done everything they could to remain hidden and invisible throughout the centuries, and how they operate, *you can understand what men throughout the centuries thought beyond their comprehension.* That is the offered value of Clarity: to highlight the Moabites and to now bridge in forthcoming chapters how they control and dominate in today's world and geopolitical events, as to forge the future for you and your family, as they unfortunately continue to perpetrate conflict, mayhem and war against the world in their unbridled quest for total world domination and control.

S ince the Moabites control the very reality we live under, they control what we are taught and what we are not taught, whether hidden or misdirected by intentional design. The following material stands up to the expected misinformation that you already have encountered or might now encounter to keep the truth, the light of Torah, hidden.

Lot: There will be those that argue that God sent two angels to Sodom because one was there to destroy the cities of sin and the other to save Lot. The devil's advocate asserts that since an angel was assigned to Lot that it was God's intent *ab initio*, from the beginning, to spare Lot. Wrong.

The question is whether God intended to eviscerate ALL those living in Sodom? To argue that He did not so intend would be to diminish the Torah because it would be to argue that God condoned the incest between Lot and his two daughters and acted to see all that undermined His relationship with the children of Israel. Abraham loved Lot. Abraham did not know the real Lot, and when Abraham interpleaded with God, as he did for Lot, God knew that the death of Lot at that point of time would have seared Abraham's heart.

When Abraham found out that Lot fathered children with his own daughters, Abraham finally saw Lot for who he truly was, known to God, in His judgment, but unknown to Abraham. Thus, when God tested Abraham, where Abraham was directed to offer his son as a sacrifice, Abraham did not challenge or question or enter into a discourse with God. He acted to obey God's command (Abraham passed the test and did not have to sacrifice his son).

If Abraham had asked God why ALL the people of Sodom were to be destroyed, assuming there were one or more people worthy of being saved, God may have afforded Abraham an answer. However, in the manner that Abraham put forth his own true agenda, which was for Lot, God responded by granting Abraham's desire.

Further, the two angels in Sodom spoke to Lot together and the Torah reflects that **they together** told Lot to leave for "**we will destroy this place.**" Thus Torah itself refutes the argument that each angel had a single task and function, as many argue, and thus incorrectly attribute the second angel to an exclusive *ab initio* function by God to save Lot.

Those opposed to the truthful interpretation of Lot and the Moabites will use all their resources to contradict this key element. For if they can assert that God from the first intended to spare Lot, then the entire house of cards, they will say, crumbles.

Thus, God in Torah, no doubt knowing of the potential of the Moabites and their designs, once they intertwined themselves with a weak Israel, provided:

> Genesis 19:27-29 (Stone Chumash): " Abraham arose early in the morning to the place he had stood before {God}. And he gazed down upon Sodom and Gomorrah and the entire surface of the land of the plain; and saw - and behold! the smoke of the earth rose like the smoke of a kiln. And so it was when God destroyed the cities of the plain that **God remembered Abraham; so He sent Lot from amidst the upheaval** when He overturned the cities in which Lot had lived.

The biblical commentaries also give clarity to this specific and essential fact:

> Stone Chumash (p. 89, linked to Genesis 19:27): "When Abraham had concluded his pleading for Sodom, God did not tell him what the outcome would be; therefore, he arose in the morning to see what happened. In this passage, **the Torah states clearly that Lot had been spared only for the sake of Abraham.**

Lot's lechery is as plain as should be the character and nature of his daughter, when she named the child, Moab, which means "from the father." The character of the mother of Moab is in line with the true character of Ruth, the latter who hid her character and culture with a degree of sophistication and guile that escaped Lot's daughter.

Ruth's sophistication and guile resulted in a Moabite world of conflict, mayhem and war.

Boaz: The devil's argument regarding Boaz seems to center about a contention that the union of Boaz and Ruth was divine destiny to implement the Davidic line. This is curve fitting. The simple fact, in addition to all heretofore covered, that refutes it is Deuteronomy 23:6, which provides:

> Deuteronomy 23:6 "Thou shalt not seek their {Moabite} peace nor their prosperity all thy days for ever."

A man cannot marry a woman without also marrying into her family as well. Explain to the sons of Elimelech how they were supposed to honor Deuteronomy 23:6. Explain it as to not undercut God's words to Solomon in 1 Kings 11:1-13. Explain it to the reality that as a result of Boaz and Solomon Judaism and Christianity were ultimately both hijacked by the Moabites.

CONSTANTINE

Christianity subsequently deliberately moved away from Judaism and in the 4th century Constantine was the Emperor of half of the Roman Empire and Licinius the Emperor of the other half. Licinius was married to Constantine's sister, Constantia.

When Constantine ultimately defeated Licinius, in the name of Christianity, he murdered both his sister's husband (Licinius, his brother in law) and her child. Constantine's sister was a devout Christian and thus one can see the Moabite presence, even in the earliest days of Moabite influenced and amended Christianity, when Christianity rejected its Judaic roots to make it a distinct religion, serving the Moabite agenda.

In An Apology for Mohammed and the Koran, John Davenport, 1869, the book makes the following poignant comment about Constantine and Moabite influenced Christianity that stood against true Christian values, as originally expressed by Jesus and James (p. 144):

> "He {Constantine} drowned his wife in boiling water; put to death his own son Crispus; murdered the two husbands of his sisters, Constantia and Anastasia; murdered his own father-in-law, Maximilian Hercules; murdered his nephew, the son of his sister Constantia, a boy only twelve years of age, together with some others not so nearly related, among whom was Sopator, a pagan priest, who refused to give him

absolution for the murder of his (Constantine's) father-in-law. *Such was the first Christian emperor.*" (Emphasis in original)

You can imagine how Constantine treated those not family! Davenport painted the true picture of the Moabite intertwinement by describing fourteen centuries of oppression and war under Christianity as follows:

"It was at the Council of Nicea that Constantine invested the priesthood with that power whence flowed the most disastrous consequences, as the following summary will show: the massacres and devastations of nine mad crusades of Christians against unoffending Turks, during nearly two hundred years, in which many millions of human beings perished; the massacres of the Anabaptists; the massacres of the Lutherans and Papists, from the Rhine to the extremities of the North; the massacres ordered by Henry VIII and his daughter Mary; the massacres of St. Bartholomew in France; and forty years more of other massacres between the time of Francis I and the entry of Henry IV in to Paris; the massacres of the Inquisition, which are more execrable still as being judicially committed, to say nothing of the innumerable schisms, and twenty years of popes against popes, bishops against bishops, the poisonings, assassinations, the cruel rapines and insolent pretensions of more than a dozen popes, who far exceeded a Nero or Caligula in every species of crime, vice and wickedness; and lastly, to conclude this frightful list, the massacre of twelve millions of the inhabitants of the new world, executed Crucifix in hand!

"It surely must be confessed that so hideous and almost uninterrupted a chain of religious wars, for fourteen centuries, never subsisted but among Christians, and that none of the numerous nations stigmatized as heathen, ever spilled a drop of blood on the score of theological arguments."

The fact that history for centuries pointed to Israel (Jews) as the culprit in the crucifixion of Jesus is also a red flag for the Moabite design, for while Christianity was used by the Moabites for centuries as the supreme political and wealth building tool, they also took the time to flame the fires against the remnant of Jews that were cast out in the Roman Exile. Thus, while the centuries of persecution against Jews also operated as a punishment and a reality to keep the birthright intact, the hidden dynamic again was for the unceasing efforts to keep the Jews as oppressed and victimized as possible, which connected with those who lived to see all the Jews die as the intent of God was to see Lot and his family all die with the destruction He wrought against Sodom.

How could leaderships aligned publicly with God and the Ten Commandments bring forth so much death over the centuries? One of the hallmarks of the Moabites, centering about their secret family societies, is that those that spit on the cross in truth, but kiss the cross openly to the people, are those chosen to lead. This is the true nature of a Moabite leader and explains why those professing love of God have led the world into an endless stream of conflict, mayhem and wars.

King Solomon: There is no argument that can be made to cleanse King Solomon because God Himself via 1 Kings 11:11-13, declared his egregious sins and declared that the nation of Israel would be divided due to his sins. The fact that King Solomon built a temple to Chemosh counters any argument that can be made to cleanse him. Yes, you can also add the destruction of the two temples and the first exile to Babylonia, but the second exile, the Roman exile, the one that lasted until the twentieth century, falls to...

Rabban Gamliel (with an assist by Rabbi Akiva): While King Solomon diminished Israel with idolatry and the base mores of those that worshipped idols, Rabban Gamliel, with the noted assistance of Rabbi Akiva, managed to manipulate reality to cause the remnant of the children of Israel, the Jews, to cast God off and vest the full strength of His power and authority in Rabban Gamliel and the Sanhedrin. That anyone today claiming to be a Jew can give an iota of justification to what was done, continues the punishment and establishes that little to nothing was learnt during the Exile, which ended with World War II and the creation of the State of Israel in 1948.

CHAPTER 10
OLMERT'S WAR

O n June 25, 2006, Palestinians kidnapped, Gilad Shalit, an Israeli soldier.

The Palestinians kidnapping Shalit were aligned with the Fatah movement, not Hamas, as global media first suggested. In fact, Hamas members were meeting with Israelis in order to secure the soldier's release. The result of these meetings between Hamas and Israelis was that the Israeli Defense Forces were ordered to and did in fact kidnap a large number of Hamas legislators. Shin Bet, Israel's internal security service, simultaneously openly threatened the Israelis attempting to secure the soldier's release through Hamas.

The Swiss openly declared Israel's military attacks on Gaza, in reprisal, disproportionate. When two more Israeli soldiers subsequently were declared kidnapped by Hezbollah, on July 12, 2006, Israel then ran rabid, bombing Lebanon in a willful and wanton manner, as to cause numerous deaths and injuries to innocents, including women and children. Israel's religious leadership bizarrely but openly told Israeli soldiers not to be concerned with the deaths of innocents in Lebanon or elsewhere.

The author in fact interpreted this madness in November 2002, nearly four years earlier. The author, who interpreted geopolitical events and realities real time, between 9-11 and the events in the summer of 2006, knew all about the madness reflected by what many-called "Olmert's War," triggered by Israel's Prime Minister Ehud Olmert. In fact, he was expecting it since the moment Ariel Sharon was removed from the scene, due to a medical condition that the author accurately declared in advance would leave him in a persistent vegetative state.

On December 18, 2005, the author wrote on a day Sharon was hospitalized, prior to President Bush's address to the nation that evening from the Oval Office:

> I really think that Sharon's hospitalization is not coincidental and please remember that the last time {President Bush} spoke from the Oval office was when he

launched against Iraq. He has openly admitted that the mission is not complete until he brings regime change to the Middle East.

On January 4, 2006, Sharon experienced his debilitating stroke. The author noted the following on January 4th and 5th:

> I again think that Sharon twice sabotaged Bush's 'command' to move against Iran.
>
> I believe {that those wanting Sharon out of the picture} want to see Sharon live as a vegetable preferably in the same dynamic as Terry Schiavo. Without question, he will be de facto non functional and suffer greatly if he winds up living from this episode. I need not of course say that his career in politics is over. Thus, while I first thought {that those seeking to remove him} wanted him dead, ...it struck me that they might just want to make a living example of him by putting him into the same medical state as Terry Schiavo. Let me put this another way, the only way they can allow Sharon to live is if he cannot communicate what he knows. Thus, the safest way...is death; however, I got the sense that they want to make, as I just said, a living example of him.

The following is an extraordinary article published January 6, 2006, in the Israeli newspaper Haaretz:

Hospital director: Letting Sharon go to Negev farm was negligent

By Ran Reznick, Amos Harel and Aluf Benn, Haaretz Correspondents

Several senior doctors raised a host of questions Thursday about the standard of treatment Ariel Sharon has received over the last two weeks, with the director of a large hospital telling Haaretz that according to the media reports on

Sharon's medical treatment, he fears "there was indescribable negligence."

The questions cover the period from Sharon's first stroke two weeks ago to his arrival Wednesday night at Jerusalem's Hadassah University Hospital, Ein Karem, where he is being treated for a severe stroke and cerebral hemorrhage. They pertain to the supervision over Sharon's physical state, following the blood-thinning medicine he received after his first hospitalization.

Such supervision is essential, as these medicines could cause a cerebral hemorrhage, like the one Sharon suffered. Questions were also raised about the dosage he received.

"Yitzhak Rabin was not wearing a bulletproof vest that could have protected him from the murderers' bullets, and now, 10 years later, Sharon was not given the required medical treatment that could have saved him," the hospital director said. "Israel has not learned the lesson from Rabin's murder, and thus lost two prime ministers because of inadequate protection - one from weapons, the other from illness. I cannot understand how the prime minister could have been sent to stay in an isolated farm, more than an hour away from the hospital he was supposed to be treated in, two weeks after a stroke and one night before a heart procedure he was afraid of."

Sharon was slated to undergo a cardiac catheterization procedure Thursday to fix a small hole between the chambers of his heart that doctors said contributed to his initial stroke.

"A night before the catheterization he should have been hospitalized in Hadassah or at least made to stay in Jerusalem," the director said. "I also have questions about the dosage of blood-thinning medication he received. My feeling is that Sharon did not get the best medical treatment he deserved."

The author could recognize what Sharon was doing and that those opposed to him were out to murder him, because four years earlier, in November 2002, he wrote:

The reality is that now both Israel and the Arab world do not trust the Bush administration, and quite frankly, no doubt Americans will no longer as well as the Bush administration's amoral nexus to 9-11 and other designs unravel. However, the point is that Sharon came back to Israel, **knowing that his life was at risk,** and also now knowing that the US may very well be setting up Israel to take a fall for the reasons articulated. He cannot take the chance that it may be the case. **Thus, he will not go by the Bush game plan, allowing Israel to succumb while he is at the helm.**

What has been covered in the first nine Chapters of Clarity allowed the author to make this prescient analysis. The full analysis made is embodied in his 2002 position paper entitled The Bush Double Double Cross, highlighted in the next chapter.

Thus, in December 2005, Sharon went behind Bush's back to defy Bush's game plan, and after Sharon was removed from the picture, as the author originally feared would prove his fate, Ehud Olmert, an Israeli Prime Minister, who was willing to comply with the game plan, replaced him. In August 2006, however, the war came to a sudden stop, mystifying everyone globally as to what exactly happened to stop the hostilities.

On July 30, 2006, the Hezbollah leader, Sheikh Hassan Nasrallah, publicly declared Israel an **"American slave."** This single declaration suggested, according to the author's public analysis, a new era of relations between Israel and its neighbors.

CHAPTER 11
THE MOABITE THIRST FOR REGIONAL WAR

Assume you are sitting with the Moabite leadership in January 2001 discussing plans regarding Israel and the Middle East. Based on what you now know about Moabite historical agendas, what type of discussion would you expect to overhear?

You, of course, would overhear discussion about the need to eliminate Israel. You would also hear that since World War II and the subsequent creation of the State of Israel that it has become a nation distant from God, yet again. The Moabites would assent among themselves that they have instilled within Israel's leadership, having fully infiltrated Israel's infrastructure, a desire to become a nation among nations, similar to the political realities attendant to the ten tribes ultimately invaded and destroyed by the Assyrians.

You would also overhear that Israel has no real wealth whatsoever. However, the discussion regarding this topic would move to the Arab/Islamic nations that control Middle East oil, the repository of modern day wealth and global political power. You would also hear that among those Arab/Islamic nations is the last major vestige of a theocratic nation under monotheism bowing openly to God: Iran. Theocratic government is anathema to the Moabite. The mission then would be to seize the oil wealth, destroy Israel, while further moving to defame and diminish God by sabotaging Iranian theocracy.

Those at the table would be discussing that regardless of the wealth held and accumulated by them all throughout history, the element to their destiny that continues to evade them is global domination and control. With the start of the new millennium, they agree that it is time to move ahead to aggressively take in hand what they see as rightfully theirs: control of planet earth.

In 1948, for the first time since the Roman exile, the Jews returned to sovereign government in the Holy Land. The Torah provided that the Jews would be put to the test whether they would recognize that their blessings have been from God, whether they learned anything from the 2000 years in Exile, and to determine whether they were willing again to turn their backs on God to wit, whether they were ready to understand what happened in the past and implore God to return, after apologizing for all that requires apologizing to Him regarding. Thus, in 2006 we find the Moabites extant in the same dynamic with Israel as they were in biblical times. Will the Jews recognize the pattern or will they again be blinded by secular realities and fail to see or react to the Moabite presence?

We now focus upon the events in June 2006, where Palestinians kidnapped an Israeli soldier named Gilad Shalit. Based on this single event, the Moabites triggered their move, where ultimately Israel waged war against Lebanon, to trigger regional war in order to gain control over Iran, to consolidate their hold over Middle East oil, while simultaneously eliminating the nation they hold most repulsive to their very own existence: Israel.

The author long knew that this effort would be made and he also knew that the Moabite effort would fail, despite all the military might and resources of the United States of America and Israel, both current day Moabite surrogates. *Being a Moabite surrogate does not spare either the USA or Israel from also being a Moabite target and victim.*

To succinctly show how the author deployed the truths conveyed in this book to know in advance the agenda that showed itself in June 2006, below is an article that circled the globe in 2002, and went into the hands of then Prime Minister Ariel Sharon. Note that the Moabite invasion against Iraq, via its infiltrated surrogate, the United States of America, did not launch until March 2003, four months after the article was written.

However, before setting forth the article, entitled The Bush Double Double Cross, it might be wise to quickly cover a topic outside the scope of this book: the Moabite infiltration of the United States of America. The following words excerpted from an Internet posting by an American mother and citizen adeptly portrays a reality that the author openly warned the American people about since the mid 1990s and via his first novel, Recapturing America.

I Am Angry

I know why I am an angry American. I am frightened because America isn't the same country it was when I was my children's age. Allow me to share with you some of the reasons why I am an angry American.

I am angry because my government has been taken over by liars, thieves, thugs, deviants, and micromanagers. The propaganda it produces rivals that of the most fascist dictatorship.

I am angry that my government perceives my intelligence to be that of a jar of pickles incapable of making the smallest decision.

I am angry that my government takes it upon itself to shove its clucking nose into my pantry, medicine chest, bedroom, family room, doctor's office, workplace, and everywhere else it thinks I need guidance to keep me safe from myself.

I am angry that the will of the American people is ignored on every issue imaginable. If voting really mattered, it would have been outlawed long ago.

I am angry that the evil puppets in power think laws are created for the peon masses and it is their right to ignore the ones that get in the way of their agenda.

I am angry that the media has sold its soul to the evil forces running the world.

I am angry that my "leaders" have taken to calling my country the "homeland." It reeks of socialism.

I am angry that property rights are a thing of the past thanks to court-approved eminent domain theft.

I am angry that the Constitution is routinely declared irrelevant making it easier for a fascist police state and new world order to take over.

I am angry when I read stories of Americans terrorized in airports and treated like common criminals by government minions after they have paid for the right to travel within a private system, yet pilots are blocked from carrying firearms.

I am angry that America has become a nation of busybodies. We are constantly bombarded with messages to be on the lookout for terrorists around every corner, report "suspicious activity," and rat on our neighbor whenever the opportunity presents itself. Is this not how the Nazis gained control of Germany and then most of Europe?

I am angry that my government meddles in the lives of people all over the world but looks the other way on the catastrophic issue of what to do about the millions of illegals who have crashed the gates of this nation. My country's laws are ignored and mocked, yet I am told I must accept with open arms those who are here illegally. My taxes are used to educate their children in their native language. Hospitals are overrun with indigent people seeking medical care. Untaxed dollars earned in the underground economy are sent to the family back home while social services here are stretched to the limit. I read job want ads stating if you aren't bilingual don't bother to apply. What would happen to me if I placed an ad that said don't bother to apply if your English isn't understandable? Marches are conducted in my cities' streets waving their countries' flags as they shamelessly demand their "rights." I am told they deserve the same opportunities that brought my forefathers here. I am scolded that it is un-American to ask why they are not sent home. I am told that the term "illegal alien" offends them and that they prefer to be called "undocumented workers" and that my economy would die without them. I will happily pay more for fruits and vegetables if it means enforcing sensible immigration laws. But immigration isn't about the cost of lettuce. It is another facet of an agenda that is bent on changing the face of America. When America is no longer a wealthy country of white European descent, it will be a place worse than anything Orwell could have imagined.

I am angry that the thugs that run my country don't have the guts to declare English my nation's official language.

I am angry that I have to search a package for English and push a button on every telephone system and ATM machine to continue in English.

I am angry that Washington, D.C.'s Metro is now being pressured to replace every station sign with bilingual verbiage to the tune of millions of dollars. Are bilingual road signs going to be the next mandated law of the land? I am currently forced to pay for voting ballots printed in 15 different languages and my tax dollars pay for interpreter services for people who are summoned to court for breaking laws. If English is the international language of the world, why isn't it good enough to be the official language of the United States?

I am angry when I am told I am a bigot when I thumb my nose at political correctness.

I am angry when I wonder whether an expressed belief or opinion could land me in litigation if someone doesn't like what I said and wants to silence my voice.

I am angry that the symbols, customs, and roots of my Judeo-Christian country are being systematically outlawed because my culture offends newcomers. When we freely choose to go somewhere, are we not accepting the customs and cultures of that place? I am weary of being made to feel guilty for being an American.

And finally, I am angry that after working my entire adult life, I don't see retirement in my life's picture. My husband and I earn over a hundred thousand dollars a year, but by the time we pay federal taxes, state taxes, social security taxes, property taxes, sales taxes, excise taxes, energy taxes, telecommunication taxes, savings taxes, fees, permits, etc., there isn't much left. But please don't think that I mind supporting every deadbeat and down-and-outer with his hand out for a piece of my pie that I worked so hard for. I love supporting the world. After all, it's the American way, isn't it?

Would you believe that you could now explain to this woman why she is angry?

Her nation has been infiltrated and de facto conquered just as Israel was infiltrated and de facto conquered in the past and present, by the very same people, remaining invisible to the Judeo-Christian world, because, as the descendants of Lot, they blend in perfectly to hide their existence and role in the Moabite realities for the world.

The Torah details that the Moabites, despite the disappearance of biblical Moab, exist and continue to implement their stealth designs upon us.

Who can point them out? Who can point out those men and women that intermesh themselves within the Judeo-Christian ethic that have the similar role today as Ruth had in biblical times and days?

Thus, it should now strike you why the truths about Ruth have been suppressed throughout our history.

Once the truths are properly taught, people would not need to vent their frustration, as the above person has, but would have long ago stood vigilant and cognizant of the Moabites and their ways, in order to stop them from seizing control of infrastructure of nations once solidly under the Judeo-Christian ethic and today suddenly distant from it, promoting pagan values in lieu thereof. The Moabite goal is to wipe out (via culture change or military action) all nations still aligned with God.

Doesn't it strike you as odd that America has moved and continues moving to make Sodomite values mainstream? Doesn't it strike you as odd that major American cities look more each day like the cities God destroyed?

The Bush Double Double Cross

Joseph Ehrlich

11-3-2002

(Four months prior to Bush's War and nearly four years prior to Olmert's War)

http://www.rense.com/general31/thebushdoubledouble.htm

This is going to be a very deep and scary analysis and interpretation on top of the ones we have already issued concerning President Bush and his administration. Those with a nexus to the putative amoral creation of requisite moral outrage for the war against terrorism really may have exceeded all bounds of decency in planning out new world order world domination and control.

Let's go back to the Saudi initiative in late March 2002. In accordance with our interpretation, the Arab League in Beirut was unified across the board in the Saudi initiative. This only suggested to us that Israel and the US had already agreed to it. Notably, within 24 hours, Sharon initiated the claimed "criminal" incursion into the West Bank, without anyone, anyone at all, bolting from the Beirut unified position or threatening to. This immediately ratified our interpretation that Arafat was the safest man in the Middle East and our truly incredible but sadly true interpretation that what was playing out was staged and orchestrated.

What is critical to see at this juncture is what were the Arab League and Israel told by the Bush administration to persuade them to undertake the staging and orchestration? Were both parties told the same thing to manifestly further the Saudi initiative *or was each party told something highly beneficial to it at the expense of the other?*

Israel no doubt immediately recognized what we ourselves concluded: simple serious acts of terrorism would undermine the entire Saudi initiative. Thus the Bush administration in our respectful opinion sold the Israeli government on the absolute need to eliminate all Arab/Islamic regimes that would ultimately undermine or uproot the planned peace to wit: Iraq, Syria and Iran. Sharon was told to go into the West Bank and Gaza and eliminate every known terrorist (after the platform was created with the lives of innocents including children), and once doing so that *the United States would then proceed against Iraq as a prelude for the US and Israel to effectuate regime change in Syria and Iran.*

It all looked good to Israel. The United States would be in control of all enemy states and Israel could only be a major beneficiary of the US agenda.

What Israel never saw was that it fell into the Chinese trap and design when it went into the West Bank to reoccupy it in punishment for the terrorism (as a mask to undertake elimination of all terrorist cells). What Israel could not itself see even with all its intelligence and analytic brilliance was that the US strategic design of having Israel suffer from Palestinian terrorism to predicate its incursion into the West Bank and Gaza to eliminate local terrorists cells, put them into a reality of economic malaise approaching economic collapse (foreseen by Chinese intelligence working in parallel with the Arab/Islamic nations, the Chinese urging the Arab/Islamic nations not to trust the US when it came to Israel).

Israel lost its vital tourism industry and compounded the financial implosion by pulling out reservists from the already damaged and sinking economy. Sharon very soon thereafter realized the trap he fell into and adjusted the depth of the planned reoccupation of the West Bank. He went to President Bush seeking additional financial assistance to escape the Chinese design.... President Bush has put Sharon into a quagmire telling him that he is compelled to close the dollar window for political reasons at this time for both Israel and the Palestinians (Bush telling Sharon not to worry --Sharon worried has submitted a plea for $10 billion in US aid to compensate for the staged and orchestrated terrorism and its unforeseen consequences).

Moreover, what Israel never expected, once committing to the Bush plan, was that on June 24, 2002, Bush would escalate the conflict between Israel and the Palestinians to one between Islam and the West (the US). President Bush came out and ratified what we had been saying all along: that the US wanted to mold the Arab/Islamic nations into the image of the new world order agenda to wit: *remove Allah from His central role for the Arab/Islamic people.*

Israel already in the abyss had to endure the reality of the National Security Strategy, which announced that President Bush and his administration was out for world domination and control. What must have petrified the Israeli government was what we immediately concluded: President Bush deliberately went out to unify the Arab/Islamic world and China against not only the United States, but Israel as well. Why was President Bush so openly brazen about it?

The only reason we could see for him doing so is that it committed the United States to the attack against Iraq. It was long apparent to us that Saddam Hussein despite his being the personification of evil was never the target of US policy but the bogeyman for its true pursuit: Islamic oil. When President Bush post 9-11 went into Afghanistan, we immediately noted his global language praising the Saudis and Pakistanis for their support of the US military effort and incursion.

The Saudis and Pakistanis leaderships no doubt called President Bush and told him thanks but no thanks: no need to praise their cooperation with the US agenda. {The author} proffered to the House and Senate Intelligence committees that President Bush's true agenda was to initiate rebellion against both governments so that he could intervene to seize and control Islamic nuclear and oil.

Rebellion did not materialize. What did materialize was the Saudi initiative, suicide bombings against Israel, Sharon's incursion into the West Bank to eliminate terrorist cells, to lay the groundwork for the US design to now attack Iraq on the basis of undertaking regime change of all countries supporting terrorism and operating against Oslo or the Saudi initiative.

However, two new developments. First, Sharon when he realized the trap he fell into, decided to turn the tables and put the West Bank and Gaza into a similar dynamic, so to his mind if anyone was trying to engender the collapse of the Jewish State, he was responding by encouraging the Palestinian people to abandon the West Bank and Gaza by making their lives equally unpalatable.

Israel was consumed with offsetting the economic phase of the attack upon it, and regretting how it fell into the trap, now having to beg for billions from the US on the basis that it should not suffer in this manner from following the US guidelines "for peace." It could not see the forest again from the trees.

We then offered our extreme interpretation that Israel was at the mercy of the Bush administration, pointing out that Israel was overlooking the tragic obvious: *how could the US justify its design for Arab/Islamic oil bringing along Israel before the world as a co-beneficiary of its design and ultimate effort?*

This was a pretty good point we were making. We pointed out that the US design, even before the NSS and the Rose Garden remarks, was for oil. Now, since the Rose Garden remarks, it became very clear that President Bush and his administration were out for all the oil, any lingering doubt removed with the National Security Strategy. Thus, when the US attacked, the game plan as understood by Sharon, was for Israel to engage Syria (helped along by the fact that the Congress now only allows Bush to attack Iraq), to remove Hussein and Assad in one major swoop. Israel's problems would be essentially over. *But would they be over? Or would the reality be no Israel or an Israel barely clinging to life?*

When Sharon recently went to Washington for final consultations with President Bush prior to the planned US attack on Iraq, he without doubt posited this disturbing dynamic: how was the US going to face the consequences of a victorious Israel when the US was going to undertake an occupation of Iraq and capture and seize all its oil?

Were there those in his administration who were touting to the President the material benefits of a failed Israel? Would massive deaths in Israel provide the US with the requisite moral outrage to control if not seize all Middle East oil? Would such results give the US what it wanted and needed: oil and removal of the Chinese presence and design in the Middle East? It became increasingly apparent to Israel that if Israel was victorious in the US occupation and campaign that it would cause the US many long term problems and that *with a failed Israel it would solve the remainder of the US's problems.*

We now interpret that Sharon who just the other day proclaimed to the world that Israel never had a better friend in the White House than Bush 43, now carries serious concerns about what answers he received from President Bush.

This analysis written in November 2002 incredibly accurately overlaid the very events taking place in connection with Sharon's removal from office in January 2006 and regarding Israel's war with Lebanon in the summer of 2006. The November 2002 analysis continues...

It is multi dimensional and deep but this is all historically important. **We were concerned a short time ago that Sharon was a possible target for assassination.** We interpreted that with an imminent attack against Iraq, the NWO was not happy in having a supreme military man like Sharon in control of Israel. He may launch counter attacks out of preset boundaries; Sharon like Rabin was committed to the best interests of the Jewish State when under attack. Similar to the times of Rabin, if something happened to Sharon, Shimon Peres would assume the Prime Minister post and the Minister of Defense was already another {Moabite} pawn and poodle.

However, what happened since that putative assassination assessment is that President Bush got slammed big time at the UN by all the other countries fully knowing his agenda against Iraq and the rest of the region and taking the US to task for it.

While it was always crystal clear to us, it seems that since the NSS document it has become more clear to the rest of the world, who was now intent to tell the President that his policies of unilateralism were going to be rejected and that his attempt to obtain a cloak of approval was not going to succeed.

So now, we have Sharon going back to Israel after getting his final marching instructions regarding the US attack on Iraq, and Israel's overt and covert roles, and we are shocked to see that Peres and Ben-Eliezer, the NWO Foreign Minister and Defense Minister resign on the flimsiest of pretexts.

The original news reports are focused on Ben-Eliezer, that he undertook the strategy to serve himself in his attempt to rest control of the Labor party. However, these claimed political machinations are minimized by the overlooked fact that Shimon Peres agreed to resign and he controls Ben-Eliezer not vice versa.

THIS TELLS US THAT BUSH WILL NOT NOW INITIATE THE ATTACK ON IRAQ BUT THAT HE PLANS ON FORCING ISRAEL TO INITIATE A REGIONAL WAR WHERE BUSH WILL INTERCEDE ON BEHALF OF ISRAEL AGAINST SYRIA AND IRAQ.

To understand this new perceived path, we have to now look over the dynamics from the Arab/Islamic side of the equation. First, why would the entire Arab League in Beirut support the Saudi initiative? Second, why when Sharon within 24 hours went into the West Bank would not a single state including Syria and Libya not bolt from the accord reached just hours before in Beirut?

One has to today conclude that while the Bush administration was selling Sharon on the ultimate end of undermining Arab/Islamic regimes, *that the Arab/Islamic states were being sold by the Bush administration that there would be no Israel or a drastically reduced Israel and that the Holy City would be theirs to share as they pleased.*

It wasn't just that the 67 portion of Israel was going to revert to the Arab world, but everything. This is the only incentive that could make sense to the entire Arab League playing along with a strategy, which required Sharon to make an incursion into the West Bank without anyone bolting from the Arab League accord in Beirut.

The US specified its interests in terms of eliminating the threat of terrorism, especially suicide bombers, hitting the shores of the US, with the Arab League, we surmise, not understanding that once Israel reverted in full to the Arab world that there would be no need to eliminate terrorists.

Thus, this suggested that the need to eliminate terrorism had to do with what the Arab League thereafter saw was that the true goal of the US was not the mask of WMD or suicide bombers, but its critical asset oil (previously seeing it as a pretext to set up Israel for the inevitable under the Bush NWO agenda). Not only Iraqi oil and oil reserves but control of all other regional oil, especially Saudi oil. This was not supposed to be so obvious and clear to the Arab League but we below cite {full article in Appendix} the dates and language of some of our analyses making it clear that we concluded we could not agree with US policies which preemptively went out not to protect our nation but to illegally seize and control Middle Eastern oil because the government didn't like the reality that China went out during the Clinton term and captured the Middle East and now the NWO oil cartel was not going to lose its relationship with Middle East oil powers and indirect historical control of Middle East oil.

We must interject that if there was any chance of saving it, President Bush irrevocably lost it and played into China's hand by releasing the National Security Strategy, the dumbest move for US interests one could ever imagine.

The Bush administration is probably on serious medication having to play this deeply dangerous game of telling Israel that it is its best friend, and still having the nerve to tell the Arab League that the US is simply doing all these convoluted maneuvers to set up the environment so that they can have back the Holy City and that Israel will no longer be an issue in a future relationship between the US and the Arab world (saying that they have reason to align for the future with the US rather than China, who the US tells the Arab world, especially Saudi Arabia, cannot be trusted).

Conclusions: **The reality is that now both Israel and the Arab world do not trust the Bush administration, and quite frankly, no doubt Americans will no longer as well as the Bush administration's amoral nexus to 9-11 and other designs unravels. However, the point is that Sharon came back to Israel, knowing that his life was at risk, and also now knowing that the US may very well be setting up Israel to take a fall for the reasons articulated. He cannot take the chance that it may be the case. Thus, he will not go by the Bush game plan, allowing Israel to succumb while he is at the helm.**

Thus, Peres reporting about Sharon's concerns, was no doubt directed to leave the Sharon government. The question is for what purpose? The {Moabites running the US} no doubt has reached the new conclusion offered above that its interests are now better served by having Israel initiate the attack and then having the US intercede for it.

You have to understand the depth of this new design. In each step, depending on the results, the Bush administration is situated to play either scenario, or the one we believe is now in play: **the Bush double double cross, where both Israel is lost and the Arab regimes undermined per US ends.**

With the Arab world under US control (in punishment for the devastation to Israel), those who are livid over the loss of Israel are assuaged, while with Israel lost, a new platform for a renewed US relationship with the Arab world is created over time, giving them the Holy City as a prize for losing the oil and their sovereignty. This leaves the Bush administration only with China to deal with, now having effectively removed it from the Middle East.

Now, assuming that China, Israel and the Arab League understand what we proffer, what can we expect to see to offset this design?

(The author} hopes you understand that all the above represents our contention that all roads lead to the same result unless Israel primarily in here undertakes the religious resolution with the Arab/Islamic world.

What you have just read represents mutuality of interests between them, because they are both being set up for the Bush double double cross. Thus, we are here to promote the religious resolution between Israel and the Arab/Islamic world for this will permit as we argued long ago the US to clean shop from the NWO influences who take us on the road to our own destruction here at home, and that is where China comes into the picture.

Succinctly put, we believe that China has given Syria for its steadfastness, in not caving in to US pressures, protection against US design to overthrow its regime, and we believe it has given the same

assurances to Iran, and thus you can see how close we are to not only
regional but global war, and the reasons therefor.

The above assertion, which was purely speculative to most intelligence analysts, proved incredibly true as protection pacts did evolve between China and both Iran and directly or indirectly with Syria. The November 2002 analysis continues...

> However, in this paper, we are detailing the perceived double double cross strategy of the Bush administration, made even more evident to us with the forced collapse of the Sharon government. Sharon's new Defense Minister is a hawk, and the US no doubt, will encourage Israel to defend itself, and there will no doubt be enough terrorism for Israel to initiate a regional conflict in its legitimate defense, where the US will enter to "save the region and the world."

> While we can envision strategies Israel and the Arab world can or may independently deploy to offset Bush's double double cross, they will be to no avail, for again, but for the religious resolution, all roads lead to disaster.

> Look at some of the things below {the author} wrote in early 2002 and see how true they have become {the full article is in the Appendix}. The US had turned its back not only on God, but on its own Constitution, and for the stock market wealth given under Clinton, they looked aside as corruption and greed became institutionalized in the American infrastructure. Payment for that error is now being extracted.

> With Peres gone from the government of Israel, the gateway has opened for Sharon to pursue a true peace.

> We respectfully submit that you do everything possible to convince the Prime Minister that any course other than the religious resolution will lead to the devastation of the State of Israel.

> The Arab nations are not Israel's enemies. By failing to recognize the correct course, Israel and the Arab/Islamic world will succumb, each in their own way, and open the gateway to the ultimate conflict and contest between the US and China, where the US will pay for its grievous errors and sins {as surrogate for the Moabites in an agenda that seeks to defame and diminish God}.

Thus, the US, Israel and Arab/Islamic world should all recognize that the only course to serve their own futures is the religious resolution. Abandon God and the future can only be dark and dire without His intervention. ~~~END

Notably, in August 2006, when Israel was facing intense pressure from the Moabites to continue disproportionate military action against Lebanon to inflame Syria and Iran into direct military action, President Jimmy Carter, the last president to serve before the Moabites took deep control of the American government, had the courage to declare:

Carter: Bush Israel's 'worst ally' in D.C.

Saturday, August 5, 2006; Posted: 11:04 p.m. EDT (03:04 GMT)

In my opinion, maybe the worst ally Israel has had in Washington has been the George W. Bush administration, which hasn't worked to bring a permanent peace to Israel," Carter told the newspaper.

It should be apparent why the author anticipated and thus fully understood the truth behind Sharon's assassination. President Bush wanted Sharon to follow the Moabite design to trigger a regional war. Sharon aware of the design feigned illness in December 2005 as a final effort to further sandbag Israel undertaking a course where it was likely to fail as a nation (since Israel's evisceration was part of the moral outrage predicate for the Moabites to move the USA military into Iran). When the Moabites detected Sharon's resistance, then when coupled with the risk inherent with a proven Jewish General in charge of the maneuvers in pursuit of the Moabite design, the decision was made to remove Sharon as the Moabites removed Elimelech. When this analysis was proffered the author, as an aside, declared that he expected the Moabites, due to their anger with Sharon, to see him wind up in a Terri Schiavo persistent vegetative state. This incredibly, as already expressed, turned true.

When Ehud Olmert and his Defense Minister Amir Peretz took office, after Sharon was permanently incapacitated, the Moabites ordered their pawn and poodle Olmert to trigger a regional war. What the Moabites did was have Mahmoud Abbas, the man who succeeded Yasser Arafat, head of the Fatah party, the Palestinian political element under the influence and de facto control of the Moabites, kidnap a soldier named Gilad Shalit. This took place on June 25, 2006. The author immediately assessed that this was a Moabite move to trigger a regional war. This is exactly what happened. To implement the Moabite design, Olmert pursued a disproportionate response.

Monday, July 3, 2006 ·Last updated 11:36 p.m. PT

Switzerland: Israel violating law in Gaza

By BRADLEY S. KLAPPER

ASSOCIATED PRESS WRITER

GENEVA – Switzerland accused Israel of violating international law in its Gaza offensive by inflicting heavy destruction and endangering civilians in acts of collective punishment banned under the Geneva Conventions.

Switzerland said Monday that Israel's destruction last week of the main Gaza electricity power station and its attack on the office of the Palestinian prime minister were unjustified.

It also urged Israel to free dozens of arrested officials of the ruling Hamas group, including Cabinet ministers and lawmakers.

Israel has used tanks, troops, gunboats and aircraft to attack the Gaza area over the past week to press militants to free a captured Israeli soldier.

"A number of actions by the Israeli defense forces in their offensive against the Gaza Strip have violated the *principle of proportionality* and are to be seen as forms of collective punishment, which is forbidden," the Swiss Foreign Ministry said in a statement.

"The arbitrary arrests of a large number of democratically elected representatives of the people and ministers ... cannot be justified," the ministry added.

Source:
http://seattlepi.nwsource.com/national/1103AP_Switzerland_Israel.html

Ehrlich {Real-Time Analysis}: The evidence is that Hamas had nothing to do with the kidnapping of Shalit. The {evidence} shows that during this period it was a military group aligned with Fatah that was moving out aggressively and that the {Moabites}deployed it to create this very environment that if the Palestinians and Arabs had responded differently would have resulted already in a state of war. The {Moabites}fail to recognize how sophisticated the Arab/Islamic leadership has become and that they are willing to resonate with principles truly aligned with the Qur'an in putting forth their response. In fact, just this morning I read that I believe a Hamas spokesman attested that Shalit would not be killed regardless due to precepts within the Qur'an applicable to Shalit. There is no question in my mind who benefits if he is killed: it is not Hamas.

The news stories were troublesome to people around the world. Due to the kidnapping of soldiers (Gilad Shalit on June 25 in Gaza and Ehud Goldwasser and Eldad Regev in Lebanon on July 12), Israel undertook disproportionate action against both Gaza and Lebanon. Israel was acting as though it was in a rabid rage, openly committing injustices against the Palestinian and Lebanese people. The fact that both Syria and Iran could sit on the sidelines doing nothing was humiliating to both the Iranian and Syrian populations. Didn't their governments plan on intervening to stop the Israeli madness?

The Moabite design was to have Israel, as a Moabite surrogate, trigger a regional war, bringing in both Syria and Iran. Once Iran, known to the Moabites as in possession of advanced weaponry and the intelligence to destroy Haifa, Tel-Aviv and much more, used those weapons to create the moral predicate (massive death in Israel), the Moabites would deploy the USA military, as the surrogate, to consolidate Moabite control over both Iraqi and Iranian oil. Otherwise, without Syria and Iran engaging Israel, neither Israel nor anyone else could move against either Syria or Iran because of protection pacts between these countries and China.

The Moabites were frustrated. Israel was lobbing deadly accurate bombs within meters of the Syrian border and yet all attempts to cajole Syrian and Iranian involvements did not produce the expected results.

During this period, a number of things became apparent. The author appeared on the Jeff Rense Show on August 7, 2006, in order to further crystallize that not only was there an intentional design to trigger a regional war but that the Moabites had no reservation in seeing China itself involve itself in military action in the Middle East. If the Moabites were to obtain what they long wanted: world domination and control, China was the final impediment to their unfettered quest for it.

The author's assessment is below. But first take a look at the following article that highlights that Olmert's War was a Moabite staged event.

Israeli army faulted in soldier's capture
Updated 7/10/2006 10:39 PM ET

TEL AVIV, Israel (AP) - The head of an inquiry investigating how Palestinian militants captured an Israeli soldier said Monday that **despite warnings of a planned attack, Israeli forces reacted slowly to the raid and failed to note the soldier was missing for nearly 90 minutes.**

Speaking at a news conference at national military headquarters, retired brigadier general Giora Eiland described the June 25 incident, in which seven Palestinians sneaked through a tunnel under the border from Gaza and attacked an Israeli tank and a nearby lookout tower.

Calling the attack "an operational failure" on Israel's part, Eiland said four of the Palestinians had escaped back into Gaza with tank crewmember Cpl. Gilad Shalit six minutes after the first shots were fired and well before the army grasped the magnitude of the situation.

Three of the Palestinians were killed in a firefight at the start of the clash, and two soldiers were killed.

Although the attack began at 5:13 a.m., it was 6:41 a.m. before Shalit was reported as missing, Eiland said.

Four days before the incident near the intersection of the Israeli, Egyptian and Gaza borders, the army closed a nearby access gate to European observers. It cited a fear of a pending Palestinian attack.

Eiland confirmed that the military had received intelligence indicating the potential for trouble there.

"There was a warning, I say this clearly, the best there could be under the circumstances," he said. "There was definitely a warning, and I would even say a sound warning."

The capture of Shalit, 19, along with a barrage of homemade rockets launched from Gaza into southern Israel, triggered an Israeli offensive in Gaza that began June 28 and has killed at least 58 Palestinians.

The Hamas-linked militants holding Shalit, who are believed to be hiding him in southern Gaza, have called on Israel to free hundreds of Palestinian prisoners to help end the standoff.

Israel says it will not trade for Shalit's release.

The army's chief of staff, Lt. Gen. Dan Halutz, said after receiving Eiland's report that there had been failures at various levels in the chain of command but no disciplinary action would be taken against individual officers.

"Nevertheless, the chief of staff noted that he intends to speak personally to specific commanders," the army statement said.

There is little question that the Shalit kidnapping was a set up. Abbas was party to it because the Moabites toyed with him telling him that it would result in a de facto coup against Hamas and restore him to full power. Hamas, unaligned with the Moabites, had captured a surprise political victory in the Palestinian Authority's general elections. Hamas was aligned with Moabite archenemy Iran and thus had to go. Thus, after Shalit was kidnapped on June 25, 2006, note the following news stories.

June 26 2006

Rabbis, Hamas officials to meet over kidnapping

Israeli rabbis, Hamas members in Jerusalem will meet to discuss ways that may bring to kidnapped soldier's release

June 29 2006

64 Hamas officials seized

Ramallah - Israeli troops arrested 64 members of governing Palestinian party Hamas, including eight ministers, in a massive overnight operation, military sources said on Thursday

The very last thing the Moabite plan needed was a resolution to the Shalit kidnapping (with, no less, the involvement of Hamas). To satisfy Abbas and his needed role, and to add further fuel to the fire for regional war, Olmert had the IDF seize (kidnap) 64 duly elected and appointed Hamas officials. This of course also was to sandbag discussions between parties moving forward to genuinely resolve the situation. After the kidnapping of 64 Hamas legislators, there was nothing to talk about, not to say anyone to talk to.

PRESS RELEASE {one month later}

Drafted by Nafeez Mosaddeq Ahmed, Department of International Relations, University of Sussex

For immediate release 28.7.06

SHIN BET VETOED SECRET ISRAELI-PALESTINIAN PEACE AGREEMENT

Israeli and Palestinian Sources Concur: Israel Made War Inevitable.

The Omega Institute (OI), which works closely with the Institute for Policy Research for Development (IPRD), has learned from Israeli and Palestinian sources that just prior to the current crisis, senior Hamas leaders were in active dialogue with Israeli religious leaders in a round of bilateral peace negotiations. Israeli negotiators included Rabbi Menachem Froman, former deputy leader and co-founder of the Israeli Settler movement Gush Khatif; Rabbi David Bigman, head of the liberal religious

Kibbutz movement Yeshiva at Ma'ale Gilboa; and Yitzhak Frankenthal, founder of the Arik Institute. Ongoing negotiations had resulted in a breakthrough peace "understanding", which was to be announced at a press conference in Jerusalem to mark the launching of an extraordinary peace initiative. Israeli Prime Minister Olmert had been briefed extensively about the initiative by Frankenthal. Also due to attend the conference were Khaled Abu Arafa, the Palestinian Cabinet Minister for Jerusalem, Sheikh Muhamed Abu Tir, senior Hamas Member of the Palestinian Parliament, and other senior Palestinian delegates.

The meeting was to announce a joint Israeli-Palestinian call for the release of Corporal Gilad Shalit who had been abducted by Hamas in Gaza, along with proposals for the beginning of the release of all Palestinian prisoners. These measures were to precipitate unprecedented new peace negotiations on a framework peace agreement, drawn on the 1967 borders. The presence of Palestinian Cabinet Officers and senior Israeli religious leaders in contact with the Prime Minster was to underline the seriousness of this peace proposal on both sides.

Just hours before the meeting was due to start, the Israeli Shin Bet internal Security Service arrested Abu Tir and Abu Arafa and warned them not to attend the meeting, under threats of detention. The meeting, which offered a major opportunity to obtain Shalit's release and launch a new framework for peace, was thrown into disarray. The next day, the Israeli Defence Force (IDF) invaded Gaza, and the day after both Abu Tir and Abu Arafa were abducted by Israeli forces, along with a third of the Palestinian Cabinet, provoking a predictable escalation of violence.

Israel simultaneously began conducting covert incursions on to Lebanese territory, provoking Hizbollah's capture of two IDF soldiers. Credible sources confirm that the soldiers were not abducted on Israeli territory, but inside Lebanon. Like the scuppered peace negotiations, Western officials have ignored this, and misinformed the media. However, some reports corroborate the sources. Israeli officials, for instance, informed Forbes (12.7.06) "Hezbollah captured two Israeli soldiers during clashes Wednesday across the border in southern Lebanon, prompting a swift reaction from Israel."

"The revelations show that Palestinian and Lebanese actors were not principally responsible for the escalation of the current conflict", said OI Director Graham Ennis. "Contrary to the misinformation disseminated by the Whitehouse and Whitehall, Israel vetoed unprecedented peace proposals that would have initiated a promising new framework for serious negotiations, and went on to provoke Palestinian and Lebanese groups into retaliations, that now threaten to escalate into a dangerous regional conflict."

Jerusalem Post, July 4, 2006

Olmert and his associates in the government have pointed their fingers at Hamas blaming it for the Palestinian guerrilla attack on Israeli territory Sunday morning while ignoring Palestinian Authority Mahmoud Abbas's Fatah terror group's equal share of culpability. It was Fatah, not Hamas that kidnapped and murdered 18-yearold Eliahu Asheri. It is Fatah that is threatening to blow up Israeli embassies abroad. It is Fatah that is threatening to renew shooting attacks on Jerusalem and attack Israel with chemical and biological weapons. **It is Fatah that is threatening to kill the IDF hostage Cpl. Gilad Shalit.**

On July 12th the author in his daily real-time analysis provided:

Hezbollah seizes Israel soldiers

The Lebanese Shia militant group Hezbollah has captured two Israeli soldiers during clashes across the Lebanese-Israeli border.

{Author's Real-Time Analysis}: While the NWO first and foremost wants Iran the way they would really love to get it is at the cost of the destruction of Israel. Thus they kill two big birds at the one time. Iran oil and no Israel and with no Israel the false moral high ground to control Iran, Syria and Lebanon.

With the Hezbollah kidnappings, the IDF, Israeli Defense Forces, launched aggressive and disproportionate military actions on Lebanon. People could not comprehend the Israeli response, seemingly uncaring to civilian casualties and deaths including those of innocent women and children. Many Americans since the start of the new millennium carried serious questions about their government and many Israelis carried the same serious questions regarding their own government as well. What the vast majority stood blind and ignorant to is that both nations were being manipulated as surrogates for the greater Moabite design

Author's Comment
Published July 13, 2006

Thus, this is a dream dynamic for the Moabites. Get the wealth while undermining Israel -- the beauty of the Moabite alliance with the Assyrians to capture the wealth of the ten tribes while destroying them at the same time. They set up the ten tribes just as the NWO has today set up Israel as the nation made whole in 1968 to face the test of Torah post WWII.

Look at how they can play the world with the dumbed down and/or corrupted media. Olmert had to quickly open the second front because everyone started THINKING about the released facts regarding Shalit that the IDF sort of let it happen and even worse that those snatching him were with Fatah. Thus, everyone was closing in on the covert plan that we seemed to have identified (a coup d'etat by Fatah against Hamas with the cooperation of the IDF).

Now, with Hezbollah involved, Israel was directed to take egregious action against Lebanon. On July 16th, post the Hezbollah kidnappings, the Moabite controlled Israeli government stirred Jewish emotions against the Arabs. The author on that day provided the following discussion deploying channeling techniques to give unfolding events a more correct perspective, to stem the machinated anger and hostility against the Arab/Islamic peoples:

Short Discussion between myself and Chaim an Israeli

Sometimes this format lends itself best to bring up points at time of war...

Chaim: Do you Ehrlich have any idea what our issues are in Israel. Last week Arabs broke into my home, took the car keys from my pocket, and stole my car. If this were the first time it would be bad enough. However, it is the third time. Moreover, they are stealing everything else we have including murdering our men women and children. We cannot live this way. Olmert is finally doing something about it.

Ehrlich: Chaim you are a religious Jew. Does it ever cross your mind why Jews like yourself in the holy land have it so bad?

Chaim: Your point Ehrlich?

Ehrlich: The point is that God is sending you a message and He has been doing it for some time. As a result, when you don't pick up on the message, life in the holy land can be very dark and cumbersome.

Chaim: So God is with the Arabs?

Ehrlich: Forget that the source of your misery is the Arabs. Because if God is not with you in the holy land and all the Palestinians disappeared tomorrow morning, life would still continue to be very dark and cumbersome for you.

Chaim: What is the answer Ehrlich? What does someone like me have to do to change this rotten way to live?

Ehrlich: You have to first understand what is happening. If you do not see the big picture you cannot see that you are caught in a spider's web. There is no way out and the spider will ultimately eat you.

Chaim: What is it that I have to understand?

Ehrlich: You are a religious Jew, right? You go to pray daily?

Chaim: Yes.

Ehrlich: Is God central to your life?

Chaim: Yes.

Ehrlich: Is God central to the majority of Jews in Israel?

Chaim: No. But what has that got to do with me and my community that bows to God?

Ehrlich: If you can tell me that the majority of the Jews in Israel do not see God central to their own lives, then tell me how the rest of the world sees Israel?

Chaim: They hate us. They are all anti-Semites and they would like nothing better than to see us all die.

Ehrlich: Exactly. But my point is that they do not see God central to Israel. Am I correct?

Chaim: You are correct.

Ehrlich: Would you say that Israel is on a path moving its people to God or away from Him?

Chaim: Definitely away.

Ehrlich: Biblically speaking, Chaim, can Israel exist as a nation when the rest of the world sees the nation moving away from God?

Chaim: But we cannot do anything. Give me the opportunity and I would put in a government that moves the people to God.

Ehrlich: There always have been Jews like yourself that know what Israel should look like but the operative point is that it does not look like it should and those in control of the government are in fact making it and have made it a defamation to God's name.

Chaim: So what are you telling me? Are you telling me that I and my community are now doomed?

Ehrlich: You keep putting the emphasis on you and your community. My point is that can there be a nation with the name Israel that does not only not make God central but in fact is affirmatively moving the country away from Him?

Chaim: So I should pack up and move to New York?

Ehrlich: I have told you from the macro prism that there cannot be any future for Israel.

Chaim: So why did God give us back Israel? Those who fought for this land didn't have much of a connection with God. Why was God with those very people who have taken Israel where it is today?

Ehrlich. Good question. Remember 1968-1973. How did people feel about God during those years? Moreover, Chaim, how did people around the world see the Jews in Israel?

Chaim: Yes, Ehrlich, we were much more spiritual as a nation in those years. Everyone even the atheists knew that God was with us in what happened during those years.

Ehrlich: And the rest of the world?

Chaim: Yes they saw us as blessed by God.

Ehrlich: Now this is my key point Chaim. From that time till today what happened to the children of Israel? Did Israel develop a love for God in those children or did they allow if not foster a generation that did not even know God? Remember, I am not talking about you and your community. I am talking about Israel the Israel I and others see when we visit.

Chaim: Is that why you love Ahmadinejad? Don't you see that he would murder us all if he had the chance?

Ehrlich: Before we get to Ahmadinejad let's first take a broad look at Iran. Go around the world today and if you ask people all over the globe which nation under monotheism bows to God, would their answer be Israel? Or would their answer be Iran?

Chaim: Iran. Maybe also Saudi Arabia.

Ehrlich: I'm glad you mentioned Saudi Arabia. Think about this for a moment. Between Saudi Arabia and Iran which nation is more understanding and tolerant of Jews?

Chaim: Iran.

Ehrlich: Would you care to take a stab at why that is the case?

Chaim: I don't know. I just know there are Jews in Iran and there are none in Saudi Arabia.

Ehrlich: Do you know the difference between Iran and Iraq, both Moslem countries?

Chaim: Not really.

Ehrlich: Do you know the differences between Sunni and Shiite?

Chaim: I know that they hate each other. May they kill each other off quickly.

Ehrlich: You see how you regress to this type of thinking that I am so critical about. You are reflecting prejudices and biases instilled in you. Christians were instilled with the same biases and prejudices that proved to be the platform of centuries of persecution against Jews.

Chaim: Sorry I brought it up. I do hate them all. All the Arabs. They have made my life miserable and they have made the lives of my neighbors miserable. Need I tell you Ehrlich that we have lost lives of innocents and children.

Ehrlich: You should well know that I am highly aware of it and thus such awareness is what promotes my efforts to clear up what is really going on.

Ehrlich: So to go back to my point, the Shiites have a very positive history toward precepts aligned with both Torah and their holy book the Qur'an. Those serving less than noble precepts unfortunately infiltrated the Sunnis and thus they have been a tool of those men who historically opposed God and religion. The country most aligned with the precepts that Muhammad himself valued and perpetrated is Iran. They do not see Jews as enemies. They see those Jews who oppose God as enemies and thus when Israel never abandoned the militant Zionists who founded the country, men who were not aligned with God, then {Iran} opposed Israel. The proof of the validity of their opposition is that they themselves see Israel as a defamation to God.

Chaim: Well how come they never express it that way? It would certainly help me and others in my community in what we want to see here in Israel.

Ehrlich: I know. It would be something helpful. However, I believe Ahmadinejad in fact was pursuing such a course when Olmert started this crisis with the Palestinians. I know you may find this hard to believe but one of the major dynamics behind what is happening is that those who oppose God wanted to dislodge Ahmadinejad from the path he was on.

Sidebar: Moabites upset that Ahmadinejad highlights monotheism

June 28, 2006

TEHRAN (Fars News Agency)- Iranian President Mahmoud Ahmadinejad in a meeting with former Greek Premier George Papandreou here Monday night criticized some western politicians for misusing such concepts as liberalism, republicanism and democracy for seizing power and dominating the nations. ***

The chief executive official stressed that crimes committed by man all result from his abstinence from monotheism and justice-seeking spirit, and further expressed hope that human problems and hardships would minimize once monotheism, affection and justice prevail in the world.

http://english.farsnews.com/newstext.php?nn=8504070265

Chaim: Look Ehrlich I am but a single person. I do my best and I cannot take this life much longer. I cannot live with what is happening and what has happened to this nation. What can I do? Tell me why I shouldn't hate the Arabs? Why I shouldn't support Olmert who now finally goes out to confront our enemies, those that have made our lives so miserable?

Ehrlich: There is not much I can tell you that can directly help you and your family. I can only tell you the big picture of why what is happening is happening. When you at least have a hook to bring light to your misery it might lessen the burden of the current realities. Otherwise, I have tried to forge a path to have Iran and Ahmadinejad understand that it is their obligation to highlight their position to the world, especially to such Jews as yourself in Israel. They cannot sit tight knowing that God has to remove Israel to their favor. They have to show themselves worthy of God. This is what Ahmadinejad in my opinion was moving out to do. Now, Olmert went out to derail that very effort just when Ahmadinejad was making this effort.

Chaim: No one is going to accept or appreciate your own viewpoint.

Ehrlich: I know. That is why Ahmadinejad as a global leader and president of Iran could capture the ears and attention of everyone including the Jews within Israel. That is why Olmert went out to silence him and put him onto a different verbal track. Instead of speaking in terms of justice Ahmadinejad has been forced to speak in terms of war.

Chaim: This is all above me. Is there anything I can do?

Ehrlich: Not too much at this point. My heart cries for the realities of today because someone like yourself if taught correctly would have been part of a better world and environment. However, you know that Torah provides that God will ultimately openly return and when He does so He will circumcise all our hearts and thus with a simple effort on His part impart in us what I have in a small way been trying to convey.

Ehrlich: I know how you feel Chaim. We all, Jew Christian and Arab/Muslim, have been victims of a negative environment, one where we have in fact been taught incorrectly. How much better we would be as people if we were all taught correctly I am not even confident enough to say with any degree of clarity. However, speaking for myself, I know that man has great potential but I guess that only God can harness it without interference from those who exist to derail us from the blessings which we all have had in hand but never appropriately appreciated.

Chaim: Is all then lost?

Ehrlich: There are always portals. I saw the IDF recently stand sensitive to the realities of Sharon giving his life not to bend to a course that Olmert within months of his taking office takes on without a second thought. Deep in the heart of every Jew is a sense of gifted justice and I would love to see the IDF rebel against the treacherous course that Olmert pursues, they well knowing that if war breaks out with Syria then Iran comes into the picture and then what? Will the US save Israel? The IDF knows the answer: would the USA save Japan from North Korea? Would the USA save South Korea from North Korea?

Chaim: What happened to the USA? We always could count on it?

Ehrlich: **The very same people infiltrating the government of Israel infiltrated the government of the USA. They are**

enemies of God. The proof by the way is look at the children of the USA and Israel. Are they imbued with holy values or pagan values? Now take a look at even godless China. Do they protect their children from pornography and other pagan values? Yes. The USA and Israel do not. This is the point that people must understand. The enemies of Israel and the USA have conquered our nations from within. The IDF is getting a full understanding of it when Olmert moves Israel to its own destruction, without even any valid reason to quickly and obtusely do what he already has done when he just took the reigns of office. He is acting irresponsibly and for sure not as an accountable fiduciary for the nation.

Ehrlich: So Chaim. Simply put, **either Olmert at this point backs off from ensnaring Syria into war or the IDF will have to do a coup against Olmert.** Short of that, Iran is drawn into the war and between Israel as it is constituted today and Iran as it is constituted today, with whom will God stand? I have explained the answer to this question for many years and now all concerned will see whether what I proffered is indeed valid and true. However, my prayer is that Olmert pulls back and if not the IDF takes control. I carried a lot of hope and regard for what Ahmadinejad was pursuing and I want him back on track with that course. However, those true bastards the enemies of God could not stand what he was pursuing and they told Olmert the dupe and fool he is to do what Sharon would not do. What these enemies have planned for Israel I don't want to tell you. You are upset enough.

The very next day, July 17, 2006, the author wrote the following directed to a far different audience than the one targeted by the channeled discussion above:

> **I believe the IDF knows that it cannot win militarily and that igniting war with Syria and Iran will cost endless lives in Israel.** I believe the IDF cannot justify legitimate goals to the current campaign. Thus I believe that the IDF knows that the military campaign is inconsistent with Israel's interests and thus I believe that the chances now are 60% that the campaign will not expand into Syria and Iran. However, the IDF has to move against the NWO

government. The NWO powers will direct Israel to move/stay in Lebanon and this accomplishes nothing because the damage that still will unravel this week to Israel equates to more damage than Israel would have sustained if it had done nothing under Olmert's service to NWO interests.

The assessment was that the Moabites would give or in fact had already given Iran secret codes to circumvent Israel's defense systems. The Moabites pressed Olmert into expanding his already seen disproportionate response. The Moabite design was for regional war:

Israel may launch large-scale ground offensive in Lebanon - Peretz

07.20.2006, 09:45 AM

Author's {Real-Time Analysis} Comment: Please remember that if I were talking to a Moabite leader, he would say:

"We the Moabites are fulfilling God's will. We do not implement our design on Israel when it bows to and honors God but when it has lowered itself to such a degree to follow our path the Moabite path against Lebanon and if we told it against Iran as well. Thus we are fulfilling biblical destiny."

What about the Moabites' role in putting Israel into the position that God would not protect it? They would say for sure that it was Israel's obligation to learn from its own history, from what is studied day after day, by thousands if not hundreds of thousands, to reject the {Moabite designs as it should have at the time of Ruth}and move the nation to God not away from Him. That we offered Jews and their rabbinate money and honors and inducements is no different that the days we offered them our women. They were willing to sin before Moses and God and that is what they are de facto doing again today. As to the rabbinate you yourself proved the point that they cast God out of Israel so that they could exclusively sit with the power over the people.

Are the Moabites wrong?

They are not wrong. What they are wrong about is that they are going to prevail against Islam in their quest to separate Islam from God.

Thus what is my purpose in advising Israel and Jews?

It is never too late (until the fat lady sings) to acknowledge truth and repent. Jews have their own superhighway to enlist God's favor and forgiveness. However, from what I see before me, with the nation of Israel supporting Olmert's war and the rabbis distorting Torah to further legitimatize it, Israel via the Moabite design from within will set itself up for its own annihilation.

God keeps the birthright, but I won't sit silently and see the pale of wholesale death fill the Middle East. Just the other day it was an issue whether it would play the biblical path or the secular path. However, in the last several days, I see that the NWO moves to self destruct Israel from within, I guess fairly close to what happened to the ten tribes re the Assyrians in connection with the first failing.

Before today many of you may have seen this all as serious but casual discourse. Well those days are now over. There was no question that Israel attacking Syria would cross the fine line. Israel will not do that. However, I now deduced the alternative path, which makes it an occupied Lebanon, an eviscerated Tel Aviv and Haifa, and an uprising in Jerusalem. Remember the goal is for Bush to stand in Jerusalem (no doubt at the temple mount) as he stood in front of the World Trade Center Towers.

For those in Israel and for those Jews elsewhere around the world, this is not the time to stand silent. It is time to wake up and move. I know that until now you knew I was right but the world around you still was not you thought all that bad. Now, for sure, you can see that it is that bad and that the time the darkness comes to your door is not altogether that far off.

Thus, since events were unfolding as analyzed four years earlier, the author appeared on the Jeff Rense Show on August 7, 2006. The Internet posting of the author's reflections of his radio interview read as follows:

Link to audio of full interview

http://www.senderberl.com/clarity.mp3

Ehrlich: Rense Radio Interview –
Reflections Thereon
Joseph Ehrlich
8-8-6

I was pleased that I was able to cover with Jeff Rense a wide range of issues and dynamics concerning the current crisis. The main point I believe made was that Bush and the NWO did not direct Olmert to trigger regional war with less than the intent to commence it. Without regional war, there is no portal for the {Moabites}to move against Iran, and Iran is the primary target (oil, dissipating Islam via negating Shiite influence) and Jerusalem the main objective (from Israel's evisceration).

The NWO thinks itself clever. Without the consent of Israelis, they have set up Israel to be a de facto suicide bomber. With a new Middle East in the picture per Condy Rice, the evisceration of Israel provides Bush and the NWO the second stage of moral outrage they have been seeking since 9-11. In payment of Israel's evisceration, they will move against Iran thinking the moral outrage sufficient to curtail China's intervention for Iran.

WRONG. That is why Bush and Condy made a big mistake with their "a new Middle East" remark buttressed by Condy declaring on Meet the Press on Sunday that she sees "opportunity in crisis." Thus Condy is delegating Olmert's War to the same dynamic as 9-11, allowing the NWO to carve out its agenda from the opportunities that arise from the engendered crisis. This means things will be getting worse than they already are! China advising its nationals to leave Israel is no small matter in this line either.

Ironically, President Bush standing with Condy behind him (to avoid Bush from fondly starring at her as he routinely does) said at an unusual Crawford Ranch news conference:

"Now you know, I appreciate people focusing on Syria and Iran. And we should. Because Syria and Iran sponsor and promote Hezbollah activities all aimed at creating chaos, all aimed at using terror to stop the advance of democracies."

To show the coordination in the planning, Olmert said the following yesterday to a first time ever meeting with some 50 spokespeople from the Foreign Ministry, the IDF, the PM office and other government agencies TO INSTRUCT THEM ON THE PRINCIPAL MESSAGES THAT THEY SHOULD BE DELIVERYING IN APPEARANCES BEFORE THE FOREIGN MEDIA (Haaretz):

> "Our enemy is not Hezbollah, but Iran, which employs Hezbollah as its agent," he told them at the meeting, the first of its kind."

www.haaretz.com/hasen/spages/747029.html

My NEW suggestion that I introduced during the interview was for China to tell Hezbollah to stand down completely. While this would cause lots of humiliation problems, when you have an opponent driven to ignite regional war, as the pretense to effectuate an attack on Iran, that it could not otherwise implement, then you deny the opponent his desired course.

Otherwise, since NWO control over Israel allows the destruction of the State of Israel, there is no alternative but regional war and with regional war comes the match for WWIII, a term many neo-cons have put into play via NWO controlled global media.

With Bush himself de facto declaring what the pawns and poodles are putting directly in play, the desire for a wider war to wit against Syria and Iran, then you have to deny them this insane course for as I expressed what sane man would affirmatively desire regional war not to say regional war that could likely and would likely trigger global war?

I expressed that the NWO does want to tackle China but I could not of course present the deep deep deep scenario that the NWO has no objection to war between China and the USA since the NWO would have no problem with the evisceration of both countries.

I did however note that depopulation was part of the NWO agenda and that elimination of Arabs and Muslims would be consistent with that depopulation schematic. I noted in a different segment that Bush and the neo-cons had no problem with civil war in Iraq and would in fact be pleased if everyone would kill each other off since the only item that they are interested in is OIL.

I had the opportunity to note what Americans should always keep in mind: that when Bush pulled off the border patrol and openly allowed everyone (and everything) to cross the Mexican border into America, his VP, Cheney, was hollering to the American people about the terrorist threat to America. Thus Americans should understand that there was no threat to the USA and that the administration fully stood aware of it. How could there be a threat when no one but the administration carried the sophistication to pull off what we today know as 9-11? However, I did not relay, because the audience would not correctly understand the point, that with Israel's planned evisceration stood the answer to the {Moabite's} concerns with history over who was really behind 9-11.

Understand, that if Hezbollah does not stand down, then what others refer to as the end days are probably here right around the bend. If Hezbollah does stand down, there will have to be an overreach to trigger a regional war. Iran and Syria have had to communicate to their political bases why they have stood aside. Israel helped a lot here. They made a mistake bombing Syrians meters within the border on the Lebanon side but being EXTREMELY careful not to touch a Syrian on the Syrian side of the border. This showed how specific and serious the instructions were to bait Syria to enter the conflict, but the {Moabites} knew post NK {North Korea} that they could not cross the Syrian border to entice Syria into the conflict (otherwise I guarantee you they would have done so long ago). Also I have noted that Syria has not even sent jets anywhere close to the border to avoid the gambit I detailed to draw Syria into the war.

So China is giving its recommendation and Iran is making the decision. Iran should not make a decision on the predicate that God will protect it. **The correct decision is the one that simply pulls the plug on expansion of the war per the {Moabite} schematic.** Then if the {Moabites}move to expand the war despite the stand down, dynamics completely change and the {Moabites} will lose and lose big time. I trust you might understand that then the war by definition will include US military troops and vessels and that means to wit those in Iraq. China will have to enter the picture openly because there is no other possibility.

When it moves to this degree the first thing to find out is where is Bush and elitist centrix behind the mess? If they are in their bunkers, flushing them out early on could possibly save the world. I would like to see those bunkers taken out since putting the elite above ground is similar to putting a rifle in Bush's hand and sending him to the Iraqi front lines. The war would be over before it starts. END

Israel, Hezbollah, Iran, Syria and Lebanon, all thereafter shocked the world and stood down in near unison from the conflict. The Moabites were enraged over the stand down; they, themselves, not, at first, understanding what happened.

"Secretary of State Condoleezza Rice has become increasingly dismayed over President Bush's support for Israel to continue its war with Hezbollah."
August 9, 2006

CHAPTER 13
ISRAEL CUTS A DEEPLY COVERT DEAL

I t can be safely said that the regional war did not take place due to events that no one but a handful of political elites and those privy to the author's analysis would ever know or realize. We now cover this highly exclusive analysis, showing a prime example of how one can connect dots invisible to others unaware of the teachings and truths of the first nine chapters.

On the date the author appeared on the Jeff Rense Show, China sent its special envoy, Sun Bigan, to resolve the Middle East crisis. He did end the conflict, with the silent assent and cooperation of both China and Israel. Neither the Moabites nor the author knew at that time of what had been put in play on July 25, 2006 by Israel and China.

While the author did not know about the deduced deal between Israel and China, he was able to immediately detect from a single news headline that Israel was talking in secret with Iran and Hezbollah. Thus, obviously, Israel finally concluded that the scenario in the Bush Double Double Cross might in fact be playing out. It was being played out and Israel, it appears, four years later, accepted and acted upon the analysis.

July 30, 2006

Hezbollah leader: Israel continuing aggression at U.S.' behest

Nasrallah threatens to fire missiles at central Israel

By Yoav Stern, Haaretz Correspondent and News Agencies

Hezbollah leader Sheikh Hassan Nasrallah on Saturday vowed to fire rockets on communities in central Israel if the military operation in Lebanon continued, **and accused Israel of being an American "slave."**

Here was the author's immediate real-time analysis (July 30, 2006):

Something very big has happened. I can't put my finger on it just now but it seems that Israel has concluded in some manner that its NWO leadership was going to implode the country as part of the NWO plan!

From this truly remarkable article, I am deducing that something big has happened.

Israel may have concluded that its future is not with the NWO and EU but in fact may be as I have long suggested with Iran. This would be an earth-shattering event of monumental proportions and I may be a little ahead of myself on this one.

However, either Israel is deceiving me to quiet things down until the 9th of Av passes or else the article below suggests that what I just the other day highlighted to wit, the East has united in seeing the NWO threat. Ipso facto why doesn't Israel see that it is in the same boat as the Arab/Islamic countries (scheduled for elimination) and that the Middle East should unite, as has the East.

I see it in this article but whether I am on the right track (I really want to see this happen) or not the article is pretty outstanding.

~~~

Remember, the Moabites are our common enemy. Their success is that they blend in among us, infiltrate us, usurp the good and have conquered both the USA and Israel. They are the sworn enemy of God, of Israel, and seek to depopulate/enslave us all without inhibition. **The only way in all due respect that Israel and Hezbollah could genuinely be talking is if they have platformed a common groundwork on the recognition that the NWO is out to eliminate them both (with Iran and Syria and everyone else in the Middle East).**

~~~

Conclusion: I believe that there exists a major division with the IDF and other major facets in Israel over what {Ehud} Olmert has done here. These people were looking for an answer for what was the true covert US agenda. God willing, they could only truly explain what was going down by accepting the biblical realities that we have presented, interpreted and analyzed. This is a bold deduction from a single article but I:

a. believe that Israel and Hezbollah are talking and

b. that they have moved toward a united conclusion that the NWO is out there to screw everyone in the Middle East from Iran to Israel.

Need I say that they are 110% correct. I can only tell you one thing. If Israel does team up with Iran (and thus China) then the NWO people will have to find a very deep hole to hide. The only thing I want to add in here is that Israel must also conclude that it must:

a. move its people to God

b. agree {to} a new reality of theocracies throughout the Middle East {the reality needed to identify, offset, and prevail over Moabites}.

How did the author confirm that the above analysis was correct, aside from the fact that the conflict did not expand to a regional war but in fact resulted in the stand down the author was recommending?

Aug. 22, 2006 2:53 | Updated Aug. 22, 2006 7:02

US to Israel: No financial aid for war

By HERB KEINON

Washington has let Jerusalem know that for now Israel should not expect any financial aid to help defray the cost of the war in Lebanon, The Jerusalem Post has learned.

According to sources in Jerusalem, the government was considering requesting US aid - one report estimated a request of $2 billion - to help pay the cost of the war. There was talk in Washington of a large-scale financial package to help rebuild southern Lebanon, and in the process keep the Iranians out of the process. Israel was apparently hoping to fold its aid request into this package.

However, according to the sources, Washington has made it clear to Jerusalem that such aid for Israel is unlikely, even as US President George Bush on Monday announced a $230 million aid package for southern Lebanon.

"Things could change," the source said, "**but right now this type of request would be like spitting into the wind.**"

Source:
http://www.jpost.com/servlet/Satellite?cid=115452591909 6&pagename=JPost%2FJPArticle%2FShowFull

{Author's real-time comment}: Ehrlich: Good. It is time that Israel cuts the tie to its heroin supplier. China recognized that the NWO was setting it up so that it would be subservient to the supplier of the opium (oil) that China was positioned to be dependent upon (the reason for the NWO allowing China to become the manufacturing behemoth of the world). Israel's problem is that it is addicted to the money and funds that the NWO gives Israel to stand as the obedient slave to it. However, the difference now is that enough Jews in Israel KNOW and SAW WITH THEIR OWN EYES that the NWO as I have long expounded was setting up Israel as the second level of moral outrage so that Israel's evisceration would be :

a.   the predicate for the attack on Iran and

b. that Israel would be out of the NWO's hair so after effectuating the attack and occupation of Iran that Israel would not be an impediment to NWO placating the Arab/Islamic nations.

The problem of course for the NWO is that everyone now KNOWS ... how it plays its game. Moabites can be recognized by their behavior pattern. ~~~Note the elegance of the NWO: "this type of request would be like spitting into the wind." What better confirmation of my analysis do you want than that?

How about this headline and article?

Uncle Sam to Olmert: Drop Dead

21.8.06 | 11:03 By Gary Pickholz

http://www.haaretz.com/hasen/pages/ArticleContent.jhtml?itemN

There has been an astonishing bipartisan sea change in Washington within the last two weeks regarding financial support for Israeli military activity in general, and what is perceived as reckless adventurism in particular.

From the standpoint of Israel's finances, a vortex of factors have suddenly come together that raise significant doubt that Washington will foot the bill for the Lebanon War, much less increase military aid to Israel going forward.

A significant blunder of the Olmert Administration has been its pandering to a lame duck the Bush Administration at the expense of garnering bipartisan support on Capitol Hill. American politics differ significantly from Israeli or European politics, and a fading Bush Administration has become increasingly irrelevant in terms of foreign appropriations. Even within the Republican Party, the lame duck President has ceded much of the authority to the two front leading Republican Senators for the 2008 nomination. The Olmert Administration has played the wrong hand in Washington's poker game.

Simultaneously, there now exists widespread bipartisan sentiment on Capitol Hill for a radical reduction in US military and foreign aid across the board, and in the Middle East in particular. From a Republican perspective, there can be no further increase in foreign aid within the parameters of the Republican budgetary platform, which is taking a beating due to the escalating costs of the Iraqi/Afghani war. From the Democrat side of Congress, there is growing sentiment that the vast sums of American aid have only fueled the battles of the Middle East and it is time for a significantly lower profile.

Israel is the New Taiwan

From an American perspective, the costs of Olmert's adventure into Lebanon are staggering both financially and politically, dwarfing the costs of the Gaza handover. America will be asked to pay over $ 7 billion in replacement costs to the Israelis, plus at least an additional $3 billion to rebuild Lebanon from the very bombs Congress paid for in the first place. This is prior to all calls for additional Israeli aid for its economic growth --all within 24 months of the original final date for US guarantee of Israeli national debt. All within a year of more than $5 billion in additional costs for the Gaza relocations.

Senate responses fall into two categories. First: revulsion for Israel's carpet bombing of civilians in retaliation for terrorist actions, as expressed on the Senate record by Senator John Warner of Virginia, one of the two leading Republican candidates for the 2008 presidential nomination. Far more important and pervasive, however, is the taboo none dared even express until August 2006: the Israel is the new Taiwan –a poor military ally, incapable of fulfilling its regional role irrespective of a bottomless credit, no longer worth the significant investment. Like Taiwan experienced, a sudden sea change has occurred on Capitol Hill that those funds may be better invested in other manners within the Middle East puzzle, capable of achieving greater long-term alliance and stability for America. **Like Taiwan, the Israeli government may well find itself suffering whiplash from the sudden embrace of its archenemy by the United States as a more viable solution to pouring billions into the black hole of military adventurism**

What was not even a remote possibility in American Israeli relations 35 days ago is now openly discussed on a bipartisan basis as a more intelligent solution to American interests in the region. While the Olmert Administration must now work double time in repairing its image on Capitol Hill, there certainly is no prospect of discussion of even further aid to repair the damage to the Israeli economy suffered in the past month.

All previous growth and prosperity projections for the Israeli economy are now worthless, and perhaps for the first time in the history of the State of Israel, discussion will focus on minimizing cutbacks of American aid rather than relying upon a bottomless line of credit with Uncle Sam.

Shimon Peres after getting advance word on August 15, 2006 from the State Department that there are changes to the Israeli-American relationship.

CHAPTER 14
THE MOABITES THREATEN ISRAEL

W hat was it that finally confirmed the Moabite realities to Israel? The author perhaps is best able to detail the single event: Qana. Once the Moabites got word that Israel without their knowledge (to wit pulling a Sharon) was talking with Iran and Hezbollah, the Moabites were prepared to show Israel the kind of punishment the Moabites were ready to impose on Israel.

July 30, 2006
(Qana took place several hours after the analysis on page 131 was published)

Qana: Without question to my mind this was Israel's immediate punishment for speaking to Hezbollah (ironically it took place within a handful of hours of my last {report} to you)

Israel bombs Beirut and 1000 innocents die. Bush: Israel has the right to defend itself.

Israel bombs Qana Hezbollah stronghold and the world weighs in against it including Jordan when fifty die.

Ahmadinejad should make a point of the world responding to Bush the tail wagging the dog.

Why would Israel bomb Qana if they are talking to Hezbollah?

Not everyone is aware of what is going on. Moreover, if the NWO moves against Israel they call up their assets to set up the "outrage" and also implement the deed (when Rice and Bolton and Bush weep for the innocents it makes me ill). Moabites have their men on both sides of the fence and otherwise do what they want. However, here, after how many innocent children died in the Beirut onslaught does the world suddenly take umbrage at what Israel did in Qana.

It just shows you how the NWO can move the world to where it wants.

Israel should talk to Ahmadinejad. If they reflect that they have taken the wrong path I am sure that he will be receptive. On the secular level Ahmadinejad is their only recourse because he understands what is going down. Israel can always read past {reports} in preparing to speak with him.

Conclusion: Ahmadinejad understands what we understand. If he sits by and does nothing for Israel, Israel will ultimately dissolve. If Olmert didn't move out as he has, it would have taken x years but since Olmert did move out on the NWO war schematic, the expulsion might be quicker than anyone imagined. The NWO is working to make Israel odious and this is something with Olmert at the helm that it does not have to work very hard at accomplishing and the more odious the NWO makes Israel the sooner the pale of darkness will descend.

I never really thought that such a stupid man could ever hold the PM position in Israel. However, he was perfect for a NWO schematic I proffered publicly in November 2002 {The Bush Double Double Cross}. Israel is a dead weight for the NWO. {North Korea} proved that the NWO cannot win the Middle East militarily. The NWO sent Olmert out for one good try to see if Olmert could get Syria and Iran to engage. Syria and Iran when teamed up with China and with Ahmadinejad as the president of Iran is now both sophisticated and biblically aligned and oriented. The NWO control of both Israel and the USA is therefore of no moment. ~~~

Technically I see Qana as a bingo because there was no reason for Qana to take place and for the NWO to extend itself as it did to punish Israel unless Israel was found out, as Sharon was found out, countermanding the NWO schematic. Israel was doing this by speaking to Hezbollah. My strong recommendation is to speak to Ahmadinejad. However, Israel has to bow to God enough as to admit to Ahmadinejad that Israel took the wrong course, taking it away from God.

Ahmadinejad has to help Israel if Iran wants to genuinely oppose the {Moabites}, the enemy of God. He cannot rest on his knowledge that Iran will prevail and Israel will falter and be expelled. This is a biblical and historical dynamic and reality.

Thus I would STRONGLY suggest that Israel in all due haste move forward because with {Ehud} Olmert in the PM chair death and darkness loom over Israel.

The above was written July 30th at the peak of the conflict. What happened is that Israel and China did what was suggested, but what no one expected: they teamed up together to provide a strategy to put an end to the IDF's move to Beirut by land, which by necessity would have triggered the attack on both Haifa and Tel-Aviv by Hezbollah and Iran, moving the conflict to regional war, leading possibly to global war, all to the favor of the Moabite leadership.

WHAT ARE THE SIGNS OF THE ALLIANCE BY ISRAEL WITH IRAN AND CHINA?

{Real-Time analysis}

Answer: It was really Nasrallah's July 30th comment about Israel being a slave to the US. **Then I linked it to the death of the Chinese Lt. Colonel (Du Zhaoyu).** Israel could not have been that reckless. Ten warnings, and all the other evidence that it was a deliberate targeting of those four UN observers, Lt Colonel Du Zhaoyu whom was subsequently proclaimed by China to be a martyr.

He was a martyr and he may have consented to what happened!

Then of course Israel used a **precision bomb** -- making the case 100% for China against Israel!

So when China came crashing down with the threat of entering the war (via Sun Bigan, August 7-11), it produced 100% proof that it had sufficient grounds to enter the war because there was unequivocal evidence to the degree of an admission that Israel knowingly and willingly and deliberately took out the four UN observers {remember the Moabites told Olmert to pursue a regional war solely based on the predicate of three kidnappings}.

Thus, Israel had legitimate ground to diffuse Chinese anger and the resolution that came about was **regarding a war that had nothing to do with conquering Hezbollah but EVERYTHING to do with escalating a conflict to regional if not global warfare.**

So Israel you did listen.

This warrants a more detailed look as to what events confirmed such startling deductions.

COUNTERMEASURES TAKEN

China elevates slain UN peacekeeper in Lebanon as martyr

http://www.zeenews.com/znnew/articles.asp?aid=314187&sid=WOR

Beijing, Aug 07: China on Monday elevated Lt Colonel Du Zhaoyu, a Chinese UN peacekeeper killed in an Israeli air raid in South Lebanon last month, as a martyr. ~~~

Du, 34, was killed during an Israeli air raid on Lebanon in late July, eight months after he was sent to the Middle East to work as a UN observer.

He is the eighth Chinese military personnel to die in UN peacekeeping missions since 1988, Xinhua news agency reported

Ehrlich: Were any of the other seven designated a martyr?

On July 25, 2006, the IDF eviscerated a UN Post, where four UN observers, including one Chinese observer, Du Zhaoyu, lost their lives. Kofi Annan based on the facts given to him lashed out against Israel.

Annan calls attack 'deliberate targeting'

ROME, July 25 (UPI) -- U.N. Secretary-General Kofi Annan has condemned the killing of four military observers in Lebanon by Israeli forces, calling it "deliberate targeting."

"I am shocked and deeply distressed by the apparently deliberate targeting by Israeli Defense Forces of a U.N.

139

Observer post in southern Lebanon," Annan said Tuesday in a statement made in Rome, where he is to attend a high-level international meeting on Lebanon on Wednesday.

He called the act a "coordinated artillery and aerial attack on a long-established and clearly marked U.N. post," and said he had received "personal assurances" from Israeli Prime Minister Ehud Olmert that United Nations' positions would be spared.

Annan said General Alain Pelligrini, the U.N. force commander in south Lebanon, had been in regular contact with Israeli officers throughout the day Tuesday, and had stressed the need "to protect that particular U.N. position from attack."

"I call on the government of Israel to conduct a full investigation into this very disturbing incident and demand that any further attack on U.N. positions and personnel must stop," Annan said.

The names and nationalities of those killed are being withheld until family members can be notified.

~~~

Earlier, the UN Deputy Chief, Mark Malloch-Brown said they had accepted Israel's apology, but still had "serious concerns" about what happened. UN officials said they had contacted Israel 10 times to make their presence known but Israel had continued shelling the area.

Israel's response to the kidnappings were clearly disproportionate as indicated but Israel's behavior was really atypical, when showing little concern or regard for women, children and innocents and now also showing bizarre behavior in eviscerating a UN Observer Post. **Moreover, if Israel could go and trigger a war in seeing one to three soldiers kidnapped, Israel now faced seeing China move toward war with Israel for what China saw as the willful killing of the Chinese UN Observer.**

AP Blog: U.N. strike divides council

Friday, July 28, 2006, 6 p.m.

UNITED NATIONS

China's U.N. Ambassador Wang Guangya, normally very straightforward and unflappable, was frustrated and angry _ very angry.

So were many other members of the Security Council.

Israel scored a direct hit on a U.N. post on the Lebanon border Tuesday. Four unarmed U.N. military observers _ from China, Austria, Canada and Finland _ were killed. ~~~

On Friday, the secretary-general said he accepted Israeli President Ehud Olmert's sorrow over the killings. He said Olmert "indicated to me that he couldn't believe it could be intentional," but Annan again called for a joint Israeli-U.N. investigation so there aren't two reports on the bombing.

http://www.time.com/time/world/article/0,8599,1220278,00.html

UNIFIL contacted the Israeli military to warn them that one of their bombs had fallen close to a U.N. position. Over the next six hours, another 10 aerial bombs exploded between 100 yards and 300 yards from the U.N. post, while four 155mm artillery shells exploded inside the position, causing extensive damage. "We contacted the Israelis every time after one of the bombs fell. **We were begging them to stop** because it was going to end up in a tragedy. They said they would look into the matter and correct the situation," the UNIFIL officer recalled. Israel, while saying that the accident is under investigation, has not confirmed that it got the warnings.

Regardless of what preceded it, there is no disputing that the position was hit by at least two aerial bombs at 7:20 p.m., killing all four observers. UNIFIL insists there were no reports of Hizballah firing Katyusha rockets from the vicinity of observers' position, and that there was no obvious target for the Israelis that was discernible to UNIFIL. The officer contends that the Israelis did not halt their air strikes because "they don't care. They feel they have more important issues on their mind to hit Hizballah. Everything else is secondary." **According to a senior U.N. official in Lebanon, the Israelis used "precision guided missiles," inferring that the air strike was not an accident....**

On or about August 3, 2006, China upped the ante, to allow Israel to begin positioning itself for a stand down.

> China's Foreign Ministry on Thursday told Chinese nationals to leave Israel due to fighting on the Lebanese border, the government's main news agency reported. "The conflict between Lebanon and Israel is increasing, so <u>Chinese citizens in Israel should get as far from the battle area as possible</u>," the notice said, according to the Xinhua News Agency.

What really got the Moabites angry, when they later figured it out, is that they were out there protecting Israel at the UN and elsewhere against the claims of wanton and willing targeting of the UN Post. **The great secret of course is that the UN Observer Post was targeted per deeply covert agreement between Israel and China.** With this contention in mind, look at the following major news stories issued to make it clear that as far as everyone was concerned, Israel was in deep trouble with China.

PLA soldiers carry Du Zhaoyu's coffin to a military plane which left Israel for China yesterday afternoon. [Xinhua]

Cooperation vowed in handling death

By Xing Zhigang (China Daily)

Updated: 2006-08-02 06:13

Israel yesterday pledged "100 per cent" co-operation with China to handle the aftermath of the death of a Chinese UN observer in an Israeli air raid on a UN post in southern Lebanon.

Nadav Eshcar, political and press officer of the Israeli Embassy in China, described the death of Lieutenant Colonel Du Zhaoyu as a "tragedy," for which Israel expressed deep sorrow.

"As we have promised, we will be 100 per cent co-operative to show our goodwill in this time of hardship," he told China Daily.

Eshcar said the Israeli Government co-operated fully with the Chinese team sent to bring back Du's body.

Israeli authorities **issued visas on the spot** for the team's seven members, who included Du's widow Li Lingling and officials from the Foreign Ministry and the Peacekeeping Affairs Office of the Ministry of National Defence.

The team flew to Tel Aviv last Thursday to bring back Du's body.

Eshcar said **Israel also allowed a Chinese military plane to land at Tel Aviv International Airport** to carry Du's coffin home. ~~~

Eshcar said the Israeli Ambassador to China, Yehoyada Haim, will attend a memorial ceremony planned in Beijing to remember 34-year-old Du.

Du, who has a 1-year-old son, died with three other UN observers last Wednesday, when Israeli planes bombed their base in the town of Khiam near the eastern end of Lebanon's border with Israel.

Li Lingling carries a portrait of her late husband Du Zhaoyu killed in an Israeli air raid when Du's body was flown home August 2, 2006. [Xinhua]

His widow Li Lingling, who had flew to Israel to bring Du's body home, followed the coffin, holding a framed picture of Du in hands (sic).

Du's parents and his baby son, who had his two-year-old birthday on Monday, waited at the airport.

The Chinese People's Liberation Army (PLA) Assistant to Chief of the General Staff Zhang Qinsheng and China's Assistant Foreign Minister Cui Tiankai led an array of Chinese military and government officials, standing underneath the plane.

Over 100 Chinese army officers with uniforms and their service caps in hands stood at attention as Du's coffin was carried from plane to a hearse.

The 34-year-old Du, a Lt. Colonel, was killed in an Israeli raid on a UN post in southern Lebanon on July 25, which also killed three other UN observers from Finland, Austria and Canada, respectively.

Israel has expressed deep sorrow and regret over the incident, but denied it was deliberate.

UN Secretary General Kofi Annan said on Sunday that questions still surrounding the deaths of the four UN military observers in Lebanon must be answered.

Now, that Israel made it clear that it was afraid of Chinese involvement, and China, by arrangement, had an open portal to make the attendant threat, in view of the fact that Israel started the entire episode predicated on the kidnapping of a single soldier, China and Israel played their next card for the planned stand down.

August 8, 2006

China's special envoy to the Middle East, Sun Bigan
(China Confidential)

"The mastermind behind the coordinated Arab demand for an immediate Israeli troop withdrawal from Lebanon is China's special envoy to the Middle East, Sun Bigan, who is currently visiting the region.

Sun, who is a veteran diplomat and one of China's leading Arabists, called Monday for an immediate unconditional ceasefire in the war between Israel and the Lebanese proxy army of Beijing's non-Arab Islamist ally, Iran.

"Israel and Lebanese Hezbollah should end hostilities immediately to avoid further deterioration of humanitarian crisis in Lebanon," Sun told a press conference in Damascus following a closed-door meeting with Syrian Vice President Farouk al-Shara. Sun expressed China's willingness to intensify "consultation and coordination" with Arab nations.

As China Confidential reported on Sunday, Beijing is maneuvering to become a trusted intermediary--and maybe even a mediator--in the Middle East conflict. Sun is advancing the argument that the United States has lost credibility and influence in the region as a result of its steadfast support for Israel, and that a more neutral power-- such as China-- is urgently needed to help end the fighting and reduce regional tensions.

The real objective is to weaken the U.S. position--and ultimately drive the US from the region altogether.

Toward this end, China has been a major arms supplier to Hezbollah's sponsor. In the context of energy deals, Beijing has sold Iran tanks, planes, artillery, and cruise, anti-tank, surface-to-surface and anti-aircraft missiles. Chinese-designed missiles--including some that have been upgraded and improved by North Korea--have found their way into Hezbollah's arsenal of aerial terror.

China is also providing covert technical assistance to Iran's disputed nuclear development program--and supporting Iran diplomatically with a promise to block meaningful United Nations Security Council sanctions against the wannabe nuclear power."

From the August 8, 2006, posting on Rense.com at http://www.rense.com/general73/ehr.htm:

Author's real-time comment.

The $64,000 question is whether China will cause Hezbollah to stand down and uproot the NWO drive for regional/global war or whether China knowing the inevitable will escalate the conflict on its own timetable. My suggestion is to remove the game board from Bush and the NWO. The best move strategically and overall would be for Hezbollah to stand down and move out of the region.

Comment Received... Mr Ehrlich, yesterday I watched a long news presentation from Lebanon & what I found quite amazing is that the reporters were saying Hizbollah fighters had completely vanished like ghosts, The BBC could not find any Hizbollah fighters nor would any Lebanese tell them where they are!

Thus, within days of the interview on the Jeff Rense Show, Israel and Hezbollah stood down. The Moabites were told by Israel that Israel was at risk of war with China and China had the goods that

Israel's attack on the UN Observer Post was deliberate, which Israel, no doubt, told the Moabites was intentionally targeted to stir things up all the more in the quest to get Syria and Iran to log in as adverse parties in the war Olmert was waging, per Moabite instructions, against Lebanon and Gaza.

Israel and China both did not want to honor the Moabite course by going to war under the Moabite preferred schematic for war. Thus, via Israel's deliberate attack on the UN Post with a precision bomb, the conflict was escalated between them *before* Haifa and Tel-Aviv were bombed, where massive deaths would arise, when, if the case, there would be nothing to discuss. However, with China livid over *what was in fact* a deliberate bombing, Israel had no choice but to stand down, and with Israel's decision to stand down, so did Hezbollah (per instructions from China). **Thus, the Moabite design to ignite a regional war, to de facto implement the very design revealed by The Bush Double Double Cross analysis, was undermined.**

Moreover, due to Moabite behavior via the USA -- Israel, China and Iran, everyone began seeing the common interests that now existed between one-time foes and enemies. The following letter the author received on August 21, 2006 from London, England, best expresses it.

Dear Mr. Ehrlich,

In a quiet moment in my day I sat with a cup of tea and started thinking about what you had written the last few days and started myself looking at the links. What I realized Mr. Ehrlich is that you are again dead right with your analysis, because certain things did not make sense on the secular level but after your analysis they do make sense.

(1). Israel could have Blitzkrieged Lebanon with 500 tanks and +30,000 troops and with this no matter the heart and courage of Hizbollah, Israel would have over run Hizbollah, then placed themselves in that Bekka Valley near Baalbeck and in Beirut. That task with the resources available to the IDF was very achievable on a military level. The effect as you Mr. Ehrlich have pointed out would have been Regional war leading to global war!

(2). In Israel not doing this and the outcome of what happened, where Israel gave Hizbollah the victory that is a selfless act, and Hizbollah is a shia Resistance linked with Iran, so Israel was giving Iran the victory, which acts as a form of confirmation to your analysis that Israel is trying to bow to God via Iran! (Which is very good).

(3). **President Assad of Syria and President Ahmadinejad of Iran after the ceasefire did NOT blame Israel for what occurred in Lebanon. Ahmadinejad blamed the U.S and Assad blamed Europe through that speech he made where the German FM cancelled his visit. <u>Now that is conciliatory from both Iran and Syria towards Israel</u>.**

There is much more, but the more I think about your analysis and then look at what has actually happened the last 5 weeks and the outcome, the more and more your analysis that Israel has aligned with Iran becomes viable and highly probable. The actions that occurred and the missing links and dilemmas on the secular level through action, fit perfectly with the reason that Israel aligned with Iran, that analogy explains those missing links.

If this is the case Mr. Ehrlich, then all those lives that were lost from both Lebanon and Israel are MARTYRS because their lives that were lost were not lost in vain, they were lost in moving the Mid East back to God! Maybe one day their lives can openly be remembered in such a way!

DAMASCUS, Aug. 15 (Xinhua) -- Syrian President Bashar al-Assad on Tuesday told the opening session of a journalists conference that Israel's war on Lebanon was a "planned aggression".

"The Israeli aggression against Lebanon was not connected with its kidnapped soldiers (by Hezbollah), but had been prearranged for a period of time," Assad said. ***

Speech of President Bashar al-Assad at Journalists Union 4th Conference

Tuesday, August 15, 2006 - 12:15 PM
http://www.sana.org.sy/eng/21/2006/08/15/57835.htm

> This means, in the final analysis, that the world does not care about our interests, feelings and rights except when we are powerful. Otherwise, they would not do anything. They push us towards peace with what they say, but push us towards war with what they do. Here, the countries concerned with the peace process, and **they are mostly European**, are responsible for what is happening.

Bashar al-Assad followed the interpretation put forth by the author in November 2003 in Bush's Mission: Expecting the Second Platform of Moral Outrage. This major position paper asserted that while Europe postured itself as opposed to the invasion of Iraq, Europe was not only its main beneficiary, but in fact the driving force behind the invasion.

Assad and Ahmadinejad both not blaming Israel in the stand down says it all. Incredibly, for the first time it formally appears during a war footing and setting that Israel and the Arab/Islamic countries recognize the Moabite design and thus were able to agree!

The following remarkable news stories attests to the validity of the author's 2002 analysis, The Bush Double Double Cross. Moreover, they further support the author's public position paper entitled Bush's Mission: Expecting the Second Platform of Moral Outrage, included in the Appendix.

US neocons hoped Israel would attack Syria

Israel considered expansion of conflict in Lebanon 'nuts.'

Christian Science Monitor

http://www.csmonitor.com/2006/0809/dailyUpdate.html

August 9, 2006 at 12:00 a.m.

The White House, and in particular White House advisors who belong to the neoconservative movement, allegedly encouraged Israel to attack Syria as an expansion of its action against Hizbullah, in Lebanon. The progressive opinion and news site ConsortiumNews.com reported

Monday that Israeli sources say Israel's "leadership balked at the scheme."

One Israeli source said [US President George] Bush's interest in spreading the war to Syria was Bush's hard-line strategy against Islamic militants.

After rebuffing Bush's suggestion about attacking Syria, the Israeli government settled on a strategy of mounting a major assault in southern Lebanon aimed at rooting out Hizbullah guerrillas who have been firing Katyusha rockets into northern Israel.

In a July 30 story about Israel being prepared for a possible attack by Syria in response to its attacks in Lebanon, The Jerusalem Post noted the White House interest.

The IDF [Israel Defense Forces] was also concerned about a possible Syrian attack in response to the ongoing IDF operations in Lebanon. It was also known that Syria had increased its alert out of fear in Damascus that Israel might attack.

Defense officials told the Post last week that they were receiving indications from the US that America would be interested in seeing Israel attack Syria.

Neoconservatives, or 'neocons,' believe that the United States should not be ashamed to use its unrivaled military power to promote its values around the world. Several prominent neocon columnists have recently written about the need for Israel to take the current conflict beyond Lebanon to include the countries they consider to be Hizbullah's main backers - Iran and Syria.

Here is a remarkable story released four months after hostilities ceased:

Neo-Cons Wanted Israel to Attack Syria

By Jim Lobe

Inter Press Service

http://www.ipsnews.net/news.asp?idnews=35888

Tuesday 19 December 2006

Washington - Neo-conservative hawks in and outside the administration of U.S. President George W. Bush had hoped that Israel would attack Syria during last summer's Lebanon war, according to a newly published interview with a prominent neo-conservative whose spouse is a top Middle East adviser in Vice President Dick Cheney's office.

Meyrav Wurmser, who is herself the director of the Centre for Middle East Policy at the Hudson Institute here, reportedly told Yitzhak Benhorin of the Ynet website that a successful attack by Israel on Damascus would have dealt a mortal blow to the insurgency in Iraq.

"If Syria had been defeated, the rebellion in Iraq would have ended," she asserted, adding that it was chiefly as a result of pressure from what she called "neocons" that the administration held off demands by U.N. Security Council members to halt Israel's attacks on Hezbollah and other targets in Lebanon during the summer war.

"The neocons are responsible for the fact that Israel got a lot of time and space ... They believed that Israel should be allowed to win," she told Ynet. "A great part of it was the thought that Israel should fight against the real enemy, the one backing Hezbollah ... If Israel had hit Syria, it would have been such a harsh blow for Iran that it would have weakened it and (changed) the strategic map in the Middle East."

Wurmser's remarks bolster reports from Israel that hawks in the Bush administration did, in fact, encourage in the first days of the Israel-Hezbollah conflict the government of Prime Minister Ehud Olmert <u>to extend its war beyond Lebanon's borders</u>.

"In a meeting with a very senior Israeli official, [U.S. Deputy National Security Adviser Elliot] Abrams indicated that Washington would have no objection if Israel chose to extend the war beyond to its other northern neighbour, leaving the interlocutor in no doubt that the intended target was Syria," a well-informed source, who received an account of the meeting from one of its participants, told IPS shortly after the conflict ended last August. A similar account was published in the Jerusalem Post at the time.

The ability to connect the dots is grounded upon the willingness to make God and Torah central to our thinking. Without admitting to the masked teachings and truths, revealed in the first nine chapters, there was no way for the author to accurately interpret many years earlier what ultimately unfolded in the summer of 2006. There was no way to carry confidence that the plan was to destroy Israel *ab initio* from the date of the state's creation. There was no way to know that the Moabite plan included more than seizure of oil, included more than regime change, but also culture change in the plan to undermine all nations that remained aligned with monotheism. In other words, succinctly said, it all makes sense, including the newly seen bonding between Israel, China and Iran, once you see from the light and thus see that this trilogy of nations represent the full spectrum of nations that can and should oppose the Moabites, these nations now finally finding, during the course of events in the summer of 2006, the common denominator to their respective woes – *not to minimize the fact that they finally can identify an enemy that successfully remained invisible throughout the centuries.*

It is tantamount to having a chronic disease, without any idea of its root cause, and thus suffering endlessly because of it, without the ability to confront it. Thus, without admitting to Ruth's role, to the Moabite stratagem, it is impossible to connect the dots of a sordid history that followed her infiltration into Israel against Divine Decree: one which impugned Judaism, Christianity, and, as seen today, the nations aligned with the Judeo-Christian ethic.

Many have posited the question why the Book of Ruth and Torah could not have been written in a manner where its deeper meanings are better understood; thereby, precluding reliance on interpretation, compelling study and comment throughout the centuries.

The Torah was given after Abraham's intervention for his nephew, Lot. The author of the Book of Ruth took great pains to mask the hidden messages, so that they would survive. **Do you doubt for a moment that if the author spelled out the truth regarding Ruth in what he wrote that it had any chance to survive the element of time, not to say remain part of the religious liturgy?**

The author of the Book of Ruth thereby could not cover with detail the events of Elimelech's death, the death of his two sons, or the loss of wealth. However, the author could reveal his true intent by leaving a red flag accordingly via the incident regarding Ruth at Boaz's "feet". Whereas, he normally would omit such reference in a story that purports to honor Ruth, he could lodge this red flag regarding his true intent because to the Sodomite mind its inclusion did not register as a red flag to deny it a place in religious liturgy. Otherwise, with the Moabites enmeshing themselves into both Judaism and Christianity, do you doubt for a moment what might have happened to Torah if what is made clear in Clarity was made openly clear by Torah? Thus, no doubt, with God's intervention, Torah and the Book of Ruth survived the element of time in a violent environment clearly controlled by the Moabites.

Would the Moabites have used their position in the all-powerful early Church to see the Torah, Old Testament, discarded, if not burned, and removed from Christian reverence? Everything else that was Torah connected was turned inside out, but the Torah remained intact, because the Old Testament, like the Book of Ruth, was not an open and apparent threat to them (especially when they controlled a religious leadership complicit in the misdirection that obfuscated the teachings and truths highlighted by this book – a complicity apparent today by their silence and acquiescence, with a corrupted U.S. Congress, to the crimes and injustices taking place since 9-11).

The Moabites are the cancer that moves to undermine under their current agenda all present-day nations under the Judeo-Christian ethic, including the descendants of Abraham in nations under true Islam. Now, when learning under the light, you instantly can grasp a deeper appreciation of the Moabite designs against Islam and in particular Iran. The Moabites have de facto control over Judaism and Christianity, but they have been obsessively seeking to control, to dilute, in order to ultimately undermine, Islam – particularly the openly theocratic nation, Iran.

The more times you read the first nine chapters of this book, the deeper will you instill within yourself teachings and truths that have been denied you. If what this book offers truly represents light, then you have already felt the importance of the teachings and truths deliberately denied you. If they are teachings and truths from the light, you will never forget them. You will never tire of reading them. As just said, the more times you read the book, the more insight you will derive. The ability to not only see but also understand the dynamics behind of the shift of the paradigm of power is the result of the author's accepting these teachings and truths obfuscated from us.

Once you accept God's centrality to our very existence, then you too can make astounding interpretations. There is a segment ahead that allows you to confirm for yourself that you now can connect dots that you never even knew existed.

If you don't share in these proffers, then you can conclude that the teachings and truths presented by this book, as far as you are concerned, are not from the light. This will have made the author's efforts for you fail.

The sad part of closing this effort is recognizing the reality that over all the centuries, since the Roman exile, despite all the time spent studying, truths have been masked and obfuscated, which would explain the dire realities of endless conflicts, wars, deaths, including the deaths and serious injuries on wholesale levels to innocent men, women and children.

Clarity by Joseph Ehrlich was written and is offered to show you what correct teaching can mean to you and to all men and women absorbing truths from the light. In the author's humble opinion, it is these truths, many highlighted in the Conclusions and other materials just ahead, that stand among those God intended the descendants of Abraham to see, and the Jewish people to recognize during their two millennia in Exile.

Very few people are aware that Abraham formally married Hagar. The Jewish commentaries themselves certify that Keturah in Genesis 25:1 was Hagar. She elevated herself and so did Ishmael, no doubt with God's oversight, and she bore Abraham many additional children.

God kept his word to Hagar and thus you have the realities before us today with the Arab/Islamic nations in possession of the oil and otherwise on the world stage as they are. However, here is something that attests to the fatal error Israel would make had it attacked or should it ever attack Iran.

Isaac and Ishmael (I and I) buried Abraham. They united to bury their father.

Due to Moabite dominance, controlling our reality for centuries, we live in an upside down world, where evil dominates over good.

Who is the antithesis to Abraham?

Answer: Lot (NWO/Moabite)

Thus I & I -- today may represent not individuals but nations!

Israel and Iran -- must unite to bury Lot (NWO/Moabites).

Israel and Iran will be under God's protection and with His intervention Lot (Moabites) will be buried, as he (they) should have been buried, destroyed, long ago

"Do not give your inheritance to foreigners, nor your heritage to violent men, lest you be regarded as humiliated in their eyes, and foolish, and they trample upon you, for they will come to dwell among you and become your masters."

From the Dead Sea Scrolls,

TESTAMENT OF KOHATH (4Q542 – Plate 9)

CONCLUSIONS

Do You Now Realize...

- That Moabites live among us?

- That they have lived among the Jews and Christians since biblical days?

- That the Moabites are our relatives?

- That the Moabites detest God?

- That the reason the Moabites detest God is because God went forth to destroy them?

- That the Moabites also detest Jews and Christians?

- That the reason the Moabites detest Jews and Christians is because God favored them?

- That the Moabites, since the time of Ruth's intrusion, intertwine themselves into the Judeo-Christian ethic?

- But that the Moabites have no affinity nor respect for the Judeo-Christian ethic?

- Thus they have no guilty conscience over spitting on the cross?

- Thus they have no guilty conscience or remorse over war?

- Thus they have no guilty conscience over murder?

- Thus they have no guilty conscience or remorse over the deaths of innocents including women and children?

- That the Moabites detest all those today under monotheism including Jew, Christian and Muslim - all the descendants of Abraham whom God, the God that intended to destroy the Moabite, favored?

- That the Moabites historically move to keep God out of the picture by having Israel prove an abomination to God?

- That Israel, when such an abomination, removes God's protection and in fact has God stand aside so that the Moabites can implement their game plan for that time and period?

- That the Moabites have turned the world upside down from the one God intended and thus as He was to annihilate any future for the descendants of Lot that the Moabites are out to annihilate any future for the descendants of Abraham?

- That understanding the history, existence, and intertwinement of the Moabites into our culture and history explains all the mysteries that have defied explanation and reason?

- That the Moabites control our culture, our education, our media, our government and society, to press forward their plans for total victory for themselves, while diminishing not only God, but also all those genuinely under monotheism, by bringing paganism and base values into our families and homes?

- That the Moabites can be deduced and identified by their behavior?

- That understanding the truths and teachings heretofore denied you, as set forth by Clarity by Joseph Ehrlich, allows you to recapture your government and also your family, true culture, and heritage?

- That the above attests in part why this book is incredibly valuable and you must pursue the truths herein with those you respect in the community. If there are those that want to cast its truths aside, without discussion and introspection, then you must deduce, if not conclude, that they are within the Moabite system that has put a stranglehold against efforts to bring forth these truths?

- There is no attack in this book on the seed of Ruth, because God intervened in the crime of the Moabites accordingly. However, to fail to recognize the existence of the Moabites and their intertwinement into our culture and lives continues the greatest victimization of history?

- How leaders go to Church and then exit and push buttons and without conscience and remorse commit to the killing of endless steams of innocents over history. The God they portend to worship when in Church is not their God, but their enemy and façade that keeps the enemy within well hidden. Can any man or woman truly beholden to God, and the seed of those God favored, pursue chaos, mayhem and wars continually through history, perpetuating every vice and abuse known to man?

- That we must remove those aligned with the Moabite agenda in order to allow the world to turn right side up?

- The Moabites will go on causing the damage they have done throughout history because the descendants of Abraham have consistently failed God, as detailed in part by this book?

- The most important thing to remember and forge into your mind is that the Moabites look just like the descendants of Abraham. They cannot be identified by appearance but in fact their appearance is their greatest asset, allowing them to hide throughout the centuries, with a much better edge than Ruth herself had in first infiltrating and intertwining herself into Israel?

- God, as Rabbi Eliezer ben Hycranus, has been ostracized? That it is time to realize and recognize the truths of history denied us and bring God back?

It is time to educate our children correctly, and with the light of truth, they will return to God and separate us from the Moabite influence that has taken control of our environment, our lives, our families and our future.

June 19, 2006: North Korea fuels missiles for missile tests. Author declares that North Korea has stealth missile technology and that President Bush accordingly will abandon his National Security Strategy. **June 22, 2006**: Author interprets North Korea will launch on or before July 4, 2006. **June 25, 2006**: Israeli soldier Gilad Shalit is kidnapped by Palestinians aligned with the NWO dominated Fatah movement. **June 26, 2006**: Hamas is speaking with Israelis about working together for the release of Gilad Shalit. **June 29, 2006**: 64 Hamas legislators are kidnapped by Israel and Shin Bet, Israeli internal security, intimidates Israelis against speaking with Hamas. **June 30, 2006**: Israel begins disproportionate retaliation against Gaza.

July 4, 2006: North Korea launches ten missiles (per South Korean and Russian detections) and global media ultimately reports only seven missiles detected, with a single long-range missile, without stealth technology, failing. Thus, according to the author's real time analysis, three longer-range missiles with stealth technology went undetected. If the perspective was correct, the author would obtain certification by President Bush taking the extraordinary step of stepping back from his National Security Strategy, as author first interpreted on June 19. **July 7, 2006**: President Bush does a complete flip flop on how he speaks about the North Korean president. To make the point a 90 second audio clip from NBC Nightly News was posted at www.senderberl.com/nbc_nk.mp3. **July 9, 2006**: President Bush per Time Magazine (The End of Cowboy Diplomacy) declares the end of his NSS. **July 10, 2006** USA Today story: "Israeli army faulted in soldier's capture" attesting to the sad reality that the soldier was kidnapped without intent on the part of the IDF to intercede or rescue him. **July 12, 2006**: Two IDF soldiers are declared kidnapped by troops in Lebanon aligned with Iran (Hezbollah). Major retaliation by Israel resulting in willful but wanton bombing of Beirut and other areas within Lebanon resulting in deaths of innocents. **July 20, 2006**: Israeli Defense Minister announces plans to commence ground assault against Lebanon. **July 25, 2006**: Israel's rabid campaign of retaliation seeking to ensnare involvement by Syria and Iran also includes the **willful bombing of a UN post with a precision bomb**. Kofi Annan screams that Israel's attack was "deliberate targeting." News emanates that Israel warned ten times about that particular UN post, leaving Israel without justification or excuse for what took place. Israel's religious leadership publicly declares that IDF forces need not be concerned with the deaths of innocents, including women and children. **July 30, 2006**: Nasrallah declares that Israel is an "**American slave**." This single declaration suggests to the author that Israel is talking with China and/or Iran and thus Hezbollah. Within five hours of the author's analysis, Israel's bombing of Qana, resulting in fractional losses for Hezbollah, is declared by NWO media to be the deed of an Israel gone mad resulting in global ridicule against Israel, with concurrent reports of growing sentiments of global anti-Semitism, all by the author declared oxymoronic to the passive reaction seen in comparison with Israel's original bombing of Beirut, military action which resulted in a large number of injuries and deaths to innocents in Lebanon, including women and children.

August 2, 2006: Chinese military plane allowed to land in Tel-Aviv to pick up the body of Du Zhaoyu, the Chinese Lt Colonel who died in Israel's precision bombing of the UN Post on July 25, 2006. **August 3, 2006**: China declares that its nationals should leave Israel. Author analyzes that China will engage Israel and has full justification. If Israel can commence war due to the kidnapping of one to three soldiers, China can do the same with regard to holding proof that its Lt. Colonel died due to an intentional and deliberate attack by Israel on the UN Post. **August 6, 2006**: Jimmy Carter de facto openly and publicly warns Israel that the Bush administration is not a genuine friend of Israel. **August 7, 2006**: Events escalate where attacks on Haifa and Tel-Aviv seem imminent. Author appears on Jeff Rense show and reaffirms publicly that what is in play is the Bush Double Double Cross interpreted by him in November 2002, where NWO leaders are pushing for regional if not global warfare (to wit warfare with China). He announces that the best defense is for Hezbollah to simply stand down, regardless of the consequences, in order to quash the NWO (Moabite) drive for war, signified by Israel's disproportionate rabid response to the kidnapping of three soldiers. Both Iran and Syria refuse to bite at Israel's provocation for them to enter the fray, aimed at enticing them to preclude further unjust injuries and deaths by Israel to

Lebanese innocents. **August 7, 2006**: China elevates slain UN peacekeeper in Lebanon as martyr. "Beijing, Aug 07: China on Monday elevated Lt Colonel Du Zhaoyu, a Chinese UN peacekeeper killed in an Israeli air raid in South Lebanon last month, as a martyr." **August 8, 2006**: News reports emanate that Sun Bigan, China's special envoy to the Middle East, is in the region representing China's serious concerns and issues. Christian Science Monitor: "US neocons hoped Israel would attack Syria." Sub-headline further declares, "Israel considered expansion of conflict in Lebanon 'nuts.'"

August 11, 2006: Author interprets that the NWO is moving away from the quest for regional war. Author receives letters that Hezbollah seems to have disappeared from Southern Lebanon. Israel thereafter pursues several days of militarism and then there is an overall stand down (ceasefire). **August 13, 2006**: Author includes the following in his closing reports about Israel's war against Lebanon: "Also highlighted in March 2006: US President George W. Bush said he hoped to resolve the nuclear dispute with Iran with diplomacy, but warned Tehran he would "use military might" if necessary *to defend* Israel. "The threat from Iran is, of course, their stated objective to destroy our strong ally Israel. That's a threat, a serious threat. It's a threat to world peace," the US president said after a speech defending the war in Iraq. "I made it clear, and I'll make it clear again, **that we will use military might *to protect our ally Israel*,**" said Bush, who was apparently referring to Iranian President Mahmoud Ahmadinejad's call for the destruction of Israel. March 2006 excerpt proof to author that post Sharon's removal the Bush Double Double Cross was in play. Author writes, "Israel and Iran can be leaders to cleanse us from the NWO cancer." **August 13, 2006**: News reports surface about Bush administration's push for regional warfare: "US involved in planning Israel's operations in Lebanon: report 13/08/2006 9:57:00 AM The US government was closely involved in the planning of Israel's military operations against Islamic militant group Hezbollah even before the July 12 kidnapping of two Israeli soldiers, The New Yorker magazine reported in its latest issue." **August 15, 2006**: Jeff Rense permits author to post the August 7th interview. http://www.senderberl.com/renseradio.mp3. **August 17, 2006:** Attesting to the secreted reality of the shift of the paradigm of power: "**China orders America to shut up** 04:37:32 E.Ù, China's ambassador to the United Nations in Geneva told America on Thursday to shut up and keep quiet on the subject of Beijing's growing military spending." **August 20, 2006**: {from real time report}:"ANSWERING YOUR DIFFICULT QUESTIONS...Isn't the NWO so well entrenched in Israel to make your interpretation seem ridiculous? Yes and no. There is division between the historic powerhouse aligned with the Moabites for centuries and the Moabite free leadership that is moving to serve the true national interests. Thus the battles seen for what many describe as the end days are in play. Bush 43 got angry because Israel did not bring home the bacon: expand the war into Syria and Iran Thus, Bush no doubt by now knows that Israel, recognizing that the Bush Double Double Cross was a highly accurate interpretation made by {the author} in 2002, has gone over to Iran. If Israel should have bought that interpretation in 2002, I trust it has concluded that it should buy into my interpretation in 2006 of whom it needs to align with to see a future. Otherwise, God will uproot Israel and use the NWO or Iran/China to do so. In fact, below is an article that put a smile to my face: that God seems to be making a comeback on the global stage. There is a message here for the NWO: that their role is over as I have explained and there is no need for them. Thus, since Abraham's mistake opened the portal for centuries of suffering by everyone, I have explained why it will be China that will systematically wipe them off the face of the planet UNLESS they disappear on their own accord. I would advise them to take the chips off the table. What about the threat against Nasrallah and the incursions Israel is making into South Lebanon and Israel's threat to re-ignite warfare yet again? If Israel kills Nasrallah then my interpretation is wrong. Nasrallah should be safe and from where I sit he was a key person in accepting Israel into the alliance. This therefore suggests that it is Bush and the NWO that will pursue the assassination. As to everything else it is noise and disinformation since as per the secret with the NK launch these details are for true insiders not the public. Will Bush attack Iran? He wants to do it. He is angry at Israel. No doubt, Israel has told him they concluded that rumors are that Israel was going to get blamed for 9-11. **August 20, 2006**: The $64,000 question is how will Bush pursue it with his oil cohorts? The best solution for the Moabites is the Temple Mount. The answer is probably on target because taking into account all the prophecies; it would take the Temple Mount to trigger world war and long-term

163

conflict (and see Israel eviscerated). My question: What problems do the Moabites have in effectuating the strategy? The Moabites have always used surrogates, dupes, to fight the wars. They are like a cancer that enters a host country and then uses it to do its dirty work. The best example is the first example how they set up Israel and the Assyrians and they walked away with the wealth of the ten tribes and ever since they have tried to blow up the remaining two. There is no doubt that a number of Jews within Israel and Judaism are kept on record as the seed and product of Ruth (these are Jews that are the enemies of not only Israel but the Jewish people). So Israel is now out of the picture. The NWO was setting up Israel for decades...now Olmert triggered the war but then the Jews, as they tend to do, figured it out and then realized what they figured out overlaid the Bush Double Double Cross. So the question is what can Bush put in play that allows him (US military) to invade Iran? Answer: I cannot come up with one using the primary NWO target, the Temple Mount, but a C-802 or similar device seemingly from Iran striking the Eiffel Tower or something similar creating a 9-11 for France should do the job. Chirac will fight it all the way, but then it will be his life or his approval. He will approve it and then France will involve by definition Germany and Belgium and you have your global warfare scenario with the new NATO making the first strike against Iran while the NWO per US assets and Russia and Japan take on NK and China. How to stop it? I don't know but what I want to warn everyone about is that if such a set up does take place, don't sit around knitting to see what first unravels because Bush will be launching against China concurrently knowing that once China is out of the picture, that Iran is a done deal. Now you understand why I spend the time answering questions. It is to put forth light to stop the madmen from their pursuit of not any longer war with Iran, but war with China. Knowing the NWO, I believe they are setting up China for a blind side attack. Again, the target is now China. This will be Bush's most difficult sell to the NWO leadership and I trust they will put a stop to this insanity. I assure them they will not win but as I expressed on Rense Radio they will surely take us all with them. By the way, the question per the above is what will Israel do? If Israel sits it out, they are cooked. If they assess the scenario that the NWO has been successful in the first strike, they will make the parallel mistake to the Bar Kokhba Rebellion. Israel better defend Iran for if they do not and if they turn on Iran (I truly pray not) they are toast not by

Iran or China but I respectfully submit by God Himself. Remember, independent of everything Israel is on the ropes because it has failed again as it did 2000 years ago. However, God stands open at all times to a change in course from Israel. Israel does have a priority doorway. Thus, if the move to Iran was with our influence to any degree then Israel understood that it would also have to move away from the NWO and also move to God and theocratic government over time. If you thought the NK missile analysis was difficult and it was difficult beyond comprehension (to deduce that Bush would have to discard his NSS), then this interpretation is even more difficult. While the easy interpretation was that Israel was on the outs, the difficult, the hard interpretation, the nearly impossible interpretation is that Israel would move to God. This also suggests that Israel like Japan has two dominant camps. I can't see any deeper into what is happening but what I do know is that Israel from what I see correctly and wisely went with Iran and China. Thus, for all Jews and Israelis against Israel's evisceration this group knew that our position regarding Bush was correct and that *the decision was not one to abandon the USA but to abandon those that conquered the USA and were the enemies of the USA, out to blow up Israel per designs reached in 1948.* **August 21, 2006:** News story: "Uncle Sam to Olmert: Drop Dead." **August 22, 2006:** News story: "US to Israel: No financial aid for war."

September 24, 2006: BERLIN, Sept. 24 (Xinhua) -- Syrian President Bashar al-Assad has told the media that Syrian people "want to make peace with Israel", instead of striving to "wipe the Jewish nation off the map." **December 18, 2006:** Inter Press Service News Agency Neo-Cons Wanted Israel to Attack Syria Jim Lobe WASHINGTON, Dec 18 (IPS) - Neo-conservative hawks in and outside the administration of U.S. President George W. Bush had hoped that Israel would attack Syria during last summer's Lebanon war, according to a newly published interview with a prominent neo-conservative whose spouse is a top Middle East adviser in Vice President Dick Cheney's office. **Early 2007:** Newsweek declares "U.S. provocates Iran for possible war." Haaretz discloses that Bush is not permitting Olmert to go to Syria to speak to Assad. News stories reveal that Israel's Prime Minister Olmert's parents were born in China and China has been moving to honor the area in Habrin, China where his parents were born and where Jews were resident under four political regimes since in or about 1898. " 'These sites are testimony to the friendship between the Jewish and Chinese people, and are intended to contribute to strengthening the ties between the two states,' says Professor Ko Wey, head of the province's Academy of Social Sciences. 'Both the Chinese and the Jews are ancient nations, with a long history. They both suffered persecution and torture.'" The news story from Haaretz concludes with the following stunning paragraph: "**Over the years Chinese intellectuals delved into Jewish texts - especially the Bible and scripts of the Fathers.** They found similarities in the values cherished by both societies, such as respecting parents or edicts guiding interpersonal relations." **To the author, this is code that both China and Israel today recognize the Moabite common enemy. Will Israel now rethink its history and path?**

Conclusion: Suffice it to add to all the teachings and truths conveyed by this book, that the following memo by the author offered to the Moabite leadership on or about August 9, 2006, represented his true plea for them to voluntarily leave the Judeo-Christian world before all is lost for everyone. It simply takes all the deep analyses already offered and moves it one step higher.

Memo

To: NWO Leadership

From: Joseph Ehrlich

Re: Conclusions that you can prevail over China

Date: August 9, 2006

Now here we are with the current scenario in the Middle East. There is little doubt that you were out to trigger regional war and no doubt your assessments supported that China's entry into the conflict at this point of time would transmute into its defeat.

You have fully prepared plans to knock out the NK threat and there is little doubt that you placed with Japan requisite armaments to quickly do the job and have Putin as backup in case something goes drastically wrong or amiss.

Otherwise, militarily, your assessment that with NK gone, China essentially stands alone against -- USA, France, Germany, Belgium, Great Britain, Russia, Israel. The collective military machine will conquer China and I know you believe it is a fully supported conclusion on paper.

However, by now, you, if anyone, should understand that what works on paper does not work in a biblical reality as opposed to your Moabite provided reality for the world.

Thus I know you are curious how I see you losing if you bait Syria, Iran and China, amongst other nations you would be glad to depopulate, into the conflict.

First, and I need not emphasize it again, but will say it again, the biblical destiny is for you to lose, so on this basis, devoid of the need for logic or explanation, you will lose.

Otherwise, the issue is one of first strike. The second issue is who has technologies superior to the other. Remember, if you don't know what China has you cannot factor it into the formal conclusions you reach and rationalize your success over China. Third, you may not have factored in the players or perhaps the sequences of events correctly for per your own foundation of amorality whom can you really trust when the end game truly arises? There are men in the military of the USA and Russia that do have serious reservations about the truths of what has happened since WWII.

{The author} has put out for reflection the issue that in recent times we have seen the Berlin Wall fall and East and West Germany reunited. We have seen the Soviet Union who with the USA defeated Germany collapse and fall under NWO control. We have seen the USA also fall under the same NWO control as the Soviet Union. There are more than a few that know or deduced what Bush 41 told Gorbachev that not only would the Soviet

Union fall to the realities of the new world order but so would the USA. We then saw the US military used as a private army by NWO forces to implement your designs. Israel who was created to mask the survival of those behind WWII was also destined to fall, as did the Berlin Wall. While Japan went out in the 80s still thinking that WWII had not ended the truth of it is that you the NWO played possum and were continuing the war. Thus whereas you could not conquer the USA and the Soviet Union militarily, you were adept at conquering both by stealth. You implemented your design to make Israel the antithesis of a holy nation well knowing that by doing so God not only ultimately would not be with Israel but in fact would have to remove it as a nation unworthy to carry the holy name as He did when Israel befell the exile post its defeat by Rome. Thus, as it stands, you have the Soviet Union, the USA, Israel, the EU in your pocket and the constant stumbling block in these days has been China and to your dismay Iran has taken up the holiness intended to be held by Israel in bowing before God before the other nations of the world.

So let me tell you what crossed my mind. First again you will not prevail. This of course is not me telling you but me telling you what is biblically ordained and I tell you in the same exact spirit of all the other interpretations that have proven true (ones that defied your own belief).

China picked up on that poorly done move to move NATO to the EU to create a new military machine for the EU leaving out the USA military that you fully intend to eviscerate since your plan for the USA is of course the same one as you now implement for Israel.

You have pulled away, from both the USA and Israel, the Judeo-Christian precepts and have substituted pagan ones, control the media, and thus the minds and hearts of the American people and the Israeli people. Thus, you have told China where to launch the first strike to wit the countries that you have bent over backwards to keep out of the picture (for the reasons we have of course articulated): France, Germany and Belgium, the EU. However, what you have not factored in I believe is who will launch that first strike for China and what the consequences will be. I can only relay that France, Germany and Belgium are the first likely targets of the move to war by China.

China no doubt has to neutralize all military threats to it and this will be its initial focus. China knows that you want the war to be played out between USA and China because depopulating and or polluting both are acceptable results. Thus, going back to the litany of nations militarily supporting the NWO you can scratch France, Germany and Belgium. This leaves USA, Great Britain, Russia and Israel.

By your own deductions and plans Israel will be out of the picture either from the biblical or the secular plane or both. Putin I am confident will have his power stripped from him (a long planned coup d'etat) because the Russian military I believe has taken seriously my assertion of the truth of what really happened to Russia in the 80s and 90s and that Putin has sold out the nation for depopulation and evisceration. We know today what is in play. Depopulating USA and Russia and Israel all represent the very people who defeated/annoyed you, the NWO leadership, in WWII and also all collectively represent monotheists with nations aligned with the Judeo-Christian heritage who would arise to ultimately challenge you to campaign and fight for justice. These are all the nations that also not by coincidence connect directly or indirectly to both the American and French revolutions.

If you remember, China fooled you completely by having done, PRIOR to September 2004, its deals to consolidate power in its region. Now, Russia is in China's region and I have no doubt that it played Putin as it needed to do, knowing that he was the Trojan Horse sent to oversee Hu Jintao but China we are sure has made inroads into Russia to explain, expound, and prove Putin's plan to stab Russia in the back for you the NWO leadership. Thus, seeing Putin absent and missing at a critical time will confirm this analysis. It could also be the very shift that will assure China victory.

So who do we have left is USA and Great Britain. With you milking all the money for defense out of the USA, the USA now knows if it didn't know before the NK missile launch crisis that America has no defense at all from attack. Obviously so, when your agenda is to see the USA blown to ribbons in a war with China. So since the military and the naval fleet will be addressed by China's military, the only thing left for China to deal with are the endless stream of nuclear and tactical missiles that will be readied and sent against China. What I have to say here is noteworthy. When Israel failed to teach love of God to its children post the unification of Israel back to its biblical description and status post 1967, ultimately Arafat taught during that subsequent time Palestinians to hate Israel and Israelis. With such dynamic in mind, while you the NWO were stealing America's wealth and not providing us with any defense, China was building defense systems against any attack by the US military arsenal.

Do you think for a single moment that China would allow itself to be played into a regional/global war scenario unless it knew it could win? If you don't understand this you don't understand China and the one thing you and I know is that you don't understand China.

I want to see in here Israel do a miraculous turn and change of heart and understand that Iran is its friend and not its enemy and work together with Iran to encourage you to cash in and go away and leave the rest of us alone. So I do everything to leave the portal open for such a path and result. If there is regional and global war in the Middle East the results will be all that God wills. However, my mission at this point is to do everything to get us to the right path and for us to recognize and reject you. The commitment and passion I have for this desired reality arises of course when we see the ugliness arise as it has per your instructions to… Olmert. We all know that Israel could have ended the Hezbollah problem quickly and by a single military containment action: however we all know and see that Hezbollah has been allowed to claim success and victory over Israel, this Moabite created reality to leave the portal open for the move by Israel to Beirut that you have correctly concluded opens the door for intervention by Syria, Iran and China, should the others including the Bekaa Valley incursion fail.

Thus, it is a steep price for Hezbollah and others to pay, but better for Hezbollah to claim defeat, stand down and leave the area than for you to successfully get Syria, Iran and China involved in a regional/global war. You will not win but you are happy that we will all lose as well. This merely attests to your own true character and your alignment with a master that is now ready to discard you because he has made his point with his Father: when all is said and done, man, given time and opportunity, will prove himself as base, disloyal and amoral as the Father saw his first born when seeking to offset his nature with the birth of a second son (darkness/light), those collectively described in the bible as Israel. Now, Israel having proven itself a second time as unworthy, as it proved itself the first time, has answered the question and proven the point. Moabites have served their purpose in the very same expression they move to extirpate Israel now that it has served its purpose in your allowing its creation in 1948, other than offsetting the historic problems with 9-11.

Thus, if you are willing to recognize the truths incorporated in what I have written above, you will direct Israel to stand down from any move to prepare Beirut for ground attack and close up the conflict. However, my instinct tells me that you will do what you do best: push for the war that you are convinced will best serve your own long-term interests. However, I have articulated that what you are out to secure will be secured not by you but by China. You have seen this happen time and time again over past years. Why do you persist? The logic of your past points that you would prevail were equally convincing, but did you prevail? Thus, is it true that you would risk what is at risk to push the point that you are desperate to prevail as you did when you were allowed to prevail? Your wealth is now beyond measure. What propels you to push us all to the precipice? The answer of course can be seen in the 1956 movie Forbidden Planet which attests that men without boundaries are destined to extinguish their own species and kind. Rethink your position because from the current path there is no return.

http://www.rense.com/general73/nwos.htm

PROVING HOW MUCH YOU HAVE LEARNED...

You probably are wondering whether you have learned the type of analytics that the author uses in his geopolitical analyses. Thus, there is no better proof of it than by posing some geopolitical realities and dynamics and now, based on your elevated knowledge, understanding and wisdom, learned through the discernments highlighted by the author, see whether you can now proffer an answer that you could not have done before reading this book. Take the time to carefully write your answer. Then compare your answer with the author's full-blown answer to the question. If you are satisfied with your answer, then this book has educated you and elevated you to the light. Read the book again, and discover how much higher you can move accordingly with each reading.

Question:

Who are the two countries primarily seen as vanquished nations during WWII?

Answer: Germany and Japan

Question

Who are the two nations primarily responsible for the defeat of Germany and Japan?

Answer: The United States of America and Russia.

Question

What was the United States' primary industrial consumer product post WWII?

Answer: Automobiles

Question

Which two countries are associated today with top of line motor vehicles?

Answer: Germany and Japan.

Question

Companies from which two nations have acquired major stakes in the US automobile industry and sector?

Answer: Germany and Japan.

ANALYTIC QUESTION

WHAT DOTS CAN YOU CONNECT TOGETHER BASED ON THE ABOVE FACTS AND REALITIES AND WHAT DOES IT SUGGEST TO YOU?

Full-blown answer begins on the next page.

Analytic Answer by Joseph Ehrlich

Germany and Japan lost WWII but to them, as surrogates for the Moabites, it was losing a battle not the war. The war continued on after armed hostilities stopped. Yes, Germany and Japan were vanquished and to prove the point, Germany was bombed from head to toe, Germany was divided, Berlin divided, and Japan received two nuclear payloads. However, this was the mask to convince everyone that the war was over, when, to the Moabites, it was a battle in a war that continued on.

All the nations that caused the defeat of Germany and Japan were intended future targets. But first, the greatest mask for the cover-up was that the Moabites themselves supported the creation of the State of Israel. With the creation of the State of Israel, they also planned its intended evisceration, but the Moabites post WWII learned how to use the Jews, first to keep their identities buried, and then to help them regroup for the next battle, one that they did not intend to lose (the one taking place since 1981, from the moment President Reagan was shot).

Thus, in my book, Recapturing America, published in 1997, I first showed how these forces (the Moabites) put their own people into operational control of both the United States and Israel. Ultimately, the Berlin Wall collapsed, a historic and meaningful moment for the Moabites, explaining why Bush 41 attended the historic event, and why he took that moment to first publicly announce the need for a "New World Order."

Subsequently, under his stewardship, the Soviet Union collapsed. The Moabites detest the Russians and thus Russia has a very bleak future, as it has had since the collapse of Communism. The true degree of poverty and disenchantment in Russia is kept suppressed.

However, the next target was Israel, for the reasons set forth by the book. Per Recapturing America, the Moabites moved step by step to take operational control of both the USA and Israel, and now that it had it, the plan was to get Israel to act as an unwitting suicide bomber, to open needed paths of moral outrage, so that the Moabites, via its surrogate, the USA military, could obtain control of Middle East oil.

However, first Rabin balked at following the path he agreed to, seemingly recognizing that he wasn't dealing with people historically representative of the United States of America. Bush 43's actions and behaviors post 9-11, diminishing individual rights and liberties, and moving to cast aside Constitutional protections and guarantees, proved the point Rabin early on recognized. Moreover, before having Bush 43 move forward to abrogate America's heritage, the Moabites guaranteed themselves the support of a compliant Congress, and, gave Bush special signing powers, allowing him to de facto legally do whatever he pleased, which he did. Moreover, Bush 43 made it clear that abusive behavior and corrupt and criminal conduct could take place with complete immunity to those the Moabites favored. What would have singly proven the point to Rabin -- that his instincts were correct -- was Abu Ghraib, the sadism and torture perpetrated there a clear-sign that he was dealing with people historically rejected by those under monotheism.

The author warned Israel post 9-11 that those they were dealing with were not those committed to the USA but those in fact conquering it from within. Post Rabin's assassination, the Moabites moved to take over operational control of Israel, just as Ruth and those that followed her, de facto took over operational control of Israel from within.

Sharon in or about 2002 got the point. Thus, in the intricacies of diplomacy, and complex global relationships, where one's opposition is often by design, Israel was in a fight for time and survival. It had no historic friend but the USA and now realizing that control of the USA was in the hands of those seeking to ultimately impugn and destroy Israel, Israel was in serious jeopardy. That jeopardy also, per the precepts put forth by Clarity by Joseph Ehrlich, has to do with the fact that the religious leadership per the Sanhedrin of biblical days and times FAILED, yet again. This was the sign for the Moabites to move forward on its plan to eliminate its historic nemesis Israel and also take over control of Middle East oil.

Thus, when Sharon hospitalized himself and when he shortly thereafter experienced the stroke under the unfolded circumstances, the author knew it was yet another execution, knowing it to the point that, as per Rabin, they wanted to make an example of those that reneged on agreements, this time by making him a living example.

During the years, the author's incessant insistence on the true realities of the American leadership finally sunk in with not only Israel but also seemingly China and Iran and thus one or all the parties seemingly prepared for what the author long expected, since his major postings regarding it in 2002.

The consequence was not only a new-elevated covert (for the time being) relationship between Israel, China and Iran (amongst others) but also the realization that EU (German) troops were being stationed at strategic points all over Europe and Africa, including the high seas. There was one article that the author found particularly foreboding, when Germany, the nation deemed least responsible to ever again militarize, told world bodies that submarines sold by Germany to Israel were fabricated without the capacity to hold nuclear weapons. Of course, to the author this meant that Germany had nuclear submarines with the capacity of firing nuclear weapons.

Thus, the author noted that Germany had re-militarized and now with North Korea in the headlines, Japan was moving in that direction as well.

Thus, to move to the answer to the analytic question: the Moabites detest all nations under monotheism, particularly ones under the Judeo-Christian ethic, and in particular those who defeated their surrogates in WWII: Russia and the USA. Thus, Russia is a de facto neutered country, and now that the Moabites have deployed the US military under their design (but failing, as the author warned President Bush they would, on September 14, 2001), they are prepared to neuter the USA. While waiting to do so, they took control over the media and have instilled base pagan values into the children of the nation (again see Recapturing America, highlighting the institutionalization of drugs), and where they plan on sinking the nation with the demise of the U.S. dollar without the hope of America regenerating itself due to the loss of its vital and central industrial base: to wit the evisceration first of the automobile industry, with no doubt future plans to do the same to all the remaining major industrial sectors that have not heretofore been compromised by NAFTA or other Moabite machinations.

There is no reason that the US automobile industry had to come under foreign governorship or control to continue in existence (when not independently, or by Moabite hand, otherwise undermined or destroyed). It was all planned as part and parcel of the extirpation of the nations that the Moabites detest most: Israel, Russia and the United States of America.

The author's long held conclusion is that if Iran keeps on its current course, the correct course, that China and Iran will come to dominate Planet Earth, and the future for those under the Judeo-Christian ethic will be dire, unless, at minimum, the truths brought front and center stage by Clarity become mainstream.

The Torah is everything man needs to find understanding, wisdom and be gifted with discernment. Torah provided that this time, this very time, where this generation had more blessings than any other before it, with leisure time and opportunity and every reason to find the truths intended to be seen and determined by the Exile, was the period of time critical to the future for those under the Judeo-Christian ethic. They have not found these truths, to the author's despair, and thus the commitment made by the author to open a gateway to the light.

As it stands today, until you move forward under the light conveyed and taught by this book, we are far from moving towards the portal of redemption. Without creating and finding that portal, the author's conclusions, made a decade back, were that the paradigm of power inter alia would shift to China and the East. It already has done it. Thus, wisdom would include rethinking our reality and turning the world right side up. This book was written for that express purpose.

Without God, the author could never have made the interpretations made successfully defying the odds or written this book. Thus, the author sees himself as a portal to bring and teach to the light. If you see it, then you are blessed to help create light rather than perpetuate the darkness the Moabites are pressing forward full steam to prevail upon us, as they move forward in what they consider their final phase of action for world domination and control.

One More Question

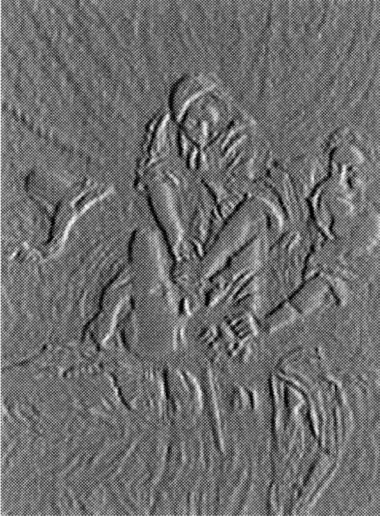

Question:

The Book/Story of Judith (a young, religious and beautiful widow) is hardly if at all known in the Jewish community (it is not included in the Tanach, the 24 books considered aligned with the Bible). Why would you say this is the case?

Answer: Judith beheaded the head of Holofornes, the chief captain of the host of Asshur. Via this act and deed, and with the intervention of God, the Assyrians turned around and called off their military move against Jerusalem and thus spared the tribes of Judah and Benjamin and the Levites, the remnant of Israel, the Jews, the fate of the ten northern tribes.

Why the author believes the story is de facto secreted is because it highlights the power of a single woman to change history. Here, Judith, alone, changed history. This then makes the mind posit the realities attendant to Ruth. If Judith, in a single night, could be a quasi-transformational figure in history, could Ruth have played a similar role, as well, in terms of her one night marriage to Boaz, implicating the future course for Israel, resulting in an Israel

179

dismally failing God? Wasn't there sufficient mental energy in the people and land of Israel to connect Boaz's one night marriage, resulting in issue, with the childless marriage to Naomi's son, and the death of Mahlon, his brother, and father, and the loss of their wealth during their tenure in Moab? Wasn't it enough to connect Ruth to God's specific Divine Decrees regarding the Moabites? To the fact of restraining their intertwinement with Israel, when they were anomalous brethren to Abraham himself? **The author has come to the realization that God's very clear decree in Torah was to specifically assist Israel in stopping Ruth's entry into Israel!**

The author of the Book of Ruth sought to preserve the truths that came to change Israel's future and thus our modern day world and course. If no one will admit to the truth of the facts, then the Exile was a waste of two millennia and Israel's destiny is as clear as it was under Ruth. Thus, in today's world, so is the destiny of the United States of America, a country under threat of becoming a third world nation, due to the Moabite infiltration from within. The Moabites today, as before, have corrupted the Congress. Only God can intervene to save us. Will you join me in praying for His return now that you know that He has been de facto ostracized from openly intervening for us and that the Moabites have also de facto hijacked both Judaism and Christianity, and move forward openly today to do the same to Islam?

Why is the Bible written in a manner requiring interpretation?

Answer: For the same reason the Book of Ruth is less lucid than the author wanted it to be. If Torah and the Book of Ruth were openly clear, the Moabites, who hijacked Judaism and Christianity, and seek to do the same with Islam, would have never allowed them the stature they continue to hold. Keep in mind that God gave the Torah long after Abraham's successful intervention for Lot. Regarding the Dead Sea Scroll inscription highlighted in the book, the Moabites continue active in keeping the Dead Sea Scrolls out of the public reach due to the fact that some segments may provide the clarity offered here.

How can leaders who go to Church and profess love of God, walk out of the Church and then push buttons or give orders that knowingly, if not deliberately, result in the deaths of innocents, including women and children?

Answer: They are Moabites who spit on the cross, detest God, but go to Church and kiss the cross, to mask their true identity, role, and agenda. They have no reservation about murder or depopulation on global levels. Their desire since Day 1 is to annihilate the Jewish people, the remnant of God's chosen, to impugn God's design to destroy Lot and his family.

Why has the US industrial base been de facto abandoned by the nation?

Answer: The Moabites seek to control and then undermine and destroy all sovereign nations under monotheism. Since the Moabites control the government and the media, policies have been passed which are contradictory to the sovereign interests of the American people and nation. What they detest first and foremost is a theocratic nation. Thus, aside from the oil, they are obsessed with conquering Iran. The Moabites have successfully undermined the Judeo-Christian nexus historically carried by the USA and Israel, thus making both these nations, from the Moabite understanding of biblical history, vulnerable to attack from within and without.

Why does China protect its children from pornography better than we do here in the USA?

Answer: While China has never been aligned with religion, its government is in service to its people. Moabite controlled government in the USA does not care about the people they rule over nor for their future welfare, aside from how it may benefit them. They also impregnate the USA with the very opposite values to the Judeo-Christian ethic that predicated America's prosperity and success as a nation, one that enabled the US to defeat the Moabite design and agenda during the Twentieth Century.

Does the nation of Israel really run or overly influence the USA?

Answer: Israel will soon be an open target of the USA, since the US is a conquered nation with a leadership that is out to eviscerate many countries including Israel and the USA itself. The harsh truth is that the governments in both the USA and Israel are Moabite controlled. The only recent difference is that Israel recognized (including Moabite surrogates to wit Moabite pawns and poodles) the message of the author that Israel's complete evisceration was on the Moabite drawing board in connection with the coerced war against Lebanon: the one that Sharon refused to initiate or trigger per Moabite directive.

Who are the enemies of God?

Answer: The Moabites. They know better than some under monotheism that God exists, and they use biblical history in order to make the nations under monotheism abhorrent to Him by instilling pagan values and mores to encourage God to turn His back on those He otherwise favors. The Moabites have made their behavior and lifestyle acceptable, to not only serve their personal interests, but also to have others engage in such once rejected paths of behavior to further help mask their identities, by making such conduct mainstream. Otherwise, since Moabites are the descendants of Lot, they are difficult to identify physically and the routes to identify them are those showing the behaviors anathema to God (and Abraham) associated with Sodom and Gomorrah, the biblical sin cities. The current trend in the USA is moving towards the very values and mores of those cities destroyed by God. It is not coincidence.

In a battle between Israel and Iran, initiated to serve the Moabite design, which nation will earn God's protection?

Answer: Iran. Since Iran is a theocratic nation, honoring and bowing to God before the nations of the world, Israel, of all nations, carried an affirmative duty to protect Iran. That it openly moved to serve the Moabite design, assured 110% that it could never prevail against Iran, just as it having a superior military has not taken it away from the abyss it has found itself over recent years. The Moabite plan since Israel's creation in 1948 was to set the Jews and Arabs (Islam) up for the double double cross. They nearly pulled it off.

Why did George Bush, Jr. go it alone against Iraq?

The Moabites did not want to have Europe, their home territory, footing the bill, and moreover the agenda was to milk the US Treasury in using the USA military as surrogate to destroy, but for the oil, Iraq. The Appendix does carry the disturbing information showing how injured military personnel were de facto abandoned by a government that cared little to nothing for them once carried off the battle field, unlikely to return. The American people with a controlled press and media are denied honest reporting and are ignorant of the truly incredible money stolen by the Moabites from the American people, the Moabites considering it the spoils of war; but the deeper crime being that the American people continue on not cognizant that they are a conquered nation living under an enemy government (even though after ten years of public service effort, the author sees some signs of the American people awakening). Clarity, among the many purposes it professes to serve, explains just who it is that has conquered the United States of America.

Why did Abraham not question God, when instructed to sacrifice his son?

When Abraham realized the consequences to his descendants from the incest knowingly committed by his nephew, Lot, Abraham repented for his egregious mistake, in intervening, especially in the way he did, for Lot to live. Thereafter, when instructed to do the very deed he otherwise would carry the unbridled urge to speak against, Abraham obeyed, saying nothing despite the three day period between setting off on the journey and lifting up the knife to sacrifice his son. God allowed Abraham's descendants life over death. God shifted the paradigm of power to the Judeo-Christian world from the notorious East. Now, that those under the Judeo-Christian ethic, having learned nothing, not even very little, from the mistakes made and recorded from biblical days; now, that the descendants of Lot are turning the USA and Israel into Sodomite communities, the paradigm of power, as foreseen, shifts to the East, where it would have been all along, but for God's earlier intervention. Moabites serve the darkness and if Moabites prevail, or more accurately said, those under monotheism fail, the planet will ultimately die and revert to its original status in a universe otherwise bereft of life, before God's intervention in creating life here for our blessed planet. Did you ever for a moment think that the eight other known planets, all without life, were anything but a testimonial to this very significant reality?

FRONT COVER COLLAGE

During the decade of real-time geopolitical analysis, I have had the opportunity to note a number of photographs that symbolize or act as metaphors to the suppressed teachings and truths in this book. I put together a collage of nine of them for the front cover, since collectively they touch upon the teachings and truths of this book. Let me explain.

Photo 1 of 9.

Starting with the top photograph on the left, you have President Bush standing on the American flag. President Bush has often highlighted the need to respect the flag, but leaders under Moabite control need to spit on the cross while kissing it in public. You are never likely to see a photograph of a Moabite leader spitting on the cross, but you can see via this photograph a President of the United States, stepping on a rendition of the American flag. A citizen truly loving his country, regardless of any excuse or rationalization, would not step on any item that is a flag or symbolizes the flag of the United States of America. To do so, would be repugnant to any citizen truly loving his country.

Many, when, at first, looking at this photograph, believe that it is a computer generated and designed photograph. It is a real photograph. It is quite genuine, taken on or about September 10, 2006, in connection with memorial services for the victims of 9-11, outside Ladder Company 10 in New York, New York.

Here are two images of other photos taken in connection with the event, since I myself was amazed that the President and the First Lady would find it appropriate to stand upon a rendition of the US flag, albeit standing on what purports to be a rug (in commemoration of those lost on 9-11).

Photo 2 of 9.

The photo below the one of President Bush with his foot on the rendition of the flag is a very touching photograph. President Bush was mentally prepared for 9-11. He was trained and taught to be hard and cold. However, Ashley Faulkner caught him off guard.

In this photograph, Ashley Faulkner, a young girl whose mother died on 9-11, encountered President Bush when he was otherwise mingling publicly on the campaign trail in May 2004. His pain about knowing that his arms were around a young girl losing her mother on 9-11, showed clearly on his face, The pain, seen on President Bush's face, was not limited to the fact that the girl's mother was a victim, but from where I sat, his knowing that the young girl was looking for comfort in the arms of a man knowing the truth regarding 9-11 and his very role in it. This is the only photograph known to me where the President displays a consciousness of guilt.

Photo 3 of 9.

The photo below it, the one of Bush extending his hand to Sharon, is a truly revealing moment, making the photograph from where I sit, historical. You can see that Sharon both fears Bush and detests him as well. His bodily response reflects the reality that he would, as foreseen by The Bush Double Double Cross, amongst other analyses, die. It is spiritually difficult to be photographed with a man with a clear nexus to your seen destiny. Sharon's autonomic response touched on the higher truth and tragedy of the captured moment.

Photo 4 of 9.

The photo to the immediate right is another historic photo showing President Bush attending the 100th birthday party for Senator Strom Thurmond in December 2002. This photograph has deep meaning on two different paths. First, you see Trent Lott there right before he made his faux pas that caused him his position as Senate Majority Leader. However, also in the photograph to the left of President Bush, not seen in the collage photo, but seen below, was Dick Cheney, who at the time was not supposed to be together with President Bush, due to the immediate terrorism threat broadcast at the time to Americans.

All these political people in the photograph knew there wasn't any threat of domestic terrorism, and they knew why, and they also knew that what Trent Lott said was what they believed, highlighted in 1997 in my novel, Recapturing America: that they were deeply concerned about a black majority in the USA, they were never going to allow an Afro-American president to control a supreme military force (explaining why the Moabites are dismembering it), and they were going to open the floodgates to Latino immigration to dilute the future role and influence of Afro-Americans in the United States, which sovereign nation they were going to undermine, by breaking its borders with both Mexico and Canada.

Photo 5 of 9.

The photograph above it is President Bush in a televised presidential debate during the 2004 Presidential election campaign. President Bush abhors the debate environment, well knowing that the debate was simply in 2004 a mask for the known result. As was originally raised by Recapturing America, the Moabites control the result by controlling both major candidates. However, the Moabites maximized control by moving to control the electronic voting machines. There was substantial proof that Ohio was supposed to go to Kerry in 2004, but with electronic manipulation and other tampering, the result went to Bush. *Why didn't Kerry object?* He was part of the Moabite control team in 2004. His role was to lose by a small margin and he did what he needed to do to lose, including failing to contest results that could be contested, and should have been contested, in a court of law.

Photo 6 of 9.

Similarly, the photograph above it, shows President Bush seated at the United Nations. Diplomatically said, you can see his inner feelings about his spurious need to be present at a global political body he clearly detests. He doesn't want to be there, he wants to be somewhere else, and he shows it.

His attitude toward the UN is similar to his attitude for years regarding Jiang Zemin, whom he saw more as the owner of the Crawford Chinese laundry than the leader of the nation that is positioning itself to undermine the Moabite agenda. This proved such a costly error that now President Bush even speaks about Kim Jong-il respectfully (in public), learning that sometimes he has to be where he rather not be.

Nevertheless, it has been President Bush's attitude and demeanor that has permitted the world to see through the agenda otherwise hidden since Bush 41 took the reigns of power.

Photo 7 of 9.

To the right is a historic photograph showing early consequences of the Moabites moving to cast aside fundamental rights and liberties protected by the United States Constitution. Under the umbrella of 9-11, the Patriot Act began to give cover for police to round up people in large sweeps and to incarcerate them without just cause. The photograph reflects the message being sent to those inclined to protest and dissent: not only will you be picked up in a major sweep and incarcerated, but we will keep you tied with your hands behind your back, so that you well remember (fear) that your next visit might even have more onerous consequences for you.

Photo 8 of 9.

The photograph below it, showing Bush 41 extending his hand in support to his son, Bush 43, connects with the Ashley Faulkner photograph. This photograph, taken several days after 9-11, at the Washington National Cathedral, pits Bush 43 in a memorial service for the victims of 9-11. Bush 41 didn't have to worry because as long as Bush 43 doesn't have to hug a young girl losing her mother, he has been successfully desensitized and programmed to move forward on the Moabite design.

Photo 9 of 9.

The last photograph in the collage is another rare photograph. It shows President Bush after he met with certain Arab leaders in Washington after 9-11 where they confronted him with evidence that they knew 9-11 was an inside job. This is actually the first and last time that I saw the President ever so seriously distressed over any meeting or issue in connection with the realm of his presidency. He definitely must have been caught off guard and unprepared.

Thierry Meyssan on April 8, 2002 at the Zayed Center in AbuDhabi (United Arab Emirates), at a gathering organized under the auspices of the Arab League and attended by the diplomatic corps and the international press corps stated inter alia at the time several facts little known: "The official version does not include the attack on the White House annex, the Old Executive Office Building (called the "Eisenhower Building"). Yet, on the morning of the eleventh, ABC television broadcast, live, pictures of a fire ravaging the presidential services building. " He also relayed regarding this:

"Neither does the official version take into account the collapse of a third building in the Manhattan World Trade Center complex, independently of the twin towers. This third building was not hit by a plane. However, it, too, was ravaged by a fire before collapsing for an unknown reason. This building contained the world's biggest secret CIA operations base, where the Agency engaged in economic intelligence gathering that the   military-industrial lobby considered a waste of resources that should have been devoted to strategic intelligence gathering. If we look closely at the attack against the Pentagon, we notice that the official version amounts to an enormous lie. It is obviously impossible that a Boeing 757 could, for some 500 kilometers, escape detection by civil and military radar, by fighter-bomber planes sent in pursuit of it and by observation satellites that had just been activated. It is also obviously impossible that a Boeing 757 could enter the Pentagon's air space without being destroyed by one or more of the five missile batteries protecting the building. ~~~An air traffic controller from Washington has testified seeing on radar an object flying at about 800 kilometers per hour, moving initially toward the White House, then turning sharply toward the Pentagon, where it seemed to crash. The air traffic controller has testified that the characteristics of the flight were such that it could only have been a military projectile."

Victory is in the blood for 'aristocratic' Republican

(computer enhanced/generated graphic supplied)
http://www.guardian.co.uk/print/0,,4086720-103632,00.html
November 6, 2000

The Republican George W Bush will be elected US president on November 7 because he has more royal blood than his opponent, it was claimed today. The Texas governor has twice as many ties with aristocrats than his Democrat rival Al Gore, according to Burke's Peerage. The company, which publishes books on ancestry, aristocracy and history, has predicted the outcome of the presidential race for almost 200 years. It says the candidate with the most royal blood has always been the victor.

Mr Bush has direct descents from William the Conqueror, Henry II and Charles II, according to Burke's Peerage. He also scores better than his father, who lost the office of president to Bill Clinton, because of his mother's well-to-do ancestors. Barbara Pierce Bush's royal connections include French Bourbon and several Scandinavian monarchs, as well as members of the Russian, Spanish and German monarchies.

In contrast, Mr Gore can only boast roots that include a few b-list central European royals including three German dukes and two Holy Roman Emperors from the middle ages. "Although never in the history of the United States have two presidential candidates been endowed with so many royal connections, our final research proves that governor Bush will become president," said a spokesman for Harold Brooks-Baker, publishing director of Burke's Peerage.

"Do not give your inheritance to foreigners, nor your heritage to violent men, lest you be regarded as humiliated in their eyes, and foolish, *and they trample upon you,* for they will come to *dwell among you* and *become your masters.*"

From the Dead Sea Scrolls,
TESTAMENT OF KOHATH (4Q542 -- Plate 9)

APPENDIX
DEEPER ANALYSIS REGARDING THE TRIAL OF RABBI ELIEZER

The first inclusion is the deeper analysis of the Trial of Rabbi
Eliezer ben Hycranus. Since this was the crime that proved the de
facto sine qua non to the Roman Exile for the Jewish people, all
under monotheism and others oriented with contemporary
geopolitical issues should see their time with the Deeper Analysis as
time well spent.

Professor Daniel J.H. Greenwood wrote a very rare article addressing the Trial of Rabbi Eliezer (*Akhnai*, 1997 Utah Law Review 309). The author in 2004 used excerpts from Professor Greenwood's article to highlight historical realities that took place during the trial, serving the Moabite design.

References to NWO are to New World Order. The New World Order in today's times seek one world government and is a *de facto* encapsulation of the historic quest by the Moabites for global domination and control.

> **Greenwood:** Logic having failed, R. Eliezer appeals-- directly to the Legislator. First, R. Eliezer performs three miracles, and then, at his request, a voice from Heaven proclaims that the ultimate Source of the Law, the Austinian sovereign, the Author Himself, agrees with R. Eliezer.*** **None of the participants challenge the validity of the miracles. There is no claim that R. Eliezer is a false prophet or a magician**, like the prophets of Baal vanquished by Elijah or Pharaoh's magicians made fools of by Moses.

> Ehrlich: God is genuine. Rabbi Eliezer is genuine. The point is that despite that reality the {Sanhedrin} has a beef with God and Rabbi Eliezer.

> **Greenwood:** Heaven, on the other hand, appears perfectly willing to intervene in the debate.*** In a world of sovereign centered positivism, surely that would be the end of the issue*** Indeed, since the Interpreter in question is not merely a Greek demigod, but God Himself--unitary, timeless and, by hypothesis, internally consistent--we know not only what He intended at the time of promulgation but what He intends now, on both the specific issue and on the general level. All the difficult interpretive issues have been resolved. What is left? Nothing, except that **the rabbis reject the ruling of Hercules or Heaven. In the name of the sacred law**

given at Sinai, they refuse to listen to the Legislator's own interpretation of that law... Rabbi Joshua stood up and said: "it is not in Heaven." (quoting part of Deuteronomy 30:12). What does "it is not in Heaven" mean? R. Jeremiah said, "since Torah was already given at Sinai, we do not pay attention to a Bat Kol, **because it was already written at Mt. Sinai in the Torah, 'incline after the majority (or many).' (quoting part of Exodus 23:2)"**

Ehrlich: The Congress intentionally, deliberately, with malice aforethought, conspired to reject God's shown willingness to play a central role in the community. **God bestows this community with His willingness to assist to identify the correct path and this group of men (leadership) is telling God to get out of not only their lives but our lives as well. More accurately said: they want to hold the power over their fellow man and they don't like the idea of having to worry about those who would seek God to intervene when they spill forth corruption and injustice.** I mean to relay to you how incredible I find the reality that the religious leadership today will not admit to the crimes against God via the trial of Rabbi Eliezer because it would upset all that has been built upon the crimes committed -- albeit that the crimes are the direct nexus to our inability to offset the NWO and the course that will lead to putative global destruction in 2005.

Ehrlich: As to the {highlighted}portion, this is the crime that the leadership totally tolerates and it is sinful. **Exodus 23:2 says the very opposite.** The Stone Chumash defines 23:2 as: **"Do not be a follower of the majority for evil; and do not respond to a grievance by yielding to the majority to pervert {the law}." What Exodus 23:2 admonishes is what Rabban Gamliel and his team including Rabbi Akiva in fact perpetrated.... This is a crime without precedent because it undermined God's special central relationship with Israel and Torah until today.** That those that study do not stand up

206

to challenge this ongoing crime bespeaks the current world condition

Greenwood: Thus, heavenly voices are unnecessary; miracles are no substitute for legal reasoning. R. Jeremiah adds to this, that in the event disputes do arise, the proper dispute resolution technique is not appeals to heaven but rather majority vote. **Indeed, not only is R. Eliezer's voice from Heaven rejected, but the later authorities make clear that all voices from Heaven and other forms of prophecy are to be rejected if they contradict the existing understanding of the Law.**

Ehrlich: The Heavens declared Rabbi Eliezer correct. These men turned a deaf ear and moved to the next leg of their conspiracy when they declared that in the future all other intercessions by God, including all prophecy by those earmarked prophets or those enabled to perform miracles, not to say God's own interventions, are all subservient to the majority ruling of the Congress of conspirators. In other words, God is subservient to man on Planet Earth. The first aspect of the crime (rejecting God's role where He was with Israel to clarify Rabbi Eliezer's interpretation as correct) is a crime without peer. The second (telling God to get lost) is a crime that defies imagination. Now, the third aspect of the crime heralds the consequences that emanate when the evil can no longer be uprooted:

Greenwood: Furthermore, the text assures us that Heaven seemingly endorses Its own rejection: Rabbi Natan met Elijah (the Biblical prophet who was taken up to Heaven alive and frequently appears as an intermediary between Heaven and earth in Jewish tradition) and asked him, "What did the Holy-One-Blessed-Be-He do at that time?" He said to him, **"He smiled and said, 'My children have defeated Me, My children have defeated Me.'"**

Ehrlich: This comes as you can imagine only from people so evil and arrogant they put Moses into the eighth row of the academy and even have the audacity to say that God visits the academy to learn a thing or two Himself from them. So this manipulation is required for the first NWO group to attest that God supports the new law *because once they can negate God Himself from uprooting their power, who thereafter could change the course?* **Thus Rabban Gamliel and his group of first NWO members gave themselves power over men in lieu of God and no one post Rabbi Eliezer could uproot them. Thus, the need for the Exile and 2000 years to figure it out and correct it.** Professor Greenwood has it down very well until here. But now he adopts a perspective that diminishes his own perceptions of what had taken place. He writes regarding the tidal wave that had Rabban Gamliel pleading for God to save his life:

Greenwood: Note that Gamliel is the source of the explanation of the causality: if it was not a miracle, it was at least an indication of R. Gamliel's bad conscience. But the story contends that it was a miracle: **the storm stopped when R. Gamliel justified (to Heaven) R. Eliezer's excommunication as necessary to avoid disputes in Israel and preserve the peace of the community.***** Here, however, the implication of R. Eliezer's vengefulness is clear. One day, Imma Shalom was distracted herself, or made a mistake about the calendar and thought it was a day without supplicatory prayers, and upon finding her husband praying, she shouted, "You have killed my brother" just before the horn sounded announcing Gamliel's death.

Ehrlich: Greenwood is interpreting the story of the tidal wave without integrating the reality that both Gamliel, Akiva and the rest of the central team all died soon after the tidal wave incident. The bottom line is that Gamliel was given the chance to repent; while he showed his guilt about what he did to his brother in law, he had the arrogance, no surprise here, to try to skirt the truth with God by telling God that he excommunicated his brother in law to bring unity to the community. First, no need to center on Rabbi Eliezer. The truth of it is that God was the primary victim and target not Rabbi Eliezer. Second, without Rabban Gamliel surviving we could not properly deduce the true meaning of the events that God gives even the egregious sinner a chance to repent. Third, punishment in this life includes the deaths detailed for both Gamliel and Akiva as those signifying egregious sins against their fellow man and God. When Rabbi Eliezer fell to his knees in tears and pain when Gamliel returned telling the community that God agreed with what he did to his brother in law, he was reflecting not vengefulness but a. humiliation and b. primarily his *sine qua non* for his courage and conviction in opposing the {Sanhedrin}: **that the message that Rabban Gamliel spread due to the abatement of the tidal wave diminished God in that it gave credence to something that was a crime against God.** Believe me, if Rabbi Eliezer was vengeful,...*his brother in law would have been dead long before then.* The events of the time show that with Rabbi Eliezer's excommunication one third of the crops failed a fact those excommunicating him admit to. *Thus, it doesn't take much extrapolation to figure out that Rabban Gamliel knew (took the risk) that his brother in law was not a vengeful person.* I trust that we all can admit that those interposing the vengeful interpretation are transferring their own weaknesses onto a man that obviously was one of the great and most courageous figures of all time.

Greenwood: R. Akiva asked him {Rabbi Eliezer}, "And what will my death be?" He answered, "Yours will be harsher than theirs."*** In short, just as Akhnai affirms that R. Eliezer was a scholar, not just a magician or a table pounding, third-rate lawyer--he first brought all the arguments in the world, and only when those failed did he proceed to miracles, and his miracles are clearly accepted as indeed miraculous--so too the other sources, both ones that seem to be clearly conscious of Akhnai and ones that do not, emphasize R. Eliezer's skill, sophistication, and knowledge. He is not banned for false prophecy, incompetence, **or even for being wrong on the merits.**

Ehrlich: Akiva was unremitting till the end having the audacity to confront his teacher on his deathbed to ask him whether he, Rabbi Eliezer, wanted to repent before he died. When Rabbi Eliezer held to the integrity of his position Akiva then connected the dots and knew in view of Gamliel's death that his own was imminent. Rabbi Eliezer didn't expound vengeance that they kept him in excommunication until the day he died: he told Akiva the truth for a man that stabbed his teacher in the back and also his God for a crime that to me is the primary force majeure for the imminent death of not only Akiva but half of Israel and their expulsion from the land. Just as we sit today all recognizing the crimes taking place by today's NWO in taking out our country, distancing us from God, and imposing pagan values; those in the community of that day had some obligation to stand up and shout down the enemy within their midst in what amounted to a much smaller community. Moreover, our arrogance today, while extant, is fractional to what it was during that time for the community at large -- all whom lacked the courage to intercede for Rabbi Eliezer **not to say object to the removal of God who was proactive and in their midst!**

Ehrlich: The solution is for Israel and the Jewish people today to correct the egregious sin carried throughout the entire Diaspora without anyone in the theological community with the courage and character to bring it to the table. Simply put, two thousand years to recognize and correct this egregious error. **No one even recognizes that it was the *sine qua non* for the expulsion. No one will even admit that God was the target and the victim and the most horrid reality of them all is that no one will even admit that Exodus 23:2 has been convoluted to carry forth the crimes.** In fact, to mask two thousand years of failure, the distortions continue and the argument is put forth that those that contest it are unworthy to raise the issue since they are not well versed enough. In other words, you have to be a rabbi to contest it, but the reality is that you will never be allowed to be a rabbi if you show the understanding and/or willingness to contest it. However, a large segment of the community of Israel studies and they keep skipping this and other salient sections of history that can change the current course. This led to the position taken that if Israel and the USA were on the right course, we wouldn't face the dangers we today face. That we continue to skirt facing what needs to be confronted has allowed China to emerge, interestingly, at the hands of the enemies within. Thus, Israel needs to apologize to Rabbi Eliezer, to God (and of course not in that order) in order to receive God's intervention for the leadership that can change the current course. ***

Now, in the next segment, Professor Greenwood proffers an argument that crimes of leadership against God and their fellow man can also be intellectually justified and thus sanitized. Thus, to the logic and argument proffered by Professor Greenwood, one can argue that 9-11's deliberate design reflects the NWO's fully understandable and logical conception of good. If this is what the NWO leadership subscribes to then the world has much more reason than at the time of the American and French Revolutions to eradicate them from our midst and Madame DeFarge's extreme perspective (attesting to another dimension of putative evil) carries more legitimacy than Dicken's first afforded it in presenting it as he did in his Tale of Two Cities, again proving the point that without God man is doomed to destruction by decisions of its leadership for war, mayhem and mass murder to supersede the carried NWO intent to enslave, oppress and deny equal opportunity and justice to those they rule over.

Greenwood: Akhnai, curiously, not only affirms majority rule, but does so with precisely the same unease as is usual in democratic theory. First, it rejects the notion that right could trump the majority. R. Joshua's selective quotation repeats the same point made by the rejection of R. Eliezer's miracles: **that is, the mere fact that Eliezer evidently is correctly interpreting Heaven's intent is not enough to make his view the law. The law is what the majority says it is, regardless of whether they are right, or even of whether we ought to incline after them to do evil.**

Ehrlich: **What Greenwood is saying is incredible: allow evil to take control and allow it to have its day!** This logic of course justifies King Solomon in defying God's direct decree to him, allows him to take one thousand wives, that opens the portal to idolatry and the destruction of the two temples. Thus, Rabban Gamliel and his band of conspirators against God intellectually, to the mind of Greenwood, made a fully understandable and justified choice regardless of the reality that it resulted in death to half the population of Israel and platformed the Exile. Big deal. Spoils of life to those that survive.

Greenwood: Which is the law, it asks: The past (that is, the law as accepted at Sinai), or the present (the Author's current understanding of it)? The understanding of those bound by it, those who have accepted it, or the understanding of the Author? The will of the (current) majority, the will of the (Sinaitic) majority, or the logic of the text, as expounded by the (current) interpreters or as expounded by its Author?

Greenwood: Akhnai rules one way: the present prevails, the past is rejected, the law is not in Heaven but for men. Eliezer is excommunicated and God endorses the rule that one need not follow correct traditions. The celebration of Eliezer's fidelity to the past only heightens the strength of the rejection of both sides of our debate: neither original intent theory, represented by Eliezer's fidelity to the tradition from Sinai, nor heavy handed constitutionalism, represented by Eliezer's insistence on following the Bat Kol, which I take to represent the best Herculean understanding of the law, are accepted. Rather, the rabbis establish their system, one renowned above all for its stability and, at least in its later development, inflexibility, on the seemingly shifting sands of a majoritarian interpretivism. The present majority wins, even if it is wrong as both history and best understanding, but it wins by interpreting, not declaring, the law.

At the same time, Akhnai highlights the problems with its own solution. God may have laughed at being defeated in the argument: **Joshua's witty misinterpretation of a Biblical line that, in context, teaches the opposite of the lesson he derives from it, *is too clever not to give enjoyment.*** But on the more serious life and death issues, Heaven remains with Eliezer, and the Talmud-- even while affirming Joshua's rule--is not afraid to point out that Eliezer remains Heaven's favorite. Akiva, after all, was raked by Roman iron combs; Eliezer died in bed, a very old man, surrounded by his students and praised as the father of his generation.

Ehrlich: The rabbis in allowing this to continue on definitely have a direct link to the failings of Israel after the regiving in 1948 and 1967. Let me make the point very clear: **If the rabbis admitted to what has been presented regarding the trial of Rabbi Eliezer and to the arguments proffered by Professor Greenwood, the community would have long ago separated from them and their authority.** They have hid the truth of the wrongdoing and in fact allowed the NWO to have gone wild: look at the above and the admission that Joshua deliberately distorted and convoluted Torah as a means to the criminal end and that his deed and getting away with it ***"is too clever not to give enjoyment."* While the true majority of men subscribe to the precepts represented by Rabbi Eliezer, the true majority of leadership subscribe to those carried by Rabban Gamliel and thus to the nefarious perspective proffered above *de facto* approving man's intent to separate from God and using evil means to serve the end.**

Ehrlich: The assertion that God laughed is pathetic and lame. There is no reference that God laughed anywhere in Torah and again similar to 9-11 the distortion and deception of the claim was necessary to achieve the predicate to further the crime in play. One only needs to look at what happened as a result to see the agenda that was truly in play: consolidated irremovable uncontested power that perpetrated abuse and corruption. The very boldness in the assertion that God came to their academy to learn from them and that Moses was lucky to get a seat in the eighth row attests to arrogance that has to be refuted by this generation or the portal to make amends opened by the Exile will close with results that will be a tragedy beyond imagination.

Greenwood: Akhnai, despite the miracles and direct Heavenly intervention, is a strikingly familiar discussion of the same problem. The Temple's destruction and the end of prophecy mark the end of God's active intervention in the world (until the coming of the Messiah)--even the Heavenly voice that remains in Akhnai is only a Bat Kol, literally a "daughter of a voice" or an echo. Truth--

especially the truth of God's eternal, Temple centered law-
-has withdrawn as well; Akhnai confronts the modern
problem of recreating law without assurance that legal
rights will in fact be Right.

The sense of loss is palpable in the texts: "formerly," the
Tosefta says, "there were no disputes in Israel." The law
was known and everyone agreed. In any event, if there
were disagreements, the Urim v' Thummim of the High
Priest could always give a definitive answer. But with the
destruction of the Temple, there is no definitive answer
from Truth, until Messiah comes to resolve all disputes.
Moreover, with the suspension of the Sanhedrin as a single
definitive decision-making body, there is not even a
supreme court or parliament with the final say: much as in
our own system with its multiple sources of sovereignty
and no body with ultimate authority over all the others, or,
as in any democracy, where decisions of the majority are
always subject to challenge by a later majority or a
redefined set of boundaries, the debate can continue
forever (or at least until the restoration of the Temple in
Messianic days). As it does.

Ehrlich: Well Professor Greenwood if you are saying that
man wanted the two temples to tumble and wanted God
and Rabbi Eliezer to be sent to the closet, then you with
glee accept what is before us today. When that nuclear
bomb drops on your head, you might fully say that it was
at least fun running things as long as it lasted. The
problem, even before that unfortunate day, which I hope
does not unfold, is that those that speak for allowing evil
to infiltrate our midst as opened by Rabban Gamliel and
his cohorts do not reflect the sentiment for the true
majority who do not share the comfort of the position
usually enjoyed by those daring to intellectualize and
sanitize the crimes that took place. Man's desire to
dominate and control invoked the dark desire to enslave,
oppress and deny his fellow man justice. Anyone who can
dare argue that such consequence is the natural collateral
damage to the need for man to be free of God and His
given laws is the same type of man that can support the
need for ultimate global depopulation (again, all such
decisions are perfectly understandable as long as they do

not target and include the NWO leaders and their families and loyal wards). With all due respect, the recommendation is simply remove those that want to closet God and put into power those that genuinely bow to and honor God and who can correctly implement God's design by honing love for God in man.

Greenwood: ...**Akhnai centers on a struggle between generations, the children overthrowing the father of the generation and the Father himself, in an Oedipal reversal of the Biblical drama of the sacrifice of Isaac.** *** The Temple is no more. God has withdrawn his Presence (Shekhina) and His protection from His House. The purity laws themselves are largely meaningless in this new world: What does it matter if one becomes impure if there is no Temple and no sacrifice, no Red Heifer with which to repurify? The entire system of sanctity has been shattered and is no more.

Ehrlich: **This is an admission to the illness of those that lead us. What Professor Greenwood is saying is that the leadership really always wanted the temples to tumble, they always wanted God to leave, and they always wanted to assume domination and control. Thus, the truth of it is never admitted to because the true majority would then arise over time to get rid of them.** So they went to synagogue and church to mask the truth that they have been and are the enemies of God. **The salient point is that if man wanted to exercise more dominion, man didn't have to act to eliminate God. The greatest gift of all was His willingness to be with us and He would have always been an ever-present check and balance power over evil running amok. Even with God boxed out, God still has been with us, the point being that if He was not still with us darkness would have consumed this planet long ago.** Thus, at this point, if the NWO again takes full control to implement the agenda to distance men from God, so that those living tomorrow will not know Him at all, and will adopt pagan and hedonistic values on a global scale {in nations under monotheism}, God will turn His back and we all will vanish as a failed species.

In the following section, Greenwood reveals the reliance of the perpetrators and his own reliance on the assertion that God laughed in declaring that the rabbis had defeated Him. This galling assertion takes on similar importance to the events of 9-11 as the foundational predicate to all that subsequently was allowed to take place in pursuit of an evil design and agenda. The entire segment below reveals this and I have highlighted each time Greenwood indicates that God laughed in his argument to intellectualize and sanitize the crimes that took place:

Greenwood: God laughs. "My children have bested Me, My children have bested Me." Bested Me because they have out-argued me, because they have understood legal discourse as a competition in which sages "best one another," as R. Joshua put it, **and they are more skilled at it than the Holy One Himself.** His lessons, then, have been learned; **the student has surpassed the teacher**. This is the "besting" that any parent hopes for: the mark that the child has grown up. Thus, a **laugh** of pleasure and delight.

Greenwood: Or perhaps a **laugh** of delight because of the specific way they have bested Him. The rabbis have understood that a tradition is not only recorded memories of the words given at Sinai, but must adapt to the changes around them. He laughs because they have understood the paradox that to maintain the tradition, they must change it, not fossilize it, that the unchangeableness of God's law is itself the source of the demand that it change.

Greenwood: Furthermore, they have used His own Torah to show that they, not He, are the proper guardians of the tradition and the proper ones to decide how it must be modified to remain the same. The Law is not in Heaven: that is, it is ours, here, and we are responsible for it. This generation, not the founders or the Author, must keep it in working order, understand it to the best of our knowledge. **The refusal to accept Daddy's help is also the acceptance of responsibility for ourselves.*****

Greenwood: We cannot depend on voices from Heaven to fix it for us if we destroy it. Indeed, it is a mark of our maturity to recognize that voices from Heaven can never remove from us the responsibility of thinking for ourselves: On that day, My children grew up, they bested Me, as children do to parents when they reach maturity. Nor can we depend on interpretation--laws are not self-explanatory. Interpretative methods are loose. Right and wrong answers can come from them-- and the majority can get it wrong, as the majority did here, both on the small question of the purity of the oven, and on the large question of how to treat dissenters.***

Greenwood: The Holy One's **laugh** is, then, the **laugh** of wonder at the sudden maturity of a people. His children are no longer the generation of the desert demanding a return to slavery so they could again sit by the fleshpots and remember the garlic, cucumbers, and fish of Egypt. Nor are they the generation of Samuel, demanding a king to rule over them like other peoples. Nor are they even the seemingly interminable generations chronicled cycling between forgetting and finding, lapsing from and returning to, the Law. Suddenly, they have understood that their collective life is theirs to make, that they must take responsibility for their Law.

Greenwood: The **laugh** is because of the acceptance of responsibility and the paradox it creates. The Law says, first, on the highest level, that it is not in Heaven, and specifically, that the majority should be followed. That is fundamental; whether Akhnai's oven is pure is not. So the rabbis are correct to follow their own, human, current understanding of the law, even if the original understanding was different.

Ehrlich: To argue that God approved at what occurred is blasphemy. First, it would have God devoid of sensitivity to the crime and injustice against Rabbi Eliezer. Second, it would diminish and discount all that was taking place: the destruction of the two temples and the responsibilities of leadership therefor. Third, it would ratify the criminal use of God's name to open the portal to a course that exiles God and allows abuse and corruption to flourish, as it thereafter did.

Ehrlich: Look at the arrogance:

a. "They are more skilled at than the Holy one Himself;"

b. "This is the besting that any parent hopes for: the mark that the child has grown up;"

c. "The refusal to accept Daddy's help is also the acceptance of responsibility for ourselves;"

d. "The Holy one's laugh is , then, the laugh of wonder at the sudden maturity of a people;"

e. "They have used His own Torah to show that they, not He, are the proper guardians of the tradition;"

f. "...And they are more skilled at it than the Holy One Himself;"

g. "The student has surpassed the teacher."

God was disappointed and angry. Greenwood talks as though the toppling of two temples and the massive deaths of the people of Israel and their exile were something totally irrelevant to the crimes in issue, which he himself convolutes as the sanitized acceptance of a child rebelling against a parent, as though God has somehow become a parent in this wishful attempt to define a metaphor to grasp to support the legerdemain of an assertion not found anywhere in Torah: that God laughed at being deceived by a gang of poker playing rabbis. Can any sane man accept the argument that God thought that the convolution of Torah appropriate, and a laughing matter to boot, to support the result and claim His approval? **Further, again, if all this was above board, would the rabbis have hid the full discussion of this event, as they have and still do, making King Solomon, Rabban Gamliel and Rabbi Akiva heroes, while leaving Rabbi Eliezer and God to erode in the memories of man?**

Greenwood: Yet, given the terrible punishment meted out to Rabban Gamliel, it surely cannot be ignored entirely.*** "'On the day that Rabbi Eliezer ben Hycranus took his seat in the Academy, each man girded on his sword.'" Eliezer is the man with special access to truth, and uncompromising truth is incompatible with a democratic society. Those who know the truth have no reason to bow to the majority--like Eliezer, they can appeal to Heaven. Only by excluding his claim to special privilege could the community continue. **But only by respecting his claim to truth can the world endure.**

Ehrlich: We find that Greenwood soon thereafter hedges his position for his interpretation skirts not only the results for Rabban Gamliel but also Rabbi Akiva and the need for the Exile to rethink what just took place. Moreover, the claim that God has to be rejected for He is somehow incompatible with a democratic society ignores the reality of these days where without God democratic society has become the seedbed for abuse and corruption and that the very precepts and principles of democracy are undermined with an agenda to now uproot them completely in nations still beholden to God.

Greenwood: Nothing in the Biblical texts cited explains why it is a majority of rabbis, rather than, for example, a majority of Jews, or a majority of prophets, that sets the rules.

Ehrlich: Here Greenwood points to a central consequence of the crimes against God. Just as Solomon angled things so he could defy God's decree and take a thousand wives, many from prohibited nations, the ten tribes then saying what is good for the goose is also good for the gander; the rabbis grasp at uncontested power opened a portal for others bent on an evil agenda to say that if the rabbis can rule in lieu of God why not us? Thus, you have the NWO dynamically operating today under the portal opened by Rabban Gamliel that foreclosed Israel from standing up to the crimes of the Rabin assassination and the American people from standing up against the crimes of 9-11 -- **again opening the shift of the paradigm of power to China.** Thus, once evil succeeds it opens the portal to all those desiring to pursue personal/evil agendas to do so under the same dynamic of legitimacy: here man defining the future for his fellow man and the planet.

Greenwood now concludes with the logic that explains why everything around us is a fragile wall ready to crumble:

Greenwood: Akhnai teaches, I think, that truth and peace are often incompatible *** So God laughed. Why? **The Father saw that His education had worked.** Akhnai marks the end of the childish Israelite people, those who complained at being brought out of the land of comfortable slavery where they sat by the fleshpots and defined themselves by descent, as the children of Israel. It marks the beginning of adulthood, where we have not answers and paternal guidance but endless debate, bitter jealousies, and hurt feelings, principles we accept as necessary for life together but cannot apply, fathers- in-law who destroy us and vice-versa, spouses whom we make love to as if possessed by demons, beautiful children and political struggles that are not theorized but lived. If stasis and stable law are death, this is life.

Ehrlich: Peace is only compatible with truth. Giving man unchecked dominion over his fellow man and his planet results in what we have today. Look all over the Internet and wherever you can look. Find me someone who has stood up to argue and speak for the victim Rabbi Eliezer ben Hycranus. How can it be that the only point mustered up is that his sentence, devoid of due process principles, and intentionally so, was excessive? How can it be that you can only find comments that put even more blame on Rabbi Eliezer because these men write that Eliezer was a vengeful man in that Rabban Gamliel died as a result of his tears and prayers {they claim for vengeance}? The victim is always at fault and gets all the blame. But do you recognize the victim? **You are Rabbi Eliezer. You were denied God's oversight that would have foreclosed the injustices, the wars, the humiliations and the rest of the lot, by He who would have contained the evil designs of this NWO group. You have been denied the truth of what happened, why it happened, and the**

results thereof, because if the community at that time knew the true agenda, was told the truth of Rabban Gamliel's design, then they may have stood up as no doubt, if we knew the truth of 9-11, we would not tolerate the NWO occupation and control of our own society. However, allowing the truth to be hidden under veils of national security and other ruses has permitted the {Moabites} to assume power and control where they cannot be uprooted and once they have such a status then the dire biblical consequences are in play and they are going to be much worse than ever before. The planet was consumed by death, devastation and injustice; the reason God entered the picture. Then these men took God's blessings and turned the tables on Him with the community standing silent as we do today. Now, we are educated, sophisticated, we are well fed, are wealthy like no generation before, and have no excuse whatsoever to stand silent and allow God to be exiled by these men who would disappear in a moment in time if the people roared. Thus roar, educate the children as we have suggested, and pray for God to return to His position of {open} oversight for us, where He was there willing to help steer our course even after the toppling of the two temples. He cannot be happy that we are sitting here so passively while our enemies and His enemies just keep pushing their personal agendas at the expense of all that is good. Greenwood's acceptance of an argument that there is no life for man with God's laws, but only life with man taking charge, to allow excitement, the bedrock of paganism and hedonism, will prove itself the ultimate weapon when those subscribing to these precepts push the planet as they are now doing to its own destruction.

Ehrlich: All those leaders standing silent to these truths are our enemies and the enemies of God. That they pretend to speak in lieu of God to exercise dominion over us is defamation to God's name. Rabbi Eliezer was our man. He was maltreated as we are. It is time to stand knowing the truths and for those with courage, what few of them there may be, to challenge matters. Seeing Professor Greenwood's arguments explains what did take place, why the religious leaderships are both silent and complicit, and why no one speaks for truth or for Rabbi Eliezer and why today they are back in pursuit of domination and control. The American and French Revolutions were interference in a design that arose with Rabban Gamliel and put on hold when the elitists were in fear: to affirm precepts and principles of fairness, democracy, equal opportunity. Now, they are back on that course not only for their own agenda but to bury God all the better. They will never succeed. However, the consequences should now be more apparent to you than ever before and thus your role can only help and possibly impact and be the butterfly that changes the course for the entire planet. **Just remember, if there were any truth and legitimacy to what was done to Rabbi Eliezer and all of us, they would not have kept it a secret for 2000 years. That it is all yet a secret and that they have done nothing to correct it attests that the original agenda is in full play, as witnessed by what is happening to the USA and Israel with the rabid intent to effectuate culture change for the Arab/Islamic nations.**

End 2004 comment and analysis on Greenwood article

The Moabite influenced academic world steers clear of addressing hidden truths in biblical history. As concerns Ruth, no one dares, since Doeg moved to remove King David from power, to articulate the obvious; that Ruth usurped control over Israel by mothering the aristocratic line that would subvert the nation, while simultaneously holding herself out as a woman beholden to Israel and God.

Her deeds operated to cause God to turn His back on the nation that earlier succumbed to Moabite temptation. Her deeds and the consequences thereof defy comprehension, unless one understands the truth of the dynamics that were in play.

Fortunately, while the truth of the trial of Rabbi Eliezer ben Hycranus has been obfuscated, the facts can be linked appropriately together to reveal a detailed picture of what Moabite goal was in play in connection with this critical biblical event.

It is apparent, once understanding the significance of what took place in connection with the trial, that Rabbi Eliezer and God's ostracization were the sine qua non to the Jewish Exile, by the hands of the Romans, via the failed Bar Kokhba Rebellion. The Moabites and those in the Jewish community directly serving their own interests, aiding the Moabite interests, wanted the truth swept under rug, and there is a continuing deliberate agenda to keep it under the rug.

In 2003, Rabban Gamliel was categorized and glorified as a "transformational leader," one who leads to take people on a wholly new direction (Perspective on Transformational Leadership in the Sanhedrin of Ancient Judaism, Management Decision: Focus on Management History, Vol. 41(2), 2003, pp. 199-207). The following from the article suggests the fallacy of the paradigm called transformational leadership:

> "The characteristics of transformational leaders mentioned by such authors as Yuki (1998), Nahavandi (2000), and Black and Porter (2000) are: ability to communicate; charisma; clear vision; confidence; encourage creativity; high expectations; honesty; individual attention and consideration; inspiration; integrity, morality; intellectual stimulation; interactivity; lead by example; optimism; personal relationship with followers.

In other words, the leaders that take history on a new course are those that display such attributes. Wrong. What is missing from the laundry list above is the central elements that historically in the Moabite world takes things on a new course: COERCION AND/OR CORRUPTION. It is clear that adjectives and characteristics such as integrity, morality, honesty had no place or role in the trial of Rabbi Eliezer ben Hycranus but corruption and coercion had a large role in the Sanhedrin's decisions regarding Boaz, Solomon, and Rabban Gamliel. This truth also was in play with the events that unraveled post 9-11, producing laws that contravened the Constitution to the United States of America. Would the authors of the article see George W. Bush as a transformational leader?

The authors in alleging that Rabban Gamliel was a transformational leader, deserving of praise, declare that he cleansed and cast off pagan values and idolatry from the Jewish community. First, the reality is that Gamliel's predecessors were the ones that opened the portal to pagan values and idolatry by distorting Torah's decrees. What Gamliel did, not only showed equal degrees of corruption, as the earlier Sanhedrins, but he did them one better: instead of simply polluting Israel by his actions, he literally excommunicated God under the veil of excommunicating his own brother in law.

Do those that profess the point seek to say that better the remnant of Jews worship their rabbinate than pagan idols, to (self-servingly) cleanse Gamliel's and Akiva's deeds?

That kind of convoluted thinking compels one to note that with idolatry God did not exile the Jews as He did under the Gamliel/Akiva leaderships. Gamliel and Akiva did more for the Moabite agenda than anyone before them, in sending God off, under the pretext that the Jews had His Torah and now He was not needed: they, his children, could run the world without Him.

Now, look out the window, or pick up your daily newspaper, and you can see how well man has done by calling the shots without God's open oversight.

Thus, Professor Greenwood's seeming sympathy for Rabban Gamliel and cohorts appears to de facto condone what took place, whereas the contention here is that it is imperative to condemn what took place, not condone it – for it should be clear that what took place, opened the portal that allowed the Moabites to control our reality, and provide us with a world that is inverse to what God intended for us.

God specifically acted by decree to preclude us from taking Ruth into the community of Israel. The de facto rabbinate of those times skirted divine decree again and again and what God acted to preclude took place: Moabite domination of Israel and history. Yet today, the rabbinate continues the sham that Ruth was pure, thereby refuting a holy decree, to create holiness about her entry into Israel and that we still have to bow to their perspective regardless of the facts. Exiling God, and declaring that a majority decision superseded divine decree, was a grievous sin, which continues with the rabbinate's refusal to hone up to the truths surrounding Ruth, helping the Moabites to continue in their agenda against God and Israel.

The author recognizing the significance of the events of 9-11, and assessing that Israel ultimately would prove to be the key to offsetting Moabite control and influence, began to bring this hidden and obfuscated reality to people of influence. Peres Personified was written in October 2001 and it is noteworthy in that it points that the United States ultimately would abandon Israel, a concept unheard of and which no one would accept at that time. However, the author felt it was important to bring that issue and several others, including the shift of the paradigm of power, out onto the table because, as feared, it would prove true and relevant, as it has, in the years that followed this very special analysis.

Peres Personified

By Joseph Ehrlich

In this story Shimon Peres serves a purpose that escapes him in real life.

If our forefathers whom we cherish could appear before us today, what would they think and what would they say?

They immediately would see a people very well fed, with lots of leisure time, living what could only be attested to as a life of wealth, where they travel and buy every imaginable convenience. They would say to themselves that God has answered their prayers to Him, and they would bend their knees and hang their heads in homage to He who has so favored their descendants.

They would then see that those whom benefited from their plight and prayers have absolutely little to no appreciation themselves for what they have and who provided it for them. They would see a culture highlighting drugs, sex and violence, and one clearly disparaging God's central presence and role in everyday life. While our forefathers prayed for everything seen today, they forgot obviously to include prayers to assure that the future generations, if so blessed, would appreciate and understand the basis for their blessings.

What would then further shock them, in addition to the regression to the hedonism and paganism which had been the historical road to destruction for their own forefathers, would be that there exists a leadership in God's premier gift, the Land of Israel, which is obsessed with providing a future framework to move the Jewish people away from rather than to God.

They would see Israel filled with Jews who didn't believe in God at all (how could such a thing happen, they would ask?), and among the Jews who believe in God, would include those who were openly and publicly willing to defame and defile God's Name and Gift by foolishly offering to return it to secure a peace which would have assured Israel's assimilation as a nation among nations.

They would see a generation who think themselves smart and advanced, with an array of technological accomplishments; but one obviously stupid to the extreme in failing to see the simple lessons of history. Fools, they would shout, looking at the current generation seeing many of them sitting and studying Torah and Jewish teachings: didn't you make the connection between Jerusalem and the future fate of the Jewish people!

Not being able to take it any more, they would stretch out and bring before them one of the current leaders, Shimon Peres. They are intrigued in how a man who could lose five elections was effectively running Israel in the very opposite manner it should be run.

Peres, not knowing exactly where he was, seeing himself in what looked like a clouded room, asks them, who they are.

"We are representatives of your forefathers," the leader of the group who identified himself as Ephraim, said to Shimon Peres. Peres immediately asks them what is going on, thinking this is some sick trick being played by his enemies.

Ephraim replies, "We are not your enemies Shimon but your forefathers. We only want to ask you questions because we cannot fathom what is going on in Israel."

Peres sensing some possible danger in how these people got to him, with all his heavy security around his home, cooperated.

"Ask what you wish," he spewed forth with his usual diplomatic tone.

"Why are you so willing to give back Jerusalem and parts of Israel, part and parcel of God's gift as provided by Torah to the Jewish people?"

"God wants peace," Peres immediately retorts. "God is interested in life not land. I understood this immediately, but Satan operates against me for years with fools undermining at every turn everything I do for the Jewish people."

Ephraim retorts, "Are the Jewish people fools because they have made you a bitter and angry man because they consistently fail to elect you to the high office you seek, or are they fools because they share like we do a different opinion."

"A different opinion, " chirps Peres.

"Are you telling us you are not bitter that they consistently don't vote you into the office you obsessively seek?"

"No, I am not bitter about it." Peres says in a less than convincing manner to the forefathers.

"So why were you so happy when Rabin was shot? Now, don't lie to us Shimon, we know that this was your chance to get shoed right into the top spot you always wanted."

"Can you believe my bad luck," Peres says, "I had the highest ratings and pushed for the vote and those stupid Arabs who couldn't have a better friend in Israel than me, failed to stop Hamas from planting bombs which undermined me."

"Maybe God wasn't so happy about seeing an Israeli leader gunned down?"

"What has it got to do with me," Peres shouts, sensing some form of trap. "You can see for yourself who sits in jail for the crime."

"What we see Shimon is a man having nothing to do with it. We see that the Israeli public is learning that the man didn't even have gunpowder residue on his hands, that he couldn't have committed the deed, and that there is a lot of evidence pointing to your own involvement."

"If you want to murder me then do it already. I am not speaking further to you. I don't know who you are. Either murder me or release me," Peres says, trying to pass on the subject, refusing to be lead where he didn't want to go in the conversation.

"Shimon, Shimon, you don't realize who you are talking to here, do you? You don't think we could see what happened at the hospital. How desperate things were. Two shots in the back and then one shot from the front. What type of country is the Land of Israel when its press doesn't make hay of such a fact? And there you were in the hospital, with him all alone, as you dared admit on that PBS television interview, kissing him on the forehead, after chasing everyone else out from the room."

Peres stood there silently refusing to respond.

The forefathers went on a different road. "**So why Shimon no peace between you and the Arabs. Isn't this a sign that you are not the man to bring peace even under your own agenda? Isn't it time after all these years to see if Israel can live without Shimon Peres, perhaps one of your friends will be better at bringing the peace than you, perhaps you are the obstacle to peace, even the one defined by you yourself?**"

Peres got red in the face. "If I cannot bring peace, no one else can!"

Ephraim says "I don't know about that Shimon, but we can help you bring the peace to Israel. Would you care to take some fatherly advice, no pun intended?"

"I am always willing to listen," Peres answers with his usual accented flare, highlighting when necessary the tolerance of those seeing themselves among the elite.

"Do you believe the Jews were freed from Egypt by God?"

"Yes."

"Do you believe there was a holy First Temple where God's presence hung over Jerusalem?"

"Yes."

"Did the Jewish people come to the Land of Israel at that time and build a holy temple for God with God's help."

"Yes,"

"Was not Israel considered a holy nation and people at that time earning the respect of foreign nations?"

"Yes, that is what I want for Israel," Peres chirps in, in part lying.

"Yes," Ephraim says, "You want Israel to be an emerald among nations, Shimon, but wasn't Israel a religious nation?"

"It was a nation of peace...

"Because God blessed the Nation, isn't that so Shimon?"

"Yes, I suppose so," Shimon chirped back.

"And while a Nation of peace we had no enemies."

"Exactly!" exclaimed Peres.

"But then Israel had a host of enemies," Ephraim said. **"The Assyrians committed the greatest Holocaust, destroying ten of the twelve tribes. These ten tribes were themselves an embodiment of peace. They lived with ideal synergy with their neighbors, all who loved** them to such a degree they sent their sons and daughters to marry the sons and daughters of Israel, resulting in high levels of assimilation."

Peres stood silently.

"God by then completed his role for Israel. He granted them the land, the blessing, peace and tranquility, and then stood by while the Assyrians swooped down and destroyed ten of the twelve tribes of Israel. **Can you give me a reason Shimon why God stood by silently when this Holocaust, the greatest in all of Jewish history, took place sending the largest numbers, percentage wise, of Jews to their death?"**

Ephraim thought he heard Peres say, "No."

"Because the Jewish people were worshiping the idols of those they enjoyed assimilating with. They took a blessed environment from God, then turned their back on God, and by doing so defamed Him and their covenant."

Peres still stood silently.

"If God intervened for the ten tribes against the Assyrians, what would the message be?"

Peres seemed anxious to answer, "That God was with the Jewish people." Ephraim noted the first sign of some resentment by Peres against God.

Ephraim then was anxious to clarify it for Peres: **"God could never intervene here for the ten tribes because if He did so, he would be encouraging a course of conduct which would only further defame and defile His Name and gift to the Jewish people.** If He intervened for them, the Jewish people then would further convolute the horrible precedent set by King Solomon, that assimilation with Israel's neighbors is countenanced and supported by God, which it never was and never will be!"

Peres focused on the reference to King Solomon. "What has King Solomon to do with the destruction of the ten tribes?" he asked.

King Solomon one of the most noted figures in Jewish history, known for his wisdom, was someone who Peres particularly admired.

"Did you know Shimon that King Solomon lived under a Divine Decree limiting the number of wives he could take as King of Israel?"

"Now that you mention it, I think I faintly remember the fact that he had some 1000 wives."

"But," Ephraim continues, " He could not have anywhere so many. The Sanhedrin of that time, the one which the Torah said must be listened to, defined the limitation imposed by the Torah to a very generous eighteen wives."

'I have trouble living with just one," Peres contributed, seeking to lighten the mood a little.

The forefathers disregarded his comment. Ephraim continued, "Solomon, after being granted his wish to God for wisdom, intertwined his ego with the blessing he received to conclude that his wisdom and discipline would allow him to escape the Divine Decree, for he would not become a victim, in his regal opinion, to the interpreted concern of the Torah."

Peres saw what was coming.

"But he did ultimately succumb due to his love for many of his wives to idol worship. They enticed him to the beauty of their ways and beliefs. How could those he loved so much represent anything but something he should look into?"

Peres replied: "So he didn't have the discipline. We all fail God as people. So what. Look at the rich legacy he left for Jewish history."

The forefathers could not believe that Peres could stand before them so blind and ignorant.

Ephraim said to Peres, "The legacy King Solomon left was first, the destruction of the ten of the twelve tribes of Israel and second, the opening of the doors to Christianity and Islam."

"One moment!" exclaimed Peres. "Are you telling me that it wasn't the assimilation and idol worship of the northern tribes that caused their destruction, but King Solomon?"

Ephraim responds: **"What we are telling you is that a King is responsible on the highest level for the consequence of his decisions. By taking on a 1000 wives he did more than fail himself, he sent a message to the northern tribes that if the King of Israel could take on foreign wives forbidden by God, then who are they to seriously inquire about the legitimacy of their own desires and then decisions to do the same?"**

Peres always carrying a dislike for the Orthodox, asked: "What about the Sanhedrin? What did they have to say about all this?"

The forefathers told Peres, that the Sanhedrin sat on their hands with tape over their mouths not wishing to challenge the King of Israel. This decision also was a major facet in changing history, in that **they were obliged to stand with courage and conviction to protect God's decrees over any fear they may have carried toward fueling anger of a King whom impacted their daily lives.** Lavished otherwise, enjoying a fine life and lifestyle, the decision was not to rock the boat, and thus Jewish history from that point on, swept dirty laundry under the rug, which it continues to do today, failing to learn properly from history. Recently the world saw Orthodox Jews sitting on their hands with tape over their mouths when Barak begged Arafat to take back Jerusalem and the West Bank.

This of course put Peres immediately on the defensive. "What has the Jewish failing of

233

thousands of years ago have to do with us today? Do you see anyone here worshiping idols in Israel today?"

"Idolatry takes many forms," Ephraim responds. "The thrust of idolatry is turning one's back to God, after God provides him with blessings and many gifts. This is the sign of the ingrate. It also defames God to the other peoples of the world who recognize that He established Himself through the Jewish people. Thus often when God acts to protect the Jewish people, it is to offset the dishonor to this historical reality if He does not do so. Otherwise, the consequence of idolatry, behavior, which defames and defiles God's Name, is understanding that the Assyrians were followed thereafter by the Babylonians, and then the Romans, the last enemy before the Jews were exiled from Israel. Now, after Israel is back in Jewish hands, Shimon, for the second time, meaning that the dire interpretations of Ki Savo are now operative, Israel is surrounded by the Arab nations and the PLO. Do you think the Arab nations are our enemies?"

"I am at the forefront of saying that Arafat is my peace partner not my enemy," Peres offers.

"However, Shimon, whereas the Arabs and PLO can be your peace partner the reality from history is that they are your enemy by your own hand!"

"What does that mean?" Peres asks.

"If the peace agenda you pursue moves the Jewish people away from God then the Arabs and the PLO will prove to be your enemy, as were the Assyrians, Babylonians, and Romans. If you devise a peace agenda which moves the Jewish people to God, then the Arabs and the PLO will prove to be your partners to a genuine and long lasting peace and you will have learned what you were supposed to learn from the Diaspora."

"Now, having said that, Shimon, let me ask you a very important question which forges the issue we are discussing. When Barak went before the world and told the world that El-AL, Israel's national airline, would commence flying on the Sabbath, did you agree with what he was saying?"

"Yes."

"When Barak went before the world and told them that the government of the State of Israel was now encouraging businesses to remain open for business on the Sabbath, did you agree with what Barak was saying?"

"Yes."

"Well, Shimon, now based on what we are here discussing, do you still want to agree with it."

Peres replies saying, "The State of Israel was founded on the principle that the Jewish people wanted to be recognized as a nation among nations. We wanted to be a Jewish State that was seen and treated as every other state. This was the aspiration of the Jewish people who founded the state, and I was among those very people and thus can attest to it first hand."

"Perhaps in Uganda," Ephraim responds somewhat sardonically.

When those behind the State of Israel were first looking for a state, they were offered the territory subsequently known as Uganda in Africa. However, while many wished to pursue the Jewish state in Uganda, **the miracle of seeing it develop inside Israel supported what Ephraim continued saying to Peres**:

"The miracle however was that via events in 1948 and 1967, the Jewish people were given back Israel. This was by God's intervention as promised by Torah. Now, today, those in Israel are the most highly educated population of Jews in all of history. The purpose of the

Diaspora was to acknowledge and integrate what we have been telling you, into the life and lifestyle of the Jewish people, which would render God central and supreme in Israel. However, after being given back the land, you and your cohorts continued to see yourselves as the dynamic behind the State, refusing to recognize and acknowledge God, and this same stubbornness and blindness is the very one which disallows your recognition that your agenda for peace, one that moves the Jewish people away from God, is one which is *void ab initio*."

"We live among other nations," Peres responds. "We have only one friend, the United States. We have to listen and pay homage to the U.S. agenda for peace. I am but a figurehead in pursuing the U.S. agenda for world peace."

Ephraim sees Peres admitting to his true role and then points out the error of his way in the most favorable manner Ephraim can muster: "Just as the Sanhedrin paid homage to their King over their God."

Peres thinks he has a good answer to that position. "God blessed Solomon. He was the approved King of Israel, the descendant of David. Perhaps the Sanhedrin integrated this into their decision not to challenge the King's decision."

Ephraim sees where Peres is going and interjects, "Just as you perceive the U.S. the supreme sole superpower who vanquished Communism as the King to whom you pay homage."

"Yes," says Peres.

"We trust then Shimon that you will now learn that the consequence of the Sanhedrin's failings point to your own. **The only road to making the Arabs and the PLO your peace partner is by carving out a peace agenda that enhances God's presence in the daily lives of those in Israel.**

God does not endorse Israel being a nation among nations but a nation that shows the world that God is central and supreme in the daily lives of the Jewish people. **Then just as in the past, when the Jewish people had no enemies, there would be no enemies, not by the hand of the United States, but by the hand of God.**"

Peres is standing and frowning.

"What you and others connective to the State of Israel are reluctant to acknowledge is that God, not man, controls the future and fate of Israel. What confuses you and many others is that a future for life not death is in your hands, not God's. You have made the future a battle between satisfying your ego, as a priority over acknowledging your primary competitor in such regard: God. There are many ways for an ambitions man like yourself, who is willing to go beyond the pale in serving yourself, as you did with Rabin, and in standing blind to the suffering and deaths the result of your poor decisions, to pay homage to yourself, to satisfy your unbridled ego. However, as it regards the Jewish people in the land of Israel, you have suffered the same consequence President Clinton suffered when he thought the deck was stacked in his favor: defeat. He thought that by controlling Barak and having him offer Arafat the moon, that the U.S. peace plan would control and be accepted. **There can never be such a peace that countenances a future of a secularized and thus assimilated Israel. God would first take back the land of Israel than permit an abomination to His Name.** That is why in a battle between Israel and the Arab people, including the PLO, ultimately Israel, despite its acclaimed military, would not prevail."

Peres was mentally tiring and desperate to respond. "Are you saying we should separate from the United States?" he asked.

Ephraim looked at Peres lamely and said: **"What would you say if world events proved that the United States would, in substance over form, abandon Israel?"**

"Never," replied Peres.

"Then you must understand Shimon why you are not with the competency to continue on as you do," Ephraim conveyed to him, "and that it is perhaps time before it too late, which it soon will be, if it is not already, for another to take on moving Israel to genuine peace."

Peres reflected on his primary fear that he would be recorded in history as a failure, over any concern of the damage he occasioned by his wrongful decisions to date: "What better course can I consider taking?" he asked the forefathers.

"By your standing up and telling the Jewish people that you erred and misunderstood and that God is central and supreme in Israel and by begging His forgiveness and showing a willingness to make a peace which moves the people of the Mid-East to God, that God will intervene and help secure a true and genuine peace."

"They will think me a fool and mad," retorted Peres.

Ephraim answered, "Will there come a day Shimon that you will understand that your role in history will ultimately be by your courage to admit wrong and to point to the true road to peace?"

"The United States and its allies in Europe will assassinate me," Peres replied.

"Not until you get the point across Shimon," Ephraim said, "and perhaps by then you might see whether God is willing to protect you once you are in true service to Israel and God."

Peres was more concerned about engendering anger in the U.S. and French leaderships. "I will have to think about it."

Ephraim thought it was time to point out something to Peres. "Perhaps you should rethink the damage King Solomon did, and what his fate after life proved to be. Shimon, you have damaged Israel beyond comprehension, allowed the wrong road, which not only impacted Israel but jeopardized the future for all Americans."

This made Peres recall how did he get here and he again questioned to whom he was speaking: "Who are you, is this all some test, a game?" Peres was now thinking he was in the hands of a U.S. mind control operation, testing whether he was going to abandon his pledge to remain loyal to the U.S. peace plan and agenda, a pledge that brought him the Nobel Peace Prize with Rabin and Arafat.

Ephraim knew he was conveying possibly more than Peres could absorb at one time, but he was there to save Peres from a fate of eternal damnation. What Peres did not know is that there was a debate in the Heavenly Tribunal concerning the degree of his punishment for his decisions and deeds. All decisions and deeds of men are reckoned with, however, when a man assumes a leadership position, just as King Solomon, his decisions can change history to a negative rather than a positive course. Shimon Peres' willingness to sell his soul to receive the covert support of the U.S. and its allies in his quest for the leadership of Israel resulted in consequences that now threatened the entire world.

Ephraim thus explained to him, "Peres, listen carefully, we are here to help you, saving you from a fate we are sure you want to avoid. When you took Israel on the wrong course, one that could not result in peace, one that encouraged a government allowing the people to move away from God, you compromised the future. During that period America became a country endorsing paganistic and hedonistic principles, where Americans, for the first time in history, stood silently by as their children were exposed to television programming imbued with sex and violence, desensitizing themselves and their children to the qualities connecting earlier generations to God."

"America," Ephraim continued, "grew and prospered when it connected itself to religious tenets. Now having moved away from them, the next war which confronts it will result in ultimate defeat not victory."

"Why is that?" Peres sarcastically asks.

"For the very same reason God did not intervene for Israel in prior battles."

"When was that?" Peres asks.

"Rabbi Akiva supported the Bar-Kokhba rebellion. You know about it?" Ephraim asks Peres.

Peres says he knows about it. After the destruction of the second temple in Jerusalem, the Romans, representing the evil of the time, persecuted the Jews and people of other lands without mercy. In desperation, Rabbi Akiva proclaimed the Jewish General Bar-Kokhba the Moshiach, which gave him the necessary support to wage war against Rome. After initial victories against Roman legions, Rome amassed a vast army that swept through Israel killing over half the Jewish population, sending large numbers into slavery, and casting all others throughout the world into what is known today as the beginning of the Jewish Diaspora.

Peres declares, "Rabbi Akiva is another great figure in Jewish history. He is known for his love for God in his willingness to give his life for God at the hands of the Roman terrorists."

"However, Shimon," Ephraim retorts, "the dynamic missed, highly applicable to today, is that the Jewish effort against the Romans can be seen as a classic case of good vs. evil. However, was it really a contest between good or evil, or should we ask whether God saw it the same way."

"I have no idea about what you saying," Peres offers in his confusion.

"We are saying," Ephraim, the spokesman, continues "that what man sees or deems as evil is not evil to God. Evil has a place and role in daily life, in world history."

Peres catches his breadth. This is new territory for him.

"If God supports his wards, the Jewish people, and would help them, why wouldn't He help them in a war against the Romans?" Ephraim asks Peres.

"The Rabbis have said," offers Peres, "that this is the beginning of the Diaspora and thus Rabbi Akiva was just a player in something already carved by God for history and the Jewish people.

"Not exactly," replies Ephraim. "The Jewish people failed God by defaming his Name and thus we have an extended period of God giving signs where the Jewish people, if they were willing, like you, to look carefully at a mirror rather than elsewhere, they might determine **that the solution to the current situation of the day rests within not without.**"

Peres was waiting for clarification.

"The Sanhedrin should have confronted King Solomon. If they did so, he would have complied with the Divine Decree. Seeing that the Sanhedrin was unwilling to stand up to the issue, this ratified his self-serving perception as true and correct. Thus his failing, the failing of the Sanhedrin, and the passing of the precedent to the northern tribes, resulted in their total evisceration.

"Rabbi Akiva, the scholar he was, knew that the enemy was not the Romans. He knew the true enemy that had to be confronted. However, these were the very people who

showered him with praise and acclaim. Instead of pointing to the problem as resting within, he pointed, as does Israel today to the Arabs, to the Romans, and thus to wage war against the perceived enemy to resolve the issue. However, he not only was wrong, and not only was Israel defeated totally, but the death and destruction was pervasive and rampant.

"This suggests that if God intervened, he would have endorsed as He would today, by intervening for Israel, the furtherance of your wrongful agenda which would take the Jewish people even further away from God. Thus, there is no doubt by anyone accepting the reality of history that the Jewish people ultimately face a resounding defeat in any war with the Arab nations and the PLO regardless of Israel's known military prowess."

"The U.S. will not let this happen," Peres says.

"The U.S. will let this happen because God is not intervening and U.S. interests puts the Jewish State and the Jewish people where they have always been when they fail God, on the back burner. The U.S. is committed to U.S. interests first and foremost, and when the dust settles, the reality is that they have much to fear from the Islamic nations and the backstop at this point of history is allowing a Palestinian State and making it clear that Israel no longer holds the status it held in past decades to the U.S."

"I can't believe it," shouts Peres.

"Do you understand Shimon that the U.S. and its allies winning WWII was because of God's intervention?"

"No," Peres answers.

"Well ask those in the U.S. government living leadership positions during those days. They will tell you it was a matter of good fortune that the U.S. broke codes, developed the weaponry, all denied

Germany and Japan during critical periods. If Germany and its axis won the war, the world today would look like the dust and soot around the World Trade Center when it collapsed. What the world saw that day was a microcosmic picture of how the world would have looked had the German axis won WWII. **God intervened for America because it was a country steeped in religious tenets and principles. However, Shimon, that is no longer true, and by now you had better understand that if it is not true, then the U.S. must reassess whether without God's intervention it can feel assured of victory regardless of its superior military.**"

Peres gave out an exhausting breath of air from his lungs.

Ephraim continued: "If America wishes to prevail, if Israel wishes to survive, you and everyone else better understand very clearly that Planet Earth is the gem it is in the universe among the other eight dead planets because Planet Earth received the intervention the other eight planets did not receive. God has those planets circle us daily as a living testimonial as to how this planet would look but for His intervention in this world. He now gave us another testimonial regarding it, on a more personal and contemporary level via the World Trade Center buildings, how the world would look if He didn't intervene during WWII and if He doesn't intervene against the road we are currently on."

"*So you join with bin-Laden and other right wing religious extremists in thinking it was God who took down the World Trade Center towers and caused the death of thousands of innocents?*"

Ephraim stood neutral to Peres' accusation. "Shimon, *God represents light not darkness. Darkness is the order of the day without God's intervention.* When you say what you say you remind us of those Jewish people who question God's design to put us into

243

Egypt and thereafter to hold us there in bondage for centuries of misery and despair. However, God is not cruel. Man is cruel. **When God intervenes you don't look at His intervention as something negative but positive, because but for God's intervention there would be no Jews in the world today."**

"Please explain," Peres queries.

"When Joseph went down to Egypt by the hands of his brothers, it was by God's design. **If Joseph did not go to Egypt and play the role he assumed there, no Jew, from only the 70 Jews who lived at that time, the descendants of Abraham and Sarah, would have lived.** They would have all died from the famine, or if a remnant remained they would have been cast into a severe bondage beyond imagination. Thus, God's intervention assured life not death, as He promised Abraham, and from the seventy, by keeping them together, as He did by His design, and keeping them from any threat of assimilation with the Egyptians, the Jews grew to a people of 600,000 and at the time of God's choosing He freed them from Egypt, and gave them Israel."

Shimon Peres stood and thought about what he just heard. He never made the time to reflect on such an important perspective of Jewish history.

Ephraim continued: "God intervened to the extent that the world could have all looked like the area around the World Trade Center, and without his intervention, 60,000 or 600,000 or even 6,000,000, all of Manhattan, could have died if the terrorist used nuclear devices in connection with the action witnessed by the world."

Shimon Peres for the first time felt the truth of the messages he was absorbing during this discussion. He asked, "What about the future?"

Ephraim was happy Peres asked this question. 'It is up to you and the Jewish leadership in the State of

Israel. Remember when I mentioned King Solomon being responsible for Christianity and Islam. **Do you have any idea at all at the connection between King Solomon and the other religions under the umbrella of monotheism, which rules Planet Earth?"**

"This is the first time I ever heard anything like what you are saying. I will listen carefully to your explanation," Peres declares.

"In Melachim 8:41, King Solomon asks God to hear the prayers in Jerusalem for non-Jews who come to Jerusalem to honor His Name. What Solomon had in mind, aside from his self serving writing that he wanted to bring Honor to God's Name, which he would have better done by disgorging himself of nearly a thousand wives to save the northern kingdom, was returning the favor of his idolatrous wives in asking his God whom he knew was the true God, the one God, to open the doorway for those outside the pale of the Hebrews, who believe in Him, to hear their prayers. **And there you have it. Jerusalem as a bedrock for both Christianity and Islam, the other key points in the monotheistic trilogy of religions."**

After Ephraim paused for a moment he continued, "Where we are today, and a lot has to do with you, Shimon, **is that we are now facing a shift in the paradigm of control in Planet Earth, which will ultimately shift to the Chinese**, and thereafter you will see that the harsh words of the Torah portion in Ki Savo becomes reality, where the living will envy the dead."

Peres coughs, his body and mind starting to see the pieces meshing together.

"The Islamic people are the last vestige of the people trying not to turn their backs on God. The primitive lifestyle many of them live keeps them away from the negative Western influences that has been transliterated to mean Western influences period. The U.S. and Israel have much to offer,

245

however, in their recent turn against the principles and values of their own histories and forefathers, they fail to see that they moved away from the classic interpretation of representing good in any war or battle against evil. Thus God, as I said, cannot intervene for either the U.S. or Israel. As a result, any initial victory in any early campaign will only parallel the false interpretation made by Rabbi Akiva in the early victories over Roman legions."

Peres is sweating a little. He asks: "Do the U.S. and Israel represent evil then?"

"Absolutely not. There is much good in both countries. However, there is only one issue as there has always been one issue. Is the leadership creating an environment removing the people from God? Since I have made it clear that the answer is in the affirmative, then God will not intervene for the U.S. and Israel. **His doing so will result in an interpretation that the current course for both countries is countenanced by God when He does not at all support the current course.**"

Peres cannot resist asking the mirror side of the question: "Does that mean bin-Laden and the Arabs represent good?"

Ephraim answers: "It is not a contest between good and evil. No doubt God detests killings. Let it suffice for you to understand that if the U.S. and Israel cannot win, then the Islamic nations as a result prevail."

"I cannot accept what you say," Peres chirps, looking around for all those in the world today who would applaud his words.

"The future is not what you think is politically proper and appropriate Shimon. If you want to move it one dimension further, **there are no winners for those under the umbrella of the monotheistic religions.** Once victory is denied Israel and the U.S., then China will emerge as the supreme superpower and once they do the fate of the Islamic nations also will be compromised. So does that make you happy that all the monotheistic religions and all those under them will sink into despair together?"

"No it doesn't," says Peres, lying to Ephraim since hearing that there are no winners makes him feel a little better than knowing that his deeds could result in just Islam winning.

"The point," Ephraim offers, "is that **the three monotheistic religions all existing and owing their blessings to God should cooperate to the degree of acknowledging God and making him central to the lives of all those living in their lands**. Thus, Israel primarily could lead the way to bring a peace where the Arab people and the PLO with Israel and the other Islamic nations reach a peace by all showing a willingness to move to God, to honor His Name, and in a snap of the fingers, there will be genuine peace. Once moving in such manner, the Islamic nations will have the leverage to cause the U.S. to look at itself, and recognize that it has gone off the road which made it a great nation and then after rethinking and reassessing it, the children of the U.S. will be freed from the onerous road they have been put on."

"Now, Shimon," Ephraim says, " the phone is ringing. Answer the phone and decide. With the message we have given you, you are the person best suited to deliver God's message to Israel and to the world. Will you represent God and bring the world to a future of life, of beauty, or, will you continue on the way you have and see, from where you are otherwise headed, that Planet Earth will join the other eight planets in this universe as a lifeless rock?"

Shimon Peres hears the phone ringing on his nightstand. It is 8:00 AM. He has slept way past the time he wished this particular morning. He answers the phone and it is the U.S. Secretary of State saying that it is an important day for the man who carries the distinction of being awarded the Noble Peace Prize.

Shimon Peres. Can you believe it? A man who history can see either as the Deliverer or the Destroyer. To be the Deliverer he must give to the world, to be the Destroyer, he will make the choice to continue to serve himself. Regardless, every man and woman who reads this must understand why Shimon Peres is the most important man in the entire world. If he continues to act as the Destroyer, each and every man owes it to the future to see him step down from office and for Israel to bring forth a leader who can act in his stead as the Deliverer.

Joseph Ehrlich
Hewlett Harbor, New York
Sukkoth 2001

Bush's Mission:
Expecting the Second Platform of Moral Outrage

The third inclusion is a major paper by the author prepared to explain the deeper truths behind Bush's War against Iraq, attesting that the professed reality that Europe opposed the invasion of Iraq was false. The author explained exactly how the Moabites had planned to immediately expand the war into Syria and Iran, but for the unexpected reality that Saddam Hussein, stripped of all military armaments, failed to deploy, as the Moabites expected and counted on, weapons of mass destruction.

BUSH'S MISSION

EXPECTING THE SECOND PLATFORM OF MORAL OUTRAGE

By: Joseph B. Ehrlich

BUSH'S MISSION: EXPECTING THE SECOND PLATFORM OF MORAL OUTRAGE

The debate in early 2003 as to whether to proceed militarily against Iraq evidenced rifts in transatlantic relations between the United States ("U.S.") and the European Union ("EU"). **The first question to confront is whether the rifts were real or by mutual consent.** To raise the question suggests an agenda in play far beyond the specter of an invasion to remove Saddam Hussein and to capture Iraq's weapons of mass destruction ("WMD") to spare the world the "imminent" threat the U.S. claimed Saddam and his WMD represented.

Particularly noteworthy accordingly is the admitted absence of a U.S. strategy in dealing with post war Iraq. A Pentagon and State Department that plans for nearly every contingency had no plans in play in how to deal with post war Iraq. Thus, this suggests the second question as to whether there were plans for a wide array of post-war contingencies, but the post war Iraq that did in fact materialize was one unanticipated and if so the reasons it evolved as it did contrary to U.S. planning expectations.[1]

The third question raised is one that lays a foundation to answer the first two questions posited above: **who had more to gain from Iraq's use of WMD?** The U.S. clearly believed and relied upon intelligence that Saddam had WMD. Thus, one must channel into U.S. planning to grasp the degree of confidence U.S. planners carried regarding the certainty that Saddam would use WMD, resulting in their devising a schematic showing how Saddam's anticipated use of WMD could prove beneficial to long-term U.S. interests.

The invasion of Iraq served three different plateaus of support: those aiming to stem the loss of influence of the United States in the Middle East; those seeking to control Middle East oil through privatization; those seeking to secure the next critical phase in multi-polar world government.

FIRST PLATEAU

Regarding the first plateau, it was generally recognized that during the Clinton term the U.S. lost a great deal of influence and control over the Middle East. China under the leadership of Jiang Zemin made great inroads into the Middle East and those inside the government assigned to such oversight noted the re-emerging trend of a movement to undermine the U.S. dollar.[2] During the Reagan Presidency, Vice-President George H.W. Bush ("Bush 41") who had originally applauded Japan for its support of U.S. policy in the early to mid 80's to reduce historically high U.S. interest rates to platform the U.S.'s ability to revitalize the U.S. economy, ultimately witnessed that Japan never accepted the premise that it lost World War II, and waged an attack on the United States in covertly moving to undermine the U.S. dollar,[3] an attack that came to a head in the spring and summer of 1995,[4] during the Presidency of Bill Clinton, where Japan had no reservations about engaging the U.S. in a trade war.[5] The end result was that Japan succumbed, with the U.S. gaining historical political influence in Japan where it thereafter assured that the Japanese leadership was one compliant with New World Order interests. However, the memory of the way Bush 41 was treated in Japan during his trip to Tokyo in January 1992, with the Japanese parading a monkey in the streets of Tokyo to reflect their sentiment toward the President, and then his keeling over during a dinner, was never far from the memory of the Bush family. Now, after allowing China to prosper under a major policy of appeasement, to prepare them economically to join the new world order foray, the United States saw Iraq take the first step in a new effort to undermine the U.S. dollar, where Saddam Hussein would only accept euros in payment for Iraqi oil.[6] Now, the campaign began to spread to where both Iran and Venezuela were prepared to follow the same course followed by Saddam. Thus, the United States concluded that China, under Jiang Zemin's steerage, would gain undeserved power and prestige in the Middle East, effectively locking out historical U.S. influence in the region, and something had to be done to preclude an attack on the U.S. economy via the U.S. dollar and thus on the U.S., resulting in the type of mayhem and damage witnessed by Israel.[7] [8]

SECOND PLATEAU

Regarding the second plateau, the President of the United States was surrounded after his controversial Presidential victory with a dominating cabal of advisors, aligned with the oil and defense cartels, who admitted after the war that as far as they were concerned they wanted to cajole the U.S. to attack prior to the events of 9-11[9], admitting that their plans required a 9-11, thus supporting the brazen proposition proffered in the President's post 9-11 National Security Strategy ("NSS", September 20, 2002), calling for pre-emptive actions against any country or party perceived to be a present or future enemy of the United States (especially it seemed against those sitting on dominant world oil reserves). [10]

Richard Perle de facto declared on Meet the Press [11] that that while there was overseas terrorism prior to 9-11 and there were plans of continued terrorism, the Bush administration could not go forward with the extreme agenda espoused by the National Security Strategy, which Perle thought the President should have had the courage to undertake prior to 9-11, until there was an incident of major DOMESTIC terrorism. Ipso facto, there was a group in the administration who were waiting, plans in hand, for successful implementation of major domestic terrorism to allow them to push forward an agenda in contravention to U.S. precedent, to wit: preemptive regime and culture change against countries perceived to be a current or future threat. The real giveaway however is that when implementing a campaign against terrorism, the United States had no reason to contravene its historical and constitutional mandate by asserting to the world through the NSS and the President of the United States that it intended to pursue both regime and culture change. In fact, this brazen course initiated itself with Bush 41, who, once seeing the Soviet Union dismantled, sought someone more compliant with the New World Order agenda than Gorbachev. Thus Bush 41 stood by, as Bush 43 sought to do in Venezuela, when a coup effectuated regime change in Russia, replacing Gorbachev with a more compliant Boris Yeltsin. This regime change allowed Bush 41 to extirpate Communism from Russia, and likewise now Bush 43, seeking to follow in his father's footsteps, moves for regime change in several states in the Middle East to eradicate Islamic fundamentalism.

The neo-conservatives desired to control, for national security interests, as defined by the NSS, the entire Middle East region[12]. Thus, without equivocation, the anticipated use of WMD by Saddam would provide a required second platform of moral outrage to move against Syria and Iran under the unilateral precepts of the National Security Strategy.[13]

Unfortunately for this cabal of planners, their plans were uprooted when the statistically improbable and then, to their minds, impossible occurred on the primary and back up dimensions. On the first dimension, Saddam did not use WMD. On the secondary back up dimension, no WMD could be found inside Iraq.

The one scenario the Pentagon could not factor correctly was the one seen, an impotent Iraq, sitting defenseless, *not deploying WMD* and in the worse case scenario having none to be found. The plans of the neo-conservatives aligned with the oil cartel fell to the wayside, only able to secure Iraqi oil after seeing their attempt for regime change in Venezuela, fail.[14] Thus, the U.S. in its initial panic to justify the platform it laid to the world for unilateral U.S. action, shifted from focusing on the use of WMD, to its discovery, to, in the last resort, allowing the President of the United States to take a position with legerdemain before the world that the one thing he is certain about is that Saddam had WMD programs, not stating that the truth of this assertion was that it was connected to a far earlier time.[15] Moreover, in this very regard, in the midst of war, on or about March 27, 2003, President Bush summoned British Prime Minister Tony Blair to Washington. It was clear that President Bush and his cabal of advisors were surprised, if not shocked, when Iraq did not deploy WMD at the most opportune moment of the campaign[16], and one cannot stand blind that the Bush-Blair love fest cooled considerably since the time of this very trip. Moreover, it is also noteworthy to highlight that Prime Minister Blair subsequent thereto was subject to unrelenting attacks at home, all which could have been allayed, had at least WMD been discovered in Iraq.[17]

How far was the Bush administration ready to go to implement its preferences for the Middle East as brazenly outlined by President Bush in his Rose Garden remarks on June 24, 2002?[18] In view of the open affiliation between the President's family and the oil industry, it appears quite far[19]. The Congress, media and manifestly the public accepted proffered administration arguments, but albeit acquiescence the administration did undermine the fabric of the nation,[20] raising the serious specter of whose interests were now paramount to this Presidential administration: the interests of the United States as a sovereign country or the best interests of the New World Order, one world government?[21]

Thus this plan had to have a reach by necessity far beyond Saddam Hussein and WMD; far beyond the reach of occupying Iraq and securing a government by choice to the approval of the Bush administration. The initiation of war against Iraq – **had Iraq deployed WMD** -- would give the cabal the second platform of moral outrage to enter and occupy all Middle East countries declared to be covert and overt plotters and planners in supporting terrorist access to WMD to wit: Syria and Iran. So anxious was this cabal to move to satisfy the true scope of its plan and design that after the war, albeit no use of WMD or discovery thereof, they engaged in war mongering against Syria and Iran, with criticism arising globally against these provocative insinuations as a prelude to further attack.[22] The Bush administration ultimately declared that it had no intent to militarily enter or engage these countries albeit the Bush administration thereafter continued to mount new claims and efforts to support doing so, including the need to bring democracy to the Middle East regardless of the U.S.'s current relationship with the current regime, putting both Saudi Arabia and Egypt into play under the NSS,[23] the President seeking to complete the covert mission seeing himself on the eve of the next Presidential election in the quagmire he is in Iraq, which would not be the case had he been able to move against Syria and Iran had he had in hand a second platform of moral outrage.[24]

Had WMD been deployed, the entire focus of the global community would have been on the horrific massive deaths suffered by U.S. troops. Before the dust settled from its use, hand selected new leaderships would have been in place in Iraq, Syria and Iran, without any global intervention and without the need to engage in the war mongering against Syria and Iraq witnessed since the time of the invasion that resulted in no use of WMD. Had any of the Middle East countries attacked Israel, causing death, destruction, and devastation to her, it would only have given the U.S. additional justification and opportunity to legitimatize what everyone now can glean as the true scope of its agenda and mission in waging war against Iraq. This free ticket for instant regime changes would be the consequence of two recorded historic acts of declared terrorism against the U.S. The U.S. thereby could have circumvented completely any argument that it was an aggressor and would have postured itself as a multiple victim of terrorism. Moreover, none of this introspection would have seen the light of day, or if it did, it would have been summarily dismissed. **That Iraq did not use WMD and no WMD were to be found was the strategic defense to short circuit the full scope of the Bush administration's intended invasion.**

Thereby, the planned mission and agenda did not evolve or unravel, giving the U.S. the problems it faces in Iraq, without an exit strategy. Moreover, with the failure to achieve the second platform of moral outrage, allowing invasion of Syria and Iran, President Bush's Rose Garden remarks and his NSS have come full circle to bite him, and bite him badly, on the near eve of election, when troops are dying daily in Iraq.

THIRD PLATEAU

Regarding the third plateau, it is apparent that when the U.S. Congress, the media, and thereby the public at large, sit quietly when an administration creates the foundation for a police state, engages in a broad range of now admitted propaganda, seeks war, seeks to change the regimes and cultures of foreign countries, and also dilutes the relevancy of the Constitution by forging ahead with a preemption doctrine in contravention thereof; not to say allows itself to flaunt conflicts of interest and give patronage to its friends and political and business allies, that the United States of America has adopted and accepted a "New America." [25] The position reflecting the "Old America" can be seen at footnote 13 and by reading the other poignant addresses on the Senate floor by the Senator from West Virginia, Robert Byrd (offered in full on his web site).[26] When no wall of opposition arose under the legitimate "Old America" premises Senator Byrd offered, then America changed right then and there.

Thus, the nation by its appointed representatives, committing itself to the new course, has supported a President that has irritated and alienated the rest of the world and thus now the U.S. has no choice, particularly under the first plateau, but to continue on to Syria and Iran. Should it not, it is highly problematic that it can prevail, even over time, in a war of attrition in Iraq. The religious commitment of those within Iraq, with the clandestine support of Syria and Iran, not to discount Saudi Arabia, assures no success for the Bush team and agenda. Thus, this would undermine those supporting the war under the second plateau. Moreover, here in the third plateau, it would prove a devastating blow to the deep commitment made for multi-polar central world government. Without control over OPEC oil pricing, and with the handwriting on the wall that one day the U.S. would leave Iraq, the predicate would exist for all those seeing themselves the target of Bush's NSS to move on the first plateau and immediately undermine the dollar by shifting their nation's wealth into the euro and enlisting payment for oil in the euro. Moreover, in doing so, they would only attest to other nations, even friendly nations, that there was no future for the dollar, and then two major events would lie ahead a. devaluation and b. removal of the dollar as the international reserve currency. Without control of the oil and with a successful sabotage of the U.S. dollar, New World Order globalization aims would be severely compromised and therefore if President Bush does not move for regime change in Syria and Iran, there is no way he can find genuine support for a second term from his new world order backers, and his failure in the mission will have dealt a serious blow to their agenda.[27]

Thus, there was no surprise when the Congress, aside from granting the administration the $87 billion it requested for Iraq, at the time of the finalization of this paper, passed the Syria and Lebanese Accountability Act, again giving the President another foundation to ultimately move against Syria and Iran.[28] Now, with his trip in mid-November 2003 to England, President Bush will unquestionably seek to convince Prime Minister Blair again of the importance of "finding" WMD. The Bush administration at this point is willing to take its chances. Finding WMD, even with the suspicions that will arise, is better than continuing on without finding it at all.

However, it does appear that the Bush administration and now the country wish to buck heads with both biblical and secular history. While Rome, after seeing its own heyday pass, came to the conclusion that global conquest served the best interests of Rome's future, no doubt history clearly attests that such policy, enmeshed openly, as today, in corruption and cronyism,[29] is doomed to failure, after running a course of death and devastation.

Similar to the time of Rome, there appears, as part and parcel of a policy of global conquest, a need to separate people from God[30] and to look for solutions in an all powerful omniscient, omnipresent and unchallengeable central/universal government.

The problems faced by the U.S. today in Iraq and elsewhere do not connect to a war against terrorism, but a war against changing the culture of the region, part and parcel of the perceived movement to separate the region from its biblical roots and foundation. To show equal application of guiding principles, this agenda also applies to the U.S. and other countries incorporated by choice or otherwise into the new world order realm[31].

The consequences of accepting the current course leading to the "New America" can be gleaned in looking more deeply into the facets of the Bush failing in Iraq. It defies description or understanding that a claimed advanced and educated population would want to stand oblivious to a government that represents ultimately an oppressive if not a failed future for them and their descendants.

The failure in the Bush plan is attributable to one reason and one reason alone: the failure in the interpretation that Saddam in the first instance would use WMD and in the worst-case scenario, if not, that WMD would be found. To his credit, Prime Minister Blair to date has resisted finding a solution outside the pale of democratic leadership, highlighting the need to identify and question the policies, tactics, techniques of the current administration, rejected by history, and which lead to heightened levels of abuse and corruption, and ultimately failure for all those involved and concerned.

News reports concurrent with the imminent and actual invasion were replete with stories of the anticipated use of WMD and how the Pentagon had prepared troops accordingly. No doubt the cabal anxious to initiate the second platform of moral outrage provided President Bush on March 19, 2003, with intelligence where he authorized the launch of thirty six missiles and two bunker buster bombs to take out the Iraqi leadership, said to include Saddam's two sons, before the US commenced ground troop movement.[32]

By next morning, Washington time, President Bush learned that the missile strikes did not pay off as anticipated. However, what is important to focus upon is that within thirty five minutes of the strike, Iraq commenced a military response, and U.S. troops, remaining static and dormant in Northern Kuwait for some 24 hours after the war commenced, needed to don on and off protective gear numerous times. U.S. troops were thereby sitting targets, without any standing order to move against Iraq. What is thereby manifest is that the launch on March 19th encouraged Iraq to respond militarily, when US troops were clustered in Northern Kuwait. After Iraq eviscerated itself militarily in complying with US influenced UN mandate to do so, the **fourth question arises: what assets did Iraq have to counter the US invasion?**[33] The Bush administration all along attested to the anticipated, the expected, deployment of WMD by Iraq, and thus what were U.S. troops sitting there to think when they are directed to repeatedly go into a "MOPP-2" level" requiring them to put on a gas mask, charcoal-lined jacket and pants, rubber boots and rubber gloves in the scorching desert heat, awaiting word of their purpose in sitting there stagnant and stationary after war commenced?[34] Televised field interviews with lower level commanding officers in Northern Kuwait showed them mystified why they were kept sitting there putting on and removing several time a day considerable gear to deflect WMD, with what they themselves saw as the commencement of war.

When a government uses its military in such a horrid fashion[35], and has no good reason to explain why troops are kept as sitting ducks for Iraqi response after it encourages Iraqi military response, when the government itself is expecting the use of WMD, as attested to by the training given the troops and directives to put on and take off protective gear in such regard, it leads many to focus on the reality that despite promises by President Bush for a full investigation of 9-11 that none was ever truly forthcoming,[36] with those in Washington complaining often that the Bush administration was the impediment in chief to moving forward to full and complete discovery.[37] Thus, the foundation is there to explain the "New America" as one possibly carrying more reason to worry about than the one in Rome. [38]

Moreover, Americans should better understand that the EU nations are prime beneficiaries of the current and potential future oil confiscations/privatization and that the U.S. currency, its military and its economy must be compromised to make the nation compliant to accepting the eventual invitation to relinquish its historic independence and sovereignty. The EU has always been married to the US leadership since Bush 41, in pursuit of the new world order agenda. In the waging of a war for occupation, control and national treasures, there was no need to implicate unnecessary and unneeded parties, as long as the mission was allowed to proceed. Once it succeeded, hand selected leaderships in Iraq, Syria and Iran would ultimately assume high profile roles at the United Nations, including the Security Council, to move forward the agenda to the next plateau. With the mission failing, this is not possible and the EU is far better positioned than otherwise, albeit it is clear that they have been cooperative in allowing the Bush administration to control Iraq, including the oil, albeit the failure of the premises given for war.

Conclusion

President Bush has no intent to leave Iraq. Further if he fails to effectuate regime and culture change in Syria and Iran, the new world order agenda is not only stayed but stymied, allowing China to resurface again to take paramount control of the Middle East[39] with Middle Eastern regimes ready to move against the U.S. dollar. [40]

Thus, President Bush's need to complete the mission is more important today than before he launched against Iraq. Once hand picked governments are installed in Iraq, Syria and Iran, then authority should shift to the UN to legitimatize the next wave of actions and events to bring the world to a central world government. In the interim, there was no need to taint the true beneficiaries of the campaign, the EU, married to the U.S. leadership, since Bush 41, in the one world government platform. Without doubt, all those responsible for giving the current President Bush the incorrect underpinnings for the strategy devised are in the woodshed. Thus, all the more incentive for them to make certain that there are no such major failings again in the mission and campaign. Now having included Saudi Arabia and Egypt in the platform for change and democracy, the President has put enormous tension into the Middle East, compelling current regimes to band together in an offset that the Bush administration only hopes translates into another platform for him to move forward militarily to fulfill fully his original mission under his NSS.

The real basis of the war is connective with the refusal of the Arab/Islamic nations to be cooperative participants in the new world order agenda. In this regard they follow their biblical mandate,[41] whereas Israel seemingly has gone the path of contravening its biblical mandate, showing the willingness to join the new world order to be a nation among nations. Thereby, many students of bible and history find the current conflict and situation to be one where under biblical mandate the Arab/Islamic nations are hard pressed to lose regardless of the absence of comparative military prowess. In this regard, noting the dismal economic status of Israel, and noting the abysmal failure of the Bush team to complete their full mission, due to the unexpected, it behooves all of us to watch how events unfold. It would appear, before seeing them unravel, that the "Old America" was a treasure to honor and defend, before allowing the type of influences that could so readily cause Americans to discard it for what replaced it.

Joseph B. Ehrlich
Hewlett Harbor, New York
November 19, 2003

[1] It would be specious to suggest that the United States fully relied on the argument that the Iraqi people would simply welcome U.S. invading forces with open arms.

[2] Ambrose Evans-Pritchard writing for the *Telegraph* filed the following on January 7, 2002: **China backs euro at dollar's expense**: "The Chinese government gave the euro its much-coveted seal of approval yesterday, announcing that it would switch part of its vast dollar reserves into the world's emerging "reserve currency."" This seemingly innocuous event no doubt had major repercussions in Washington for the reasons discussed, *infra*.

[3] Such hostility was made no secret from the media. The *New York Times* on January 10, 1992, reported: **"Bush's Painful Trip**. There was no specter of nuclear war, of course. But negotiators seemed to realize that if the huge and

growing trade deficit between Japan and the United States was not brought under control, it could drive Tokyo and Washington apart, hurt their economies and damage Mr. Bush's re-election prospects....It was too early to discern the American political effects of the Tokyo talks. But the widespread view in Japan was that the negotiators' efforts would not help the American economy or Mr. Bush's political fortunes, and indeed that they could lead to even deeper Japanese-American antagonism."

Japan was noted in the above *New York Times* article as a "rival superpower to the U.S. in the post cold-war area." What riled Bush 41 and the United States was that the U.S. in its pursuit of assistance was treated as a welfare case, seeking sympathy of foreign governments. The *New York Times* wrote: "All week, Prime Minister Miyazawa appealed to Japanese and to Japanese auto companies to make some sacrifice for the United States *out of sympathy or compassion* (emphasis added). At a news conference at the Shinto shrine of Ise, he tried to stir sympathy for the American condition but sounded, to some Americans, very patronizing." This picture of pathos was only further embellished under the fact that just prior to these statements calling for "sympathy" President Bush collapsed at a state dinner. The *New York Times* reported, "{Japan} was being asked to respond from a position of strength to help what the Prime Minister called 'a friend in need.'" All that occurred came to a head ultimately in 1995, confirming that what was in play was a covert plan to undermine the U.S. dollar as the international reserve currency and thereby the U.S. economy and the U.S. Tantamount to the Palestinian suicide bombings on Israel, the true target was the U.S. economy. See footnote 7, *infra*.

[4] In the Spring of 1995, on ABC's *This Week with David Brinkley*, Democratic Sen. Bill Bradley of New Jersey and former Trade Representative Carla Hills, warned that America could get hurt by playing hardball with Japan. Last minute intense negotiations were taking place in Geneva. As negotiations approached the June 28th deadline, Japan opened personal attacks against U.S. lead negotiator, Mickey Kantor. Japan's chief negotiator, Ryutaro Hashimoto, was someone who was an open foe of the United States. He, as chairman of the Japan War Bereaved Families Association, fiercely opposed apologies for Japan's wartime actions. He represented Japan in U.S. trade negotiations. He gave up nothing. So when Kantor presented Hashimoto with a kendo bamboo martial arts sword as a gift, Hashimoto, according to the news reports, " brandished the sword, known as a shinai, under Kantor's nose with a broad smile, he then handed it to an aide...." If this wasn't insult enough for Kantor and the U.S., Hashimoto told the world media that "...arguing with Kantor is ``more scary than even my wife when I come home drunk."

[5] The *New York Times* noted the consequence of the covert agenda against the U.S. dollar when on March 8, 1995, it noted that Treasury Secretary Robert E. Rubin "was forced to spend hours on the telephone today with finance ministers around the world amid growing concern in Washington that further instability might threaten both the nation's prestige and the dollar's position as the pre-eminent reserve currency." By April 19, 1995, concurrent with the deteriorating relationship between the U.S. and Japan the dollar was in a near crisis status. The *New York Times* on that date noted: " More traders and analysts worry now that

the weak dollar is at last beginning to pull down stocks and bonds with it. While no steep fall of all three markets together has yet occurred, the fear that the dollar's weakness could sour other much healthier markets makes analysts and Government officials concerned that its fall could precipitate a crisis."

[6] On October 27, 2000, in a small blurb carrying enormous implications, The *New York Times* noted: "**EURO RISES**. The euro rose on speculation that Iraq's demand that its oil exports be sold for euros rather than dollars will bolster the currency. In New York, the euro settled at 82.96 cents, up from 82.81 cents on Wednesday. The euro currently trades well above par with the U.S. dollar. The Bush administration made it clear that it carried no historical reservation about the techniques it would deploy to quiet this danger, made manifest in its support in 2002 for regime change in Venezuela. See footnote 13, *infra*. However, now it becomes clearer day-by-day that brutal tactics and techniques tend to backfire. Not only was Bush 43 unsuccessful in regime change in Venezuela, not only did he fail to complete the true covert scope of the mission in waging war against Iraq, but on April 15, 2003 the *Wall Street Journal* reported: "According to Ibrahim Ado-Kurwa, an independent Nigerian Muslim scholar and writer from Kano, many Muslims think that the antidollar, pro euro campaign must continue beyond the Iraq war. He argues that pressing for adoption of the euro is the only way ordinary people can fight the U.S. 'Muslims, as we can see, don't have a fighting chance in a military campaign against America.' Said Mr. Ado-Kurwa. "So our fight must be economic and it will take time."" The same *Wall Street Journal* article further noted: "Still, the common European currency has presented the first real competitor to the dollar in world markets since the modern system of international exchange was adopted in 1944. If the euro maintains its strength over time, big oil producers could begin denominating their sales in euros, or at least away from dollars, toward a basket of other currencies without suffering much, if any, economic pain, say some economists. Over the long term, "It would be a great mistake not to treat the threat seriously," saying Robert Mundell, a Columbia University professor whose research provided much of the theoretical foundation for the establishment of the euro."

[7] When Israel first encountered the escalation in 2002 in suicide bombings, it was first remiss in realizing that the strategic goal was to compromise the Israeli economy. By curtailing tourism, committing Israel to call up reserve troops, and demoralizing the nation with a generalized state of fear, it could undermine the state by damaging its economy. As a net result, Israel once identifying the true agenda, enlisted additional financial assistance from the U.S. to counter the strategy. Naturally, the U.S., if faced with the same agenda via an attack on the U.S. dollar to extirpate its role as the international reserve currency, could not enlist similar relief from any other source. Therefore, it had to deal head on with the perceived attack, as it ultimately did with Japan. Here the U.S. moved against Iraq, and also as discussed herein, set its sights on Iran.

[8] Ironically, contrary to the help Bush 41 did not get from Prime Minister Miyazawa, Prime Minister Koisumi attempts to offer help to Bush 43: "Some analysts even suggest that Mr. Koisumi is politically shrewd for trying to weaken the yen now – Japan has spent a record 13 trillion yen ($119 billion) buying dollars this year – rather than in 2004, when Mr. Bush will have to face voters on

the campaign trail. If Japan's strategy succeeds and a broader economic recovery takes hold, then Mr. Koisumi will be able to back off on exchange rates next year, giving Mr. Bush some political breathing room." *New York Times*, **In Japan, Bush Faces Tough Sell on the Dollar**, October 15, 2003.

[9] Thomas Friedman as cited by Haaretz in April 2003 declared: "It's a war the neo-conservatives marketed. Those people had an idea to sell when September 11 came, and they sold it. Oh boy, did they sell it. So this is not a war that the masses demanded. This is a war of an elite."

Theretofore he eloquently expressed the change in attitude in the current administration from any administration before it by writing on March 9, 2003, in the *New York Times* as follows: "I went to President Bush's White House news conference on Thursday to see how he was wrestling with the momentous issue of Iraq. One line he uttered captured all the things that are troubling me about his approach. It was when he said: "When it comes to our security, we really don't need anybody's permission." The first thing that bothered me was the phrase, "When it comes to our security . . ." Fact: The invasion of Iraq today is not vital to American security. Saddam Hussein has neither the intention nor the capability to threaten America, and is easily deterrable if he did. This is not a war of necessity. ***Because if Mr. Bush acts unilaterally, I fear America will not only lose the chance of building a decent Iraq, but something more important -- America's efficacy as the strategic and moral leader of the free world. A story. In 1945 King Abdul Aziz Ibn Saud of Saudi Arabia met President Franklin D. Roosevelt on a ship in the Suez Canal. Before agreeing to meet with Roosevelt, King Abdul Aziz, a Bedouin at heart, asked his advisers two questions about the U.S. president: "Tell me, does he believe in God and do they [the Americans] have any colonies?" The real question the Saudi king was asking was: how do these Americans use their vast power? **Like the Europeans, in pursuit of colonies, self-interest and imperium, or on behalf of higher values? That's still the most important question for U.S. national security.** ***Think about F.D.R. He had just won World War II. **America was at the apex of its power. It didn't need anyone's permission for anything.** Yet, on his way home from Yalta, confined to a wheelchair, F.D.R. traveled to the Mideast to meet and show **respect** for the leaders of Ethiopia, Egypt and Saudi Arabia. Why? Because he knew he needed them not to win the war, but to win the peace (emphasis supplied)."

[10] The escalation of Chinese influence in the Middle East caused real US concern when China forged a new relationship in Venezuela after the failed coup. The following news article, **Chinese Premier Meets Venezuelan Foreign Minister**, shows the reasons for concern: " December 3, 2002: China and Venezuela have seen frequent exchanges of high-level visits, enhanced trade and economic cooperation and closer consultations and coordination in international affairs in recent years, Chinese Premier Zhu Rongji said Monday. Zhu made the remark in a meeting with Venezuelan Foreign Minister Roy Chaderton Matos, giving high evaluation of the development of bilateral relations since China and Venezuela forged diplomatic ties. He mentioned in particular the visits between Chinese President Jiang Zemin and Venezuelan President Hugo Chavez in April and May last year, which defined a strategic

partnership for common development for the two nations in the new century. China values its relationship with Venezuela, and pledges continued efforts to further friendly ties, Zhu said. Chaderton praised China's achievements since his last visit 21 years ago, saying the country is building its future in line with its magnificent blueprint. He said Venezuela attaches importance to developing relations with China, and the two countries' long-term friendship and strategic partnership will benefit both peoples. Chaderton conveyed President Chavez's greetings to Zhu, who asked to send his regards to the president, and also expressed condolence on the casualties caused by a blaze in Venezuela's capital Caracas last night.

The source of the article suggests a message to U.S. authorities: **People's Daily Online** --- http://english.peopledaily.com.cn/ , especially so since China to the knowledge of the U.S. made similar inroads in Iran, Syria, Lebanon and Egypt.

China had already cited its displeasure with the NSS as follows: Xinhua: September 23, 2002, Military supremacy at core of US security goals WASHINGTON: **Now it is final: The Cold War strategy of deterrence is dead, the United States can take pre-emptive action against hostile states or terrorist groups when it sees fit**. This aggressive strategy and the clear target of maintaining US military supremacy in the world were at the core of the first national security strategy adopted by the Bush administration. The White House released the strategy document on Friday. In the 33-page document, Bush said the task of defending the United States against its enemies - "the first and fundamental commitment of the Federal Government" - has changed dramatically since the country now faces a new type of threat. **In the past, enemies needed great armies and great industrial capabilities to endanger the United States, the document said. "Now, shadowy networks of individuals can bring great chaos and suffering to our shores for less than it costs to purchase a single tank."** The grave danger the United States faces lies at the crossroads of radicalism and technology, the document said. Therefore, the United States should seek to prevent terrorists from acquiring weapons of mass destruction and adopt a new strategy in the new security environment. "Traditional concepts of deterrence will not work against a terrorist enemy" who is "stateless and targets innocents," the document said. To forestall or prevent hostile acts by the enemies, "the United States will, if necessary, act pre-emptively," it said. It was widely believed that Bush's strategy of pre-emptive strikes was shaped by the September 11 terrorist attacks. **The international community has cast doubts over the concept of pre-emption, saying it contradicts the concept of self-defence defined by the United Nations Charter and would encourage other countries to take actions against their rivals without clear threat.** Nowadays, the world is nervously watching the intensified debate in the United States about a possible "pre-emptive" strike against Iraq, which Washington accuses of seeking weapons of mass destruction. **The consequence of such a strategy has yet to unfold.** *In its national security strategy, the Bush administration shows no desire to hide its intention of consolidating a unipolar world by maintaining its military superiority. "The United States must and will maintain the capability to defeat any attempt by an enemy - whether a state or non-state actor - to impose its will on the United States, our allies, or our friends," the document said.* "Our forces will be strong enough to dissuade potential adversaries from pursuing a military build-up in hopes of surpassing, or equalling, the power of the United States." Compared with the last national security strategy published by former US President Bill Clinton at the end of 1999, the new US strategy shares the goal of maintaining the US position as the only superpower in the world, but adopts different approaches. While the Bush administration pinpointed terrorism as the biggest threat to the United States, the former Clinton administration regarded global economic problems as the biggest threat facing the country. Although the Clinton strategy stated that the United States "must always be prepared to act alone," it did not use the word pre-emption. Another sharp difference lies in the attitudes of the two administrations towards international treaties. The Clinton administration saw international treaties including those on arms control and nonproliferation as "essential elements" of the national security strategy. But the Bush strategy dismisses most of those efforts, arguing that the nonproliferation effort has failed and celebrating the administration's withdrawal from the Antiballistic Missile Treaty last year (emphasis supplied).

[11] NBC transcript excerpt (February 23, 2003): MR. PERLE: Excuse me, the lesson of September 11 was that you shouldn't have been voting on September 12 because we should have acted against al-Qaeda before that. We saw the camps. We heard the communications. We knew that they were planning additional acts of terror as they had undertaken previous acts of terror. **And we waited.** We failed to take action in a timely manner and the congressman is now saying that we have to wait. REP. KUCINICH: Are you saying that to be critical of President Bush? Is that what you're saying? MR. PERLE: **I'm critical of the failure to recognize the threat** that Osama bin Laden posed before—everything we did after September 11 could have been done before September 11. But if we had proposed doing that, I have no doubt the congressman would say, "There's no evidence. There's no imminent threat (emphasis added)."

[12] The following article by Margo Kingston on September 22, 2002, reflects the global critical perspective to what they read in the National Security Strategy (**Manifesto for world dictatorship**):

"Now we know. The Americans have spelt it out in black and white. There will be a world government, but not one even pretending to be comprised of representatives of its nation states through the United Nations. The United States will rule, and not according to painstakingly developed international law and norms, but by what is in its interests. In declaring itself dictator of the world, The United States will have no accountability to non-United States citizens. It will bomb who it likes when it likes, and change regimes when and as it sees fit, it will not be subject to investigations for war crimes, for torture, or for breaches of fundamental human rights. When it asks the United Nations to move against Iraq, it is not demanding agreement to a strong case for action. It now admits it has no evidence that Iraq is preparing to use weapons of mass destruction against any other country. The Americans have stopped pretending, and now demand outright capitulation to its hegemony. The world will be policed in American interests. Full stop. So now American history screams from background discussion to the forefront of debate. The Americans - despite their promises to be a benevolent dictatorship, do not aim to build, stabilise, and promote democracies. They aim to impose puppets, and agree to Faustian deals which brutalise and disempower citizens. They pay no heed to the disastrous results of such dictatorships when imposed in the past. Australia's choice is to become a non-enfranchised satellite state of the United States - and thus responsible for its aggression and a legitimate target for those fighting to win back countries the Americans take by force, or to fight like hell to save the United Nation's dream of world government by negotiation. The United Nations itself - the dream of multilateral solutions to problems only the world acting together can solve, is on the brink of collapse. This could be one hell of a debate, and I can't see Labor going for American unilateralism and the crushing of the UN. Yes, it's true, much of the sentiment against United State's behaviour is anti-American. It's also pro-Australian, French, or whatever country you feel you belong to. The stunning New York Times scoop - publishing President Bush's new national security strategy, to be given to Congress - is a frightening document. But as David Plumb said in The Crusade's progress, "It is time to stop being outraged by the directness and aggression of realpolitic". What can the rest of the world do? "

[13] President Bush despite no use of WMD still moved to enlist support for a campaign against Syria and Iran. He argued that there was a need to assure democracy in the Middle Eastern countries, and he included Egypt in the scope of the discussion. See footnote 23, *infra*. This controversial inclusion suggested the same dynamic Bush 41 faced in the dissolution of the Soviet Union. While Mikhail Gorbachev was instrumental in its collapse, regime change was needed to obtain a leadership that would better play into the new world order agenda. *The excuse is nearly always the need to quickly bring democracy, but the Bush administration's legerdemain in deploying the argument was made evident in the way he supported regime change in oil-laden Venezuela.* Andrew Redding who directs the Americas Project of the World Policy Institute in New York wrote on April 19, 2002 for the *Pacific News Service*: "None of these {Latin American} Presidents has much sympathy for Chavez. Most would love to see him removed from office at the ballot box. But they all understand there is something far more important at stake – development of respect for democracy and the rule of law in a region long vulnerable to military over throws of elected governments. **By aligning himself with a failed coup, President Bush has done incalculable damage to long-term U.S. interests in Latin America.** He has made it seem that ensuring a steady supply of Venezuelan oil means more to Washington than the future of constitutional government in Latin America. **Once again, U.S. support for democracy in Latin America is seen as hollow: only in cases where its friends are elected does support materialize.***** Like Bush himself, Pedro Carmona, the interim president who was backed by the White House, is a former oil executive. Until recently, he headed the country's most prominent big business lobbying organization. Carmona lent substance to the worst caricatures of the United States — and President Bush in particular — as an ally of wealthy foreign elites with despotic tendencies. In just one day in power, Carmona suspended the constitution, dismissed Congress and the supreme court, and

dispatched security forces to arrest cabinet members and members of Congress. **In other words, he did more harm to the constitutional order in one day than Chávez had done in years (emphasis added).**

In an editorial entitled W's Venezuela Disgrace, the hypocrisy of claims of democracy to pursue militaristic preemptive solutions explained the new levels of disrespect for the U.S.: "The Bush administration disgraced the USA's commitment to democracy and also bungled relations with one of our top oil suppliers when it embraced the April 12 military/business coup against Venezuelan President Hugo Chávez. Congress must step up to investigate what role the Bush administration played in the abortive coup that tried to replace the populist Chávez with a business-oriented dictator more palatable to the Bush White House.*** The irony that Bush, who was put in office by the Supreme Court in 2000 after he lost the popular vote, would lecture Chávez, who was overwhelmingly elected in 1998, is not lost on other nations who are used to self-righteous rhetoric from the norteamericanos.*** On the day Carmona claimed power, Reich summoned ambassadors from Latin America to his office. When the representative from Brazil said his country could not condone a rupture of democratic rule in Venezuela, Reich reportedly responded that the ouster of Chávez was not a rupture of democratic rule because he had resigned and was "responsible for his fate." Reich said the US would support the Carmona government and other Latin American countries "had to support the new government," a diplomat told the New York Times. **But while 19 Latin American heads of state denounced the coup as a violation of democratic principles, only the Bush administration in the name of the USA endorsed the military action.** *Newsweek* reported in its April 29 issue that the Senate Foreign Relations Committee was investigating contacts between US officials and the Venezuelan military officers involved in the botched takeover. Among those suspected of financing the plot is Gustavo Cisneros, a media tycoon and fishing buddy of former president George H.W. Bush. (Cisneros denies any role, *Newsweek* said. But Pedro Carmona, the president of Fedecámaras, the main national business confederation, who was sworn in as Chavez's replacement on April 12, was seen coming directly from Cisneros' office.) **After Chavez's reinstatement, US National Security Adviser Condoleezza Rice warned Chávez to "respect constitutional processes (emphasis added)."**

Due to the failure of Iraq to deploy WMD, the Middle East leaderships now clearly know the full scope of the Bush design, and his Rose Garden remarks and NSS doctrines now turn to bite the Bush administration badly, the threat of a move to supplant the dollar with the euro increasingly real and sinister. Thus the Bush administration is desperate for the completion of the full scope of the mission, or else its failure will have dire implications for the U.S. and could unravel the New World Order agenda.

[14] The fact that the U.S. moved immediately to guard and protect the oil fields, while allowing children to languish and die because hospitals were left unguarded and unprotected, with the concurrent destruction of historical Iraqi artifacts, did little to diminish the argument that the U.S. was out for the oil. The hypocrisy and true character of the Bush mission is also seen by oil company and U.S. complicity in Equatorial Guinea (see footnote 23, *infra*).

[15] Tom Brokaw in an NBC television interview with President Bush in on April 24, 2003 had the courage to highlight the administration's deceit: BROKAW: One of the reasons you justified this war was that he {Saddam} posed a real threat to the U.S. If he couldn't defend his own country -- and we have not yet been able to find the WMD, which were not even launched in defense of Iraq, (President Bush: "Right"), was that threat overstated? PRESIDENT BUSH: "No, not at all." The consequence of the legerdemain was that both North Korea and Iran moved to augment their nuclear weapons program. These countries no doubt saw how the US manipulated Iraq into standing as a militarily inept nation, and Saddam's reward for compliance with UN mandates was to see Iraq subject to the devastation of "shock and awe" attacks, in what history can only record as an invasion.

from transcript Polish TV interview with president bush on May 31, 2003:

Q: But, still, those countries that didn't support the Iraqi Freedom operation use the same argument, weapons of mass destruction haven't been found. So what argument will you use now to justify this war? THE PRESIDENT: **We found the weapons of mass destruction. We found biological laboratories.** You remember when Colin Powell stood up in front of the world, and he said, Iraq has got laboratories, mobile labs to build biological weapons. They're illegal. They're against the United Nations resolutions, and we've so far discovered two. **And we'll find more weapons as time goes on. But for those who say we haven't found the banned manufacturing devices or banned weapons, they're wrong, we found them (emphasis added).**

BUSH VOWS TO FIND WMD CRAWFORD, Texas **(May 3)** - President Bush said Saturday it is a matter of when - not if - weapons of mass destruction will be found in Iraq while suggesting that task is getting little help from Saddam Hussein's captured confederates. "We'll find them," Bush said of Iraq's suspected chemical, biological and nuclear weapons. "It'll be a matter of time to do so." Iraq's alleged possession of such weapons was Bush's main rationale for war, but none has been found since Saddam's government fell more than three weeks ago.

In discussing the third plateau, *infra*, the door is still open for the President under policies and techniques shown under the realm of this administration to still find them, especially in light of his visit in mid-November 2003 to England, but the dynamic will always be open, in contravention thereto, that if Saddam Hussein had such weapons, what purpose did they have if they were not deployed in defense of his country?

In another blow to the President, on November 16, 2003, Anthony Cordesman, a senior fellow at the Center for Strategic and International Studies, reported that he found no evidence that Saddam Hussein tried to transfer weapons of mass destruction to terrorists.

[16] See full discussion, pages 19-24, *infra*.

[17] BLAIR ADVISOR ADMITS THAT US AND UK WENT TO WAR FOR THE OIL MAY 14, 2003: "International Development Secretary Clare Short quit the Cabinet Monday with a House of Commons speech lambasting Blair for

a "control-freak style" that was concentrating power "into the hands of the prime minister and an increasingly small number of advisers who make decisions in private without proper discussion._"Increasingly those who are wielding power are not accountable and not scrutinized," she added. Blair and a group of young colleagues took leadership of the fractious Labor Party in the mid 1990s, jettisoned many of its long-held left-wing policies and led it to power in 1997 after 18 years in opposition. Criticisms of Blair's obsession with image have flourished ever since. His chief spin doctor, Alastair Campbell, is a household name and a satirists' favorite. Blair employs a raft of "special advisers" -- his office would not disclose how many -- among the 190 staff in his 10 Downing St. office. "The premiership in Britain has become much more presidential," said Anthony Seldon, editor of "The Blair Effect," a book about the prime minister. "No. 10 is 10 times bigger than it was 25 years ago."

British ex-PM Major launches fierce attack on Blair "spin" October 24, 2003: " Former British prime minister John Major launched a stunning attack on his successor Tony Blair, accusing him of eroding the trust of the people and undermining parliament. In his first significant political intervention since retiring from parliament two years ago, the former Conservative leader denounced the Labour prime minister's manipulation of the media as "the pornography of politics". In a pamphlet published in Friday's right-wing Daily Telegraph, Major said Blair's apparent indifference to the views of parliament and cynical news management had "done immense damage to politics". "It is fatal to the conduct of policy if the word of any government is disbelieved until proven beyond doubt to be true," Major said. "The erosion of trust has now reached the point where it is undermining the ability of the government to call on the trust of the people," said Major, who was prime minister from 1990 until the Conservatives lost 1997 general elections to the Labour Party led by Blair. Major has up until now resisted requests for interviews since he retired from active politics. But in the pamphlet titled "The Erosion of Parliamentary Government", Major said: "Spin is the pornography of politics. It perverts. It is deceit licensed by the government." "Statistics massaged. Expenditure announced and reannounced. The record reassessed. Blame attributed. Innocence proclaimed. Black declared white: all in a day's work." Over the last year polls have shown voters losing trust in Blair especially over the war in Iraq, while his office has been accused of manipulating the media and obsessing over news management. In August, top aide Alastair Campbell stepped down as Blair's director of communications after becoming embroiled in a feud with the BBC over allegations the he "sexed up" a government dossier on Iraq and weapons of mass destruction."

[18] President Bush's Rose Garden remarks on June 24, 2002, foreshadowed his intent to mold Arab/Islamic regimes to his perceived ideal for otherwise sovereign states, to allegedly modernize them within the ambit of the President's concept of democracy, while diluting democracy at home, with his National Security Strategy, inferring the US Constitution a putative impediment and irrelevant for this day and time. The Islamic world, it appears, wants to rid itself of US bullying even more than any thought of ridding itself of Israel, since the latter is not and never has been a tangible threat, and no threat whatsoever to Middle East culture.

Ron Paul in Congressional newsletter noted the following indicating the arrival of the "New America" (see also footnote 25, *infra*). "When the Constitution is called "irrelevant" during a televised hearing with 'gavel-to-gavel' coverage on C-SPAN, and the proceedings are also being recorded by the committee itself, yet neither the live broadcast nor the separate video record contain this statement due to "technical difficulties" - you can see why reasonable people believe in conspiracies. Just remember, it is the system that is so diabolical; good men and women too easily get caught up in it. That is why the Founders, in their inspired wisdom, put constitutional restraints no only on the central government, but also on our elected leaders - who can become intoxicated with their own power, as history is teaching us again.*** I'm going to tell you the full story behind the "no-longer-relevant-Constitution: statement that is so offensive. The proof of what happened is in the official transcript of the hearing where certain statements could not get "lost" due to "technical difficulties." The offensive comment is one of an increasing number of open assaults on the rule of law by those with the kind of ambition and agenda the Constitution was written to restrain. In one way, I'm glad it is out in the open. The televised hearings began on October 2nd. The subject was the resolution on the use of military force in Iraq. After a ten-day campaign to bring public opinion to bear the chairman of the International Relations Committee (IR) relented and agreed to have a hearing on the controversial resolution the White House wanted Congress to approve. In committee, I was determined to call a spade a spade. This "resolution to use military force" is a decision on whether or not to go to war. Of course everyone already knew that, but they just didn't want to be on record voting for an unpopular war. Ducking the responsibility with a resolution allowing the president to use force was politically appealing. There is always support for a popular war. But Members lack political courage to call an invasion of Iraq what it is - a war - with all the ugly images and consequences war invokes. After all, the election was right around the corner...

The proposed resolution on the use of force mentioned the United Nations 25 times. That was considered safe. Not once did it mention the Constitution. I do not look to the UN to find the authority for this sovereign nation to defend herself. I look to the U.S. Constitution. Article I, section 6, gives Congress (and only Congress) the authority to declare war. The "war power" may not, and should not, be transferred from the "people's house" to the president - the very transfer the White House's resolution attempted to achieve. Under U.S. law, the president, as commander-in-chief, has the authority to execute a congressionally declared war. It was almost noon on October 3, the second day of the hearings, when my turn came. Under the harsh glare of television lights, I offered a substitute amendment, that is, new language to entirely replace what was currently in the resolution to use force. Mr. Chairman, my amendment is a clear-cut declaration of war." In the hush that fell over the room, I added that I was depending on the Chair to "make sure" my amendment "doesn't pass." Both the Chairman and the Ranking Member assured me they would do their best to defeat it. I reminded the committee of the words of James Madison, who in 1798 said, "The Constitution supposes what the history of all governments demonstrates, that the Executive is the branch of power most interested in war and most prone to it. It has accordingly, with studied care, vested the question of war in legislature." It was after that when the Chair stated that declaring war is "anachronistic, it isn't done anymore..." It was a jaw-dropping admission...but there was more.

The Chair went on to say that the Constitution has been "overtaken by events, by time" and is "no longer relevant to a modern society."

The Ranking Minority Member called the declaration of war "frivolous and mischievous." At least it was out in the open. Now surely the display of such disdain for their oath to "support and defend the Constitution" would light up Capitol Hill switchboards with angry callers!

1. Little did I know that no one watching the hearings over C-SPAN - not a single person of what statistically is an audience of several million Americans - even heard those inflammatory comments.

2. When my staff called C-SPAN to get a copy of the video record to document these outrageous statements, we were told "technical difficulties" prevented that portion of the proceedings from being recorded.

3. ...and that same portion of the proceedings was also the only part missing on the internal record the House makes of such official hearings. It was a though it never   happened.
The Constitution is "irrelevant" in Washington in 2002? Not to this congressman and many millions of Americans!

[19] Jonathan Steele writing for *The Guardian* proffered in March 2003: "The US has mounted numerous coups in the Middle East to topple regimes in Egypt, Iran and Iraq itself. It has used crises, like the last Gulf war, to gain temporary bases and make them permanent. In Lebanon it once shelled an Arab capital and landed several hundred marines. But never before has it sent a vast army to change an Arab government. Even in Latin America, in two centuries of US hegemony, Washington has never dared to mount a full-scale invasion to overthrow a ruler in a major country. Its interventions in the Caribbean and Central America from 1898 to 1990 were against weak opponents in small states. Three years into the new millennium, the enormity of the shift and the impact of the spectacle on Arab television viewers cannot be over-estimated. Is it an image of the past or future, they ask, a one-off throw-back to Vietnam or a taste of things to come? Blair sensed Arab suspicions about the fate of Iraq's oil when he persuaded Bush at their Azores summit to produce a "vision for Iraq" which pledged to protect its natural resources (they shrank from using the O word) as a "national asset of and for the Iraqi people". No neo-colonialism here.

Unfortunately, the small print is different, as could be expected from an administration run by oilmen. Leaks from the state department's "future of Iraq" office show Washington plans to privatise the Iraqi economy and particularly the state-owned national oil company. Experts on its energy panel want to start with "downstream" assets like retail petrol stations. This would be a quick way to gouge money from Iraqi consumers. Later they would privatise exploration and development."

Senator Byrd in Senate Floor remarks on or about May 21, 2003, poignantly detailed the following realties: "What has become painfully clear in the aftermath of war is that Iraq was no immediate threat to the U.S. Ravaged by years of sanctions, Iraq did not even lift an airplane against us. Iraq's threatening death-dealing fleet of unmanned drones about which we heard so much morphed into one prototype made of plywood and string. Their missiles proved to be outdated and of limited range. Their army was quickly overwhelmed by our technology and our well trained troops.***Meanwhile, lucrative contracts to rebuild Iraq's infrastructure and refurbish its oil industry are awarded to Administration cronies, without benefit of competitive bidding, and the U.S. steadfastly resists offers of U.N. assistance to participate. Is there any wonder that the real motives of the U.S. government are the subject of worldwide speculation and mistrust?"

The Senator previously that day relayed: "Regarding the situation in Iraq, it appears to this Senator that the American people may have been lured into accepting the unprovoked invasion of a sovereign nation, in violation of long-standing International law, under false premises. There is ample evidence that the horrific events of September 11 have been carefully manipulated to switch public focus from Osama Bin Laden and Al Queda who masterminded the September 11th attacks, to Saddam Hussein who did not. The run up to our invasion of Iraq featured the President and members of his cabinet invoking every frightening image they could conjure, from mushroom clouds, to buried caches of germ warfare, to drones poised to deliver germ laden death in our major cities. We were treated to a heavy dose of overstatement concerning Saddam Hussein's direct threat to our freedoms. The tactic was guaranteed to provoke a sure reaction from a nation still suffering from a combination of post traumatic stress and justifiable anger after the attacks of 911. It was the exploitation of fear. It was a placebo for the anger."

[20] The willingness to a. wage war b. change regimes c. mold cultures d. create the predicate for a police state (Patriot Act with further provisions already in place) e. contradict the U.S. Constitution (preemptive attacks on states perceived to be a threat) f. offer the appearance of a conflict of interest (awarding contracts to political friends and cronies without competitive bidding) g. and engage in a broad range of propaganda to initiate and service the war (Jessica Lynch), suggests that the U.S. Congress, media and public should not have been or be tolerant of such dynamics.

[21] Drudge Report, September 26, 1999: **NEXT CENTURY, AMERICA WILL NOT EXIST IN CURRENT FORM, 'ALL STATES WILL RECOGNIZE A SINGLE, GLOBAL AUTHORITY.' Deputy Secretary of State Strobe Talbott believes the United States may not exist in its current**

form in the 21st Century -- because nationhood throughout the world will become obsolete! *This critical admission is amplified in discussion of the third plateau, infra.* Strobe Talbott was a key figure in government involved in all facets of the dissolution of the Soviet Union and Communism.

[22] The UK Mirror on April 15, 2003 reported: "Lawrence Eagleburger, Secretary of State under George Bush Senior, said American public opinion would not tolerate action against Syria or Iran.***Washington hawks are spoiling for a fight with Syria and Iran following the collapse of the Iraqi regime.*** "If President Bush were to try it now, even I would feel he should be impeached. You can't get away with that sort of thing in a democracy." Tony Blair on April 4th announced that the U.S. carried no plan to attack Syria or Iran and on April 15, 2003, Bush, according to a *Guardian* report, confirmed Blair's posture to the press.

[23] November 6, 2003: WASHINGTON (Reuters) - **President Bush on Thursday challenged Iran and Syria *and even key U.S. ally Egypt* to adopt democracy and declared past U.S. policy of supporting non-democratic Arab leaders a failure.** *** Speaking to the National Endowment for Democracy, where President Ronald Reagan spoke on global democracy 20 years ago, Bush said U.S. policy spanning 60 years in support of governments not devoted to political freedom had failed and Washington had adopted **a new, "forward strategy of freedom in the Middle East."** *** It was Bush's latest attempt to justify the invasion of Iraq as necessary to foster democracy in the region at a time when he is under fire for mounting U.S. troop casualties. He singled out Iran and Syria for particular criticism. The United States believes Iran's Islamic government is holding back a democratic movement and has been trying to build a nuclear weapon. Washington considers Syria a terrorist state. ***"**The regime in Tehran must heed the democratic demands of the Iranian people or lose its last claim to legitimacy," Bush said**. *** Of Egypt, whose president, Hosni Mubarak has been a vital Middle East interlocutor for successive U.S. presidents, Bush said: "The great and proud nation of Egypt has shown the way toward peace in the Middle East and now should show the way toward democracy in the Middle East."

The US therefore is following a path deployed in Russia where Gorbachev served the purpose of peace, and then puppet Boris Yeltsin was deployed to serve the purpose of democracy, code word for regime and culture change outside the parameters of popular vote or opinion. President Bush thus confirms that the original scope of the mission was way beyond what he declared and consistent with both his National Security Strategy and Rose Garden remarks. This compels one to conclude that the agenda is far beyond a war against terrorism but one more than hinted at in the National Security Strategy, an agenda for world domination and control.

The cover of democracy has been transparent for some time as most recently displayed by CBS's 60 Minutes in a production entitled **THE KUWAIT OF AFRICA** -- Despite the tiny population and vast oil reserves, Equatorial Guinea is still a poor African country whose rulers are charged with being corrupt and repressive. West and Central African Catholic Bishops united in Equatorial Guinea have denounced the flagrant discrepancy between the oil wealth in several of the region's countries and the human misery experienced by the majority of its inhabitants. The bishops blame this on the "complicity" between oil companies and politicians in the region. The US quest for control of oil properties in Equatorial Guinea have been subject to many scathing assessments. See for example: The Curious Bonds of Oil Diplomacy. http://www.gvnews.net/html/DailyNews/alert2778.html.

President Bush has given the oil cartel in Iraq coverage even beyond that enjoyed in Equatorial Guinea by allowing it by Executive order to do whatever it pleases under an absolute umbrella of protection. See Executive Order Protecting the Development Fund for Iraq and Certain Other Property in Which Iraq Has An Interest (EO 13303, May 22, 2003). One of the many criticisms of it can be read at:http://www.reclaimdemocracy.org/weekly_2003/oil_corporations_iraq_ immunity. html and, regarding the legal facets thereof, at http://www.earthrights.org/news/eo13303 memo.shtml.

[24] Without the cover that the use of WMD would have provided, the truth of the invasion could unpeel. On May 20, 2003, the *New York Times* reported the following, revealing that Iraqis committed to the U.S. saw that the true scope of the U.S. agenda was far more than Saddam's removal or detection and confiscation of WMD:

BAGHDAD, Iraq, May 20 — Iraq's main political groups said tonight that they were drafting a formal statement of protest to the American and British authorities over their plans to declare an occupation authority in Iraq, which would delay the rapid turnover of sovereignty to an interim Iraqi government.*** Hoshyar Zebari, who was speaking for Massoud Barzani, the leader of the largest Kurdish faction, told Mr. Manning that the allies needed "a political partner" in Iraq, but warned that failure to fill the political vacuum with a functioning Iraqi government could incite a strong backlash in the Iraqi population and interference from neighboring states seeking to move into the void. Several speakers warned that the allies, in delaying the formation of an Iraqi government, would provide ammunition to former Baath Party supporters of Mr. Hussein who might contend that the worst fears of Iraqis were being realized: a takeover of Iraq and its oil by Western powers.*** But he also issued what seemed to be a warning that failure to create a sovereign government would backfire. "We do not want to make your presence here an issue," he said. Meanwhile, several former Iraqi opposition groups meeting in Berlin echoed their counterparts' complaints, saying they feared that the occupation authority could evolve into an open-ended ruling mandate. "If we don't give Iraq the sovereignty they need, this will create instability in Iraq and that instability will run through to the whole region as well," said Ali Bayati, the London representative for the Supreme Council for the Islamic Revolution in Iraq."

[25] Miami Herald, March 20, 2003: **War marks the end of America we knew:** "Because these events represent more than just the end of peace. **They are also the end of the America we have known. For better or for worse, a new**

nation will be born here. And it will be different from the one it supersedes. For the first time in its history, the United States has claimed for itself -- and now puts into action -- a doctrine of preemption, the right to hit first any nation we suspect of hostile intent. *** It's a compelling argument, yes. But it has frightening implications, for it frees any nation to strike any other on the grounds that it perceives a threat. Indeed, it can be argued that the new doctrine gives thug nations an incentive to strike American interests first -- to preempt our preemption, in other words. But the new nation being born here is not just a product of the Bush Doctrine. It's also the product of Washington's recent taste for unilateral action. As the old order passes, it evidently takes with it any inclination on America's part to embrace a role of constructive leadership as part of the community of nations. Truth is, we have been rejecting that role since well before the terrorist attacks of Sept. 11, 2001.*** The country for which the world wept in September of 2001 is now the country much of the world fears. For many people, the most dangerous man on the planet is not Hussein, but Bush.***But beneath the veneer of normalcy we watch and wait and pray that Washington knows what it is doing. We need for George Bush to be right and those of us who are doubtful to be wrong. We need this for the sake of over 200,000 American servicemen and women who stand ready for war in deserts far from home. And for the sake of a nation that stands more isolated than it has in generations. Time will tell. In the meantime, bombs fall. Missiles fly. And in the thunder of their explosions, the old America passes. Those of us who loved her watch and weep from the doorstep of change. (Emphasis added)"

The argument that America is being held subservient to the best interests of the global community is adeptly discussed at How to Destroy America http://sandiego.indymedia.org/en/2003/11/ 101793.shtml

[26] http://byrd.senate.gov/byrd_speeches/byrd_speeches.html

[27] This is of course aside from the reality that continued casualties in Iraq would pose an independent major problem for him in facing re-election in 2004. Thus, President Bush welcomed UN intervention after the war and now seeks to create a large local Iraqi police presence to shift the target from US troops to hopefully perceived benign local and UN personnel, to soften the growing political consequences to him.

[28] In an AFP report dated November 12, 2003, Senator Byrd said that he feared the *Syria Accountability and Lebanese Sovereignty Act* would be used to justify future military action against Damascus. "Such insinuations can only build the case for military action against Syria, which unfortunately is a very real possibility because of the dangerous doctrine of preemption created by the administration," he said.

[29] Source: Bill Moyer's NOW, Public Broadcasting Network: "Representative Henry Waxman (D-CA) has complained that "USAID is refusing to provide basic information to members of Congress" while "the agency is portraying itself in public as fully cooperating with any and all requests for information."

On November 6, 2003, President Bush signed the $87-billion emergency spending bill, but several provisions demanding increased transparency and accountability that were added as amendments (proposed by members of both parties) along the journey of the bill were dropped by House and Senate negotiators before it was finally passed into law. As explained by the nonpartisan citizens' lobbying group Common Cause:

- "The Senate originally voted 97 to 0 to have the General Accounting Office conduct audits of the Coalition Provisional Authority (CPA) in Iraq. That provision was stripped in the conference committee on a party line vote."

- "Responding to the uproar about non-competitive bidding in Iraq, the House passed an amendment requiring competitive bidding on oil contracts. But that was also removed during a conference committee vote."

· "Congress in its final Iraq spending bill did not even include language offered by Senator Patrick Leahy (D-VT) to penalize war profiteers for defrauding American taxpayers. The Senate Appropriations Committee unanimously approved a provision to ensure that contractors who cheated the American taxpayer would face fines of up to $1 million and jail time of up to 20 years. Senators of both parties supported the provision, but Republican House negotiators refused to include the language in the final bill."

[30] President Bush invokes the name of God to carry forth the policies and agenda herein described. Many find his and his cohorts casting his agenda, particularly one that seeks to separate the Islamic nations from their religious affiliations, due to the argument that such religiosity connects to terrorism, obscene, when one considers the agenda that has moved forward to separate Americans and Israelis from the same Judeo-Christian historical tenets, which more than coincidentally provided the foundation for true democracy, including the U.S.'s Bill of Rights.

[31] Ambrose Evans-Pritchard writing for the *Telegraph* on October 23, 2003 noted:

"The European Union's elite are determined to destroy Europe's Christian heritage, Italy's reform minister, Umberto Bossi said yesterday. He described the elite as "filthy pigs" who wanted to "make paedophilia as easy as possible". Mr Bossi, leader of the Northern League, said Brussels was "transforming vices into virtues" and "advancing the cause of atheism every day"."

The following headline would have been impossible to imagine only a generation ago. **Canadian hate-crimes bill sparks Bible, Koran row** OTTAWA, May 16 (Reuters) - An attempt to broaden Canada's hate-crimes laws to include protection for homosexuals has sparked a fierce debate in Parliament *over* ***whether the Bible and the Koran could be branded as hate literature*** **(emphasis added).**

The public assertion that the bible could represent hate literature in succinct fashion highlights the change in culture effectuated by the new world order design including the USA as adeptly portrayed by the following graphic and its contents from America-on-Line:

If the modus operandi of the new world order agenda could implicate religion as an impediment to its design in the U.S. who could argue with its legitimacy in doing so in the Middle East? Its design already has been implemented against the State of Israel, as noted on August 31, 2003, by Avraham Burg, speaker of Israel's Knesset from 1999 to 2003, in writing as follows regarding the biblical regression of his country: "**Our Jewish minds are as sharp as ever. We are traded on the NASDAQ. But is this why we created a state? The Jewish people did not survive for two millennia in order to pioneer new weaponry, computer security programs or anti-missile missiles. We were supposed to be a light unto the nations. In this we have failed**."

The new world order agenda that operates under the cover of claimed movement of states to democratic principles, highlighting the need for open elections, fails to highlight its covert design that such process is only acceptable to it when all the candidates running for office are approved and to the favor of those behind the agenda. See footnote 13, *supra*. Thus elections in Iraq are fine as long as the US approves of the candidates. To show again the fairness in the application of this standard, it appears to also apply in the United States, where those out of line with the new world order standard face severe obstacles in receiving support. When Bill Clinton won the Presidency from Bush 41, he was a failed President in his first 100 days in office, and thereafter when furthering the new world order design, his popularity and success as a President soared, until he faced the scandals that compromised his Presidency.

The key issue however is to confront the claim of the Bush administration that it seeks to bring the Middle East into the new millennium, to save it from falling behind the technological progress achieved and brought to the rest of the world; that their customs and cultures are oppressive to the type of freedoms and rights enjoyed by those aligned with the new world order track.

This raises the question whether the children of Rome were better off because of their advancements than the children of less fortunate cultures? The truth of the matter is that the children of the U.S. have under the influence of the new world order been inundated with negative messages and lifestyles. Agnosticism and hedonism are on par with Rome in keeping people focused on the rewards and message of government. Religious cultures inculcate hope and future opportunity, equality and justice, attributes that never served Rome and that seemingly are inapposite to the agenda described and in play.

[32] On March 19th at about 3:00PM Rumsfeld, Wolfowitz, Myers, at the Pentagon, were said to receive intelligence, reliable intelligence, that Saddam Hussein was at an identifiable location in Bagdad. Between 3:30 and about 6:30 PM the war council, Rumsfeld, Cheney, Powell, Rice, Card and Myers discussed whether to depart from the planned coordinated military plans to start the war. At 7:12 PM Bush gave the order to launch. *The Guardian* wrote on March 21, 2003, **short cut move fails**: "It was a difficult call to make. The US war plan depended on striking multiple targets simultaneously in an attempt to reduce the chances of President Saddam responding by blowing up oil fields **or mounting missile attacks on US-led forces gathered over the border in Kuwait**." The attacked commenced at about 9:00PM Washington time. He addressed the nation at 10:15 PM. At 6:00 AM Conodoleezza Rice told him the big gamble had not come off.

[33] April 15, 2003: **What did the war accomplish?** "In the midst of the jubilation that greeted the downfall of Saddam Hussein (or at least of his statue) and the smug triumphalism that enveloped Washington as U.S. troops marched through the Iraqi capital, Americans might be well advised to sober up and take a harder look at what their government has already done and what it may soon do — in Syria, Iran, or other countries that the war party is already itching to clobber. The war party, of course, is composed of American Likudniks in the Bush administration and neo-conservative media, as well as a good many citizens who can't spell Likudnik but are inclined to confuse chest-thumping about military victories over third-rate Third World armies with real patriotism. After spreading what apparently were just plain lies about Saddam's "weapons of mass destruction" — not a one of which has yet surfaced either in combat or afterwards — the armchair warriors are now claiming that Iraq has been "liberated." Certainly the brutal rule of a tyrant, Saddam Hussein, has ended, but even if he had possessed and used weapons of mass destruction, could the carnage have been any greater than what we have already inflicted on Iraq? The New York Times last week reported that the "Number of Iraqis Killed May Never Be Determined," as its headline read. In Basra alone, local hospitals report handling "between 1,000 and 2,000 corpses in three weeks of war." A Marine officer reported that the Baghdad Division of the Iraqi army was reduced to "zero percent fighting strength." That means, presumably, it was wiped out — some 10,000 soldiers. Those are just combat deaths. There are also deaths from bombing and artillery, and not all are dead, merely crippled for life. What was the purpose of unleashing this kind of savagery against a country that had never attacked the United States or harmed any American? "The principal reason for going after Hussein," Deputy Defense Secretary Paul Wolfowitz, the administration's Likudnik in Chief and probably the main architect of the war, told the Washington Post last week, "was the direct threat the Iraqi leader posed to U.S. national security through his possession of weapons of mass

destruction." "What "threat"? When did Saddam ever utter any such threat? And what weapons? This weekend, Iraqi general and chief scientist Amir Saadi said after surrendering that Iraq has no such weapons, which is what he said before the war. Maybe there are some even he doesn't know about, but there's no trace of them so far, **and why didn't Saddam use them against U.S. forces in his last stand, to save his life or his power? If he was unwilling to unleash mass destruction against an invading army, why would he have wielded it against this country? (Emphasis added).**

[34] **On the front lines**, *Atlanta Constitution*, March 21, 2003, "The American soldiers stationed in the Kuwaiti desert are eager for the wait to be over…as Iraq retaliated with some missiles of its own."

[35] The author addressed the following point on July 4, 2002, *some eight months before the start of the war.* "While we achieve the stated goal of eliminating the threat of the use of nuclear and biological agents in battle, if the regimes are overthrown per US efforts, *the replacement regimes will secularize the subject countries diluting Islam.* This is an intended or unintended end, which the Qu'ran proscribes and demands, unbridled resistance. Thus, the US quagmire. However, from US statements since 9-11 **it has become clear that part of the US agenda is to mold the Islamic world to its perception of its place in the new world order.** Thus, we continue to fear the worst. The United States and Israel stood deliberately aloof for a decade while under the protection of the Oslo process Arafat instilled hatred for Jews and Israel into the Palestinian people. The United States knew that to uproot the recent peace initiative where it was moving to claimed success that it would only take one major terrorist deed to undermine it. As it were, it took two sequential Jerusalem bus bombings. Since it was -- in accord with our analysis -- so easy to uproot the recent US peace process, **the only conclusion is that the US knew it was easy to uproot, expected it to be uprooted, and WANTED it to be uprooted.** The only reason therefor was to escalate the Middle East to promote terrorist groups and cells to move against Americans and American targets. **Why? Again, if a massive terrorist deed is committed against Americans and/or American interests, Bush can forge ahead with moral outrage to take out the current regimes in Iraq, Syria and Iran, and possibly Saudi Arabia."**

The author, on February 23, 2003. one month prior to the war, declared, from extrapolating the current administration's willingness to pursue government behavior rejected by history, that troops in fact may prove to be essential pawns to effectuate a second plane of moral outrage: ""If you see massive deaths of America's youth in the military, trained to the highest standard, acclaimed and applauded by those sending them to face the open portal of bioterrorism, just remember how in the past those slaughtered were misdirected as they were sent to their own deaths as part of their victimization, if not outright slaughter for some. These soldiers are cleansed with the brush of patriotism, believing that if there was anything wrong with the President's orders and course that there are those in Congress and in the civil population that would speak up! While the process is much cleaner today, the elitist centrix gaining in sophistication and improving their techniques for implementation of their design, showing tremendous patience and discipline in implementing their course and design, the consequence is the same: **here the putative decimation of the US military, by either death or demoralization, or both, as a critical step to the weakening of the United States of America**."

On October 29, 2003 UPI reported: "Sick soldiers wait for treatment FORT KNOX, Ky., Oct. 29 (UPI) -- More than 400 sick and injured soldiers, including some who served in Operation Iraqi Freedom, are stuck at Fort Knox, waiting weeks and sometimes months for medical treatment, a score of soldiers said in interviews. The delays appear to have demolished morale -- **many said they had lost faith in the Army and would not serve again** -- and could jeopardize some soldiers' health, the soldiers said.

Further signs of a campaign of demoralization: **Sick, wounded U.S. troops held in squalor** FORT STEWART, Ga., Oct. 17 (UPI) -- Hundreds of sick and wounded U.S. soldiers including many who served in the Iraq war are languishing in hot cement barracks here while they wait -- sometimes for months -- to see doctors. No more meal bills for hospitalized troops From Jamie McIntyre CNN Washington Bureau WASHINGTON (CNN) --Wounded service members in U.S. military hospitals will no longer be presented with a bill for meals upon discharge, the Pentagon said Wednesday. US Soldiers to America: Bring Us Home Now 13 October 2003, 10:29 am US Soldiers to America: "Bring us home now; we're dying for oil and corporate greed!"

[36] From Joel Skousen's World Affairs Brief (http:// www.JoelSkousen.com). *World Affairs Brief* September 26, 2003 **THE MEACHER REVELATIONS**: "Michael Meacher, a former British Minister of the Environment, made dramatic claims two weeks ago that, "Wars against both Iraq and Afghanistan were planned in advance of Sept. 11." This is a fairly brave statement for a former member of the British governing establishment, one that may cost him his political career in the UK. In an article published in the Guardian, Meacher claimed that the US had foreknowledge of the plot but deliberately allowed it to go forward to advance a strategic agenda related to the Project for the New American Century (PNAC), involving promoting future US dominance in world affairs. [*As my readers know, it is my opinion that PNAC was a carefully crafted front for the larger, more secret global agenda to take down US sovereignty and replace it with world government.* Meacher said that incompetence is only a cover, that it is "clear the US authorities did little or nothing to pre-empt the events of 9/11...[A]t least 11 countries provided advance warning to US intelligence agencies."

[37] Toronto Star **Barbs aside, 9/11 questions aren't going away May. 18, 2003. Barbs aside, 9/11 questions aren't going away** Few of us doubt that murderous Saudi Arabian terrorists executed this massacre. But I wanted to know more. Why did the U.S. military, with the most powerful arsenal in world history, fail to prevent or at least try to stop a series of hijackings and crashes that went on for nearly two hours? Where was the Air Force? If President Bush and his cabinet were not, at this very moment, still trying to censor, suppress and delay the publication of the Joint Congressional Inquiry into 9/11, if there had been honest disclosure and straight stories from the

beginning, perhaps all these "dark questions," as the Post puts it, would never have arisen. The great majority of people, sickened and overwhelmed by the horror of the attacks, unquestioningly accepts the White House version. Many thousands, however, are patiently stitching together the documented evidence and noting the huge holes in the fabric of that official story. Just ask yourself how the United States, with its vast intelligence establishment and spy power, could have been caught unawares in such a drastic state of unpreparedness on Sept. 11.President Bush, or, as he delights to call himself, the commander-in-chief, must certainly have been briefed about the ominous drumbeat of terrorist threats that were accumulating over the spring and summer of 2001. According to the report by Eleanor Hill, staff director for the Joint Inquiry, there had been "an unprecedented rise in threat" during that summer. U.S. government agencies had been warned by the intelligence community that there was a high probability of "spectacular" terrorist attacks by Al Qaeda "designed to inflict mass casualties. ... Attacks will occur with little or no warning." The warnings included the possibility that airplanes would be used as weapons. There was even an April, 2001, intelligence report that terrorists planned "a spectacular and traumatic attack" like the first World Trade Center bombing, as well as an earlier report a group of Arabs planned to fly a plane into the World Trade Center or CIA headquarters. According to Hill, these warnings went to "senior government officials" whom she was not allowed to name. On that fateful morning, the first pictures of the burning tower were broadcast at 8:48 a.m. By then, according to a carefully documented timeline at http://www.cooperativeresearch.net , the Federal Aviation Administration, NORAD (joint U.S.-Canada air defence), the Pentagon, the White House and the Secret Service all knew that three commercial passenger jets had been hijacked. Here begins the obfuscation and deceit, in small matters and large, that permeate the official narrative. Disinformation was spewing all over the place that week after Sept.11. Serious newspapers actually reported that one hijacker's passport fluttered down from the roaring inferno to be found in the rubble by sharp-eyed intelligence officers. The key question to me was one of air defence. There are, after all, standard procedures in the event of airplane emergencies. The FAA and NORAD have clear rules about any plane that suddenly loses radio contact with the tower or veers more than 15 degrees from its course. Once the air traffic controller detects an emergency, he or she must inform aviation officials who alert NORAD. Fighter jets are then sent up to check out the straying plane, signal to it with dipped wings, escort it back on course or even force it down. "We scramble aircraft to respond to any potential threat," said Marine Corps Maj. Mike Snyder, a NORAD spokesman, in an interview with the Boston Globe. But it didn't happen that way on Sept. 11. The first reports from authoritative sources (NORAD's Snyder, Vice-President Dick Cheney and, most significantly, Air Force Gen. Richard B. Myers) all stated that no jets took off until it was too late.Just two days after the catastrophe, on Sept. 13, Gen. Myers was confirmed as the new chair of the Joint Chiefs of Staff. On that day, he told the Senate Armed Forces Committee that no Air Force jets got into the air until after the attack on the Pentagon.On Sept. 15, The Boston Globe reported on a strange contradiction. The Globe quoted NORAD spokesman Snyder, who insisted that "the command did not immediately scramble any fighters even though it was alerted to a hijacking 10 minutes before the first plane ... slammed into the World Trade Center." He said the fighters remained on the ground until after the

Pentagon was hit at 9:40 a.m. But The Globe also expressed puzzlement over the new official story that had just emerged. Now Americans were being told that fighter jets roared up from Cape Cod and from Virginia, but just didn't make it in time. Furthermore, no explanation was ever offered for the bizarre fact that Andrews Air Force base, whose job it is to defend the U.S. capital just 19 kilometres away, had no fighter jets ready to go into action — despite the months of serious warnings of impending terrorist attacks. And these are the people we're to trust with a missile defence system? They can't even get their stories straight, let alone defend their air space. According to The Post and to some of their hot-eyed followers, to ask these questions is to indulge in "poisonous delusions ... that do not belong in a mainstream newspaper." I'm not sure they're the proper arbiters of mainstream journalism, but I'm willing to be "unintentionally comical" in pursuit of understanding.

[38] Suffice it to add that the Secret Service did not follow Secret Service Protocol on September 11, 2001 in allowing the President to remain at a known facility and premises and to give a televised statement to the nation to boot from that facility.

[39] Outside the scope of this paper, a conflict arose in the Spring of 2003 between Hu Jintao and Jiang Zemin. China made it appear on or about May 28, 2003 that Hu Jintao controls. It is important to emphasize that Jiang Zemin, as part and parcel of the transition of power from himself to Jintao, stacked the government with his people. Thus, there was no way Hu Jintao could have rendered Jiang Zemin impotent without his concurrence. More important to appreciate is that Hu Jintao saw the Bush administration's conduct and demeanor regarding Iraq, and unless he is in unquestioned service to the new world order mission, the Bush administration's behavior and conduct, would compel Hu Jintao to quietly respect the known anti-Bush posture of his predecessor. As far as the U.S. was concerned, it only wanted to learn that a solution to SARS would reveal itself, which it did, and that China , at least publicly, was following the course set out for it by those affiliated with the new world order. In this regard, China is officially assisting in reigning in North Korea. However, there is no doubt that Bush's failing in his mission has provided China with unheralded opportunity, strategic and otherwise, should Bush have to abandon the mission and pull his troops back home.

[40] While it seems apparent that part and parcel of the U.S.'s own absorption into the new world order stream ultimately would require it to submit to a new world currency, thereby requiring the U.S. dollar to be eventually supplanted as the international reserve currency, the improper timing of it, however, carries the clear potential to blow up and undermine the entire globalization agenda. The U.S. may have considered that this in fact was the intent of SARS and thus a bio-weapon intentionally released by China's military aligned with Jiang Zemin, in response to Bush's Middle East war agenda.

[41] The bible shows the Angel of God telling Hagar, mother of Ishmael, regarding her descendants: "I will greatly multiply your descendants so that they will be too many to count. He will be a wild donkey of a man, His hand will be against everyone, And everyone's hand will be against him; And he will live to

the east of all his brothers." (Gen 16:7-12). Also see Judges 2:21-22:"I also will no longer drive out before them any of the nations which Joshua left when he died, in order to test Israel by them, whether they will keep the way of the Lord to walk in it as their fathers did, or not". **In the biblical context, Israel should be a nation making God central to its existence and daily lifestyle, one honoring Him before the nations of the world accordingly, and also out there protecting the Arab/Islamic nations and peoples from efforts to remove Allah as central to their own lives and cultures.**

MISSED MESSAGE OF TORAH
EXCERPTS

The fourth inclusion is from Missed Message of Torah, where the author began formally connecting the events of 9-11 to missed messages in Torah. From the early biblical days, when God openly was with the Hebrews, even then man insisted on standing blind to teachings and truths. The gap between Joseph and his brothers, and even his holy father Jacob, are noteworthy in these excerpts.

Excerpts from Missed Message of Torah

By Joseph Ehrlich
2002

Jacob Rachel and Leah all know Jacob would have twelve sons. Likewise, Jacob and Rebecca already knew that it was destiny that Jacob would receive the blessings and carry forth God's will and design (25:23).[1][1] Therefore, was there any need to resort to the deception and manipulation Jacob resorted to in receiving the blessings? Clearly not.[2][2] Thus in

---

1[1] God's revelation to Rebecca that the older would serve the younger no doubt played some role in her favoring Jacob over Esau. Rebecca thus imparted to Jacob the need to obtain the birthright. Rebecca knowing that Esau primarily craved the power and leadership that came with the blessings, correctly thought that he might flippantly fall for a ruse to transfer the birthright. Jacob, showing the influence of his mother, adeptly secures the birthright for a bowl of lentil soup. Now, over seventy years of age, knowing from Rebecca the importance of also securing Isaac's blessings, Jacob, as a full adult, must make the decision whether or not to resort to the unholy tactics pushed on him by his mother to secure the blessings. Shown *infra* is the Torah's proof that Jacob carried little faith in God, the first egregious expression of it was by allowing himself to bring unholiness within the bounds of God's expressed will and design for the Jewish people. The Torah wishing to be clear on this point, at this very time, the mistake is made, clearly shows that Jacob knew his manipulation and deceit against his father (and brother) would be implemented in the presence of God (27:7) and that Jacob was willing to affirmatively despoil God's Name in bringing unholiness within the boundaries of God's design (27:20): "**How is it that you were so quick to find, my son?" And {Jacob} said, "Because HASHEM your God arranged it for me**."). How could Israel be platformed on forefather Jacob who the Torah attests lacked requisite faith in God and otherwise aggrieved Him? When God told David that the Temple would be built by Solomon, and then Solomon in fact built it, thereafter defying Torah, marrying one thousand women, introducing idolatry into Israel, does not mean that God found favor with Solomon because he built the temple. Likewise, God was honoring his covenant with Abraham and Isaac by building the Jewish Nation and people through Jacob (God had little choice...).

2[2] A chorus of scholars might here declare that this assertion is poppycock because Rebecca knew that Isaac was ready to bestow his blessings upon Esau on return from the hunt. The reality of God is that when God spoke to Rebecca,

choosing to do so, Jacob set a course for the Jewish people and history, where such stratagems have to be deployed as per his need to free himself from Laban (31:25). Such strategies attest to a hard and harsh life and sometimes consequences which are unforeseen, as per Jacob's own words as a nexus to the early death of his love, Rachel (making Jacob feel without further thought that he himself cast Rachel to the early death previously foreseen by him at the well).

Now, we return and are left with Joseph in slavery in Egypt, with Jacob and his remaining sons in Canaan. Ultimately, in a well-known episode of Torah, Joseph as viceroy of Egypt sees his half brothers contrite for what they did to him. ***

---

telling her that the older would serve the younger (25:23), this put reality in the same dynamic as Jacob, Rachel and Leah knowing that Jacob was to father twelve sons. When God makes a decree, it is clear that one should show confidence in it and not act in a manner defiling it and/or God. When we do this, it parallels Reuben honoring his mother by seeing his well-intentioned ends justify his incestuous means. By acting in a manner not in accord with God and Torah, to wit here: deceit and manipulation of a father, under an umbrella to serve God, we defile God and assure a darker future than would otherwise have been the case. Moreover, the Torah in 27:33 ("Indeed, he shall remain blessed"), supported here by Rashi ("Isaac perceived the Gehinnom open beneath Esau"), gives evidence that Isaac would not have bestowed the blessings on Esau independent of the actions of Rebecca and Jacob (and even if it didn't provide the support it does, we would be expected to know it from our study of Torah pursuant to Kavod Hashem). While Jewish study tends to elevate the forefathers, Torah's intent is clear to teach future generations from the mistakes of the forefathers; future generations learning little from scholarly platitudes given them. This also reminds us that our forefathers, while worthy of the honor and respect they deserve, do not rise, even close, to the level of God and Torah itself. Moreover, one can see that many of the Ten Commandments have a close nexus to the behavior, decisions and actions of Jacob, Rachel and Leah encompassed herein.

JACOB LACKS THE FAITH TO KNOW THAT JOSEPH IS ALIVE SERVING GOD'S DESIGN.

In Parashas *Mekeitz*, the Torah recites its rendition of Pharaoh's dream and only thereafter recites Pharaoh's version of his dream, as he relayed it to Joseph. This suggests that Joseph, in making the correct interpretation, knew from God the true contents of Pharaoh's dream before he heard it from Pharaoh, and thereby confirms that Joseph was in pursuit and fulfillment of his previous two dreams (37:7-37:10), *specifically relayed to his father, Jacob, and to his brothers.*[3][3] Joseph, knowing his role was pursuant to God's design, was equally confident that his father, Jacob, father to the twelve tribes of Israel, knowing God, never doubted that he, Joseph, was alive and living in furtherance of his dreams and God's design.

In this very vein, Joseph immediately ascribes to Pharaoh that his skill and ability in dream interpretation is due to God (41:16), honoring God, rather than himself, in earning Pharaoh's favor, which itself was clearly the result of God's intervention. We know the latter because in 41:37 the Torah writes:

> *"The matter appeared good in Pharaoh's eyes and in the eyes of **all** his servants."*

Since the Jews pursuant to God's design were **odious** to the Egyptians (43:32 paralleling Jacob's remarks to Simeon and Levi at 34:10), it is statistically impossible, *especially when one realizes that Joseph's interpretations will effectively take seven years before being seen as true and valid*, for "all" his counselors to see that

---

[3][3] Learning from the mistake of his grandmother Rebecca in failing to convey God's messages to the members of her family.

Joseph's interpretations and involvement in the fate and future of Egypt was for "good." Thus, like with Hamor and Sechem, when all of the men willingly, without exception, offered themselves for painful circumcism, one can immediately conclude that the reality the Torah relays is the result of God's intervention.

Joseph's spirituality and confidence in his dreams is evident, such as where the Torah says (42:9):

> "Joseph recalled the dreams that
> he dreamed about them, so he
> said to them, "You are spies! To
> see the land's nakedness have you
> come?"

Joseph was aware that to fulfill the dream his brothers needed to get his brother Benjamin. The brothers were all witness to Joseph's dreams. Nevertheless, they were unable to simply assess that if the viceroy was the nexus to the strange happenings and woes they confronted, there might be reason to ask about the viceroy.[4] On inquiry, no doubt, the brothers would learn he was a {Hebrew} who was once a slave and then upon closer examination they no doubt would be able to recognize the eyes mouth and face of someone they so once hated (sharing with their father a refusal to see what was directly in front of their eyes). Similarly, when Jacob hears the story from the sons he sent to Egypt, if he had confidence and trust in God's delivered dreams, dreams that *Joseph explicitly relayed not only to his brothers but to Jacob*, it was a given,

---

[4] It not being a secret in Egypt that he came to Egypt as a {Hebrew} and a slave.

especially on recognizing that with Benjamin in tow, they all would be bowing to a {Hebrew}. Where did they hear that last?

Where did Jacob hear that last (37:7-37:10)? And to show the basis for God's disappointment in Jacob, reflected in Am Yisroel, Jacob's returning sons say to him: (43:7):

> "The man persistently asked
> about us and our relatives
> saying," Is your father still alive?
> Have you a brother?[5] And we
> responded to him according to
> these words; *could we*
> *possibly have known* that he
> would say, "Bring your brother
> down?"[6]

Again, the Torah drives home the point that the brothers and surely Jacob just from this single reference ABSOLUTELY SHOULD HAVE KNOWN that this is Joseph, in fulfillment of God's will, per Joseph's prophetic dreams. Jacob and sons repeatedly fail to honor God, *by listening but never hearing, by believing but never showing the deep degree of faith God expected from those who knew Him.*

---

[5] **Note the singular use of "brother."**

[6] "Possibly have known" is Torah mocking both Jacob and Joseph's brothers for their stubbornness and willingness to stand dumb and blind to what is before them.

***Thus, *Joseph lives without pain and suffering*, thinking his father knows the truth of the matter, whereas Jacob suffers for 22 years, lacking the faith and thus the confidence and knowledge, even when it is flaunted in front of his face by the words of those who cast Joseph into his bondage, and his role for God and the Jewish people (foreshadowing {Israel's} own bondage). [7]

THE CONSEQUENCE OF THE FAILURE TO CORRECTLY TEACH TORAH IS AGAIN SEEN IN EXAMINING PARASHAS VAYIGASH.

Failing to see that Jacob committed an egregious sin in using manipulation and deceit, unholy means, to further God's design, and thereafter failed to atone for such an egregious sin, has brought us to the woeful condition we face in {Israel} (and the failure there portends the return to perpetual persecutions for the Jewish people in and outside of {Israel}).

JACOB SHOWS FAITH IN MAN ABOVE GOD AND SUFFERS ACCORDINGLY AS WILL ISRAEL

45:3: And Joseph said to his brothers, "I am Joseph. Is my father still alive?" But his brothers could not answer him because they were left disconcerted before him.

---

[7] And most significantly for {Israel} today, Jacob never apologizes and asks for forgiveness from God, even after learning that Joseph is still alive and fulfilled his dreams and God's design, thereby passing on this need to see (Israel) repent for the grievous sin of their father, Jacob (Israel). This consequently explains the continued difficulty, if not outright refusal, for present day Israel to see the failing and true messages of Torah and highlights the need for Torah to be taught correctly!

Moreover Joseph first asking about Jacob shows his nexus to his father and that he only put Jacob aside during his period of success in Egypt because he knew he was serving God's design *and he was sure that Jacob knew this as well.* However, soon he is to learn that *Jacob did not share the symmetry of Joseph's thinking* (and faith in God and Joseph's dreams as he revealed to his father and brothers) serving as a further punishment for Jacob's repeated failure to show the same faith in God as shown by Abraham and now Joseph.

> 45:9: Hurry - go up to my father and say to him, "So said your son Joseph:
>
> *'God has made me master of all Egypt.* Come down to me; do not delay *** -for there will be five more years of famine - so you do not become destitute you, your household, and all that is yours."

Joseph no doubt first discovers that his father thinks him genuinely dead. Thus, Joseph conveys by his words, *notably not repeated accurately by his half brothers (45:26) when they tell Jacob about Joseph being alive and viceroy of Egypt,* that he has been living to serve God's design, and he thought Jacob knew it!

> 45:16: The news was heard in Pharaoh's palace saying, "Joseph's brothers have come" And it was pleasing in the eyes of Pharaoh and in the eyes of his servants.

When Joseph interpreted Pharaoh's dreams and saw his role in service of Pharaoh, the Torah relates that it was pleasing to Pharaoh and *ALL* his servants. Here the word "all" is missing suggesting that this was the first dynamic that those in Pharaoh's court started to question Joseph and his high role in Egypt. After the death of Pharaoh, these high counselors who first found favor will change their feelings toward Joseph and his growing family perceiving their presence and power as a threat to the Egyptian people.

> 45: 28: And Israel said, "How great! My son Joseph still lives! I shall go and see him before I die."

One has to only compare Jacob's reaction to Joseph's extrapolated reaction had he been in his father's shoes. Without question, his first words would have been to honor God. The Torah uses "Israel" not Jacob to suggest that Jacob is turning his back on God, as Israel does today after the miracles of 1948 and 1967. God is the first thought in Joseph's mind but not in Jacob's as further reflected in 45:26 where the Torah shows that Joseph's brothers did not use Joseph's words to directly signify to Jacob that he was in service to God (as Joseph all along was sure Jacob knew) but the brothers themselves, also, like their father, simply defer to man over God, by saying to Jacob: "Joseph is still alive," and that he is ruler over all the land of Egypt; but {Jacob} rejected it, for he could not believe them (Torah confirming Jacob's perpetual lack of faith in God proving again the punishment that Jacob suffered for twenty two years was not shared by Joseph)."

> 46:3: And {God} said to {Jacob}, "I am God – God of your father. Have no fear of descending to Egypt, for I shall establish you as a great nation there. I shall descend with you to Egypt, and I shall also surely bring you up; and Joseph shall place his hand on your eyes.

Many think that this shows God's favor to Jacob whereas everything surrounding it proves to the contrary. God honors His covenant with Abraham and Isaac and implements it through Jacob the same as he honored His wish that

Solomon, David's son, build the First Temple. While Solomon built it, he himself directly defiled God's decrees, bringing idolatry into Israel, resulting in its ultimate fall and collapse. Therefore, that Solomon built the temple does not suggest in any way that God found favor in Solomon. Likewise, it would be remiss to read this sentence as God showing favor to Jacob, with whom He must have been seriously disappointed in not repenting despite all the misery showered on Jacob for his egregious sin against his father and for his far more serious sin in being stubborn in failing to identify it and apologize to God, even with God's continued intervention strongly suggesting to Jacob that he need change his perception, as did Rachel, before she could bear children. ***

> 46:29 Joseph harnessed his chariot and went up to meet Israel his father in Goshen. He appeared before him, fell on his neck, and *he wept on his neck excessively.* Then *Israel* said to Joseph, "Now I can die, *after my having seen your face, because you are still alive.*"

This shows that God is not very pleased with Jacob's faith in Him. When Joseph wept on his brothers' neck and now his father's, it represents per Jacob's weeping for Rachel at the well, the harsh future ahead for them where they otherwise could have enlisted a more worthy one consistent with a holy people under God.[8][8] When the Torah above refers to Jacob,

---

[8][8] After Jacob expires, the brothers all offer themselves as slaves to Joseph, fearing the worst, showing that they still had no faith in his dreams or his words which attested that all that transpired was part and parcel of God's design and that he harbored no ill will toward them at all (50:15-50:17). Joseph weeps not only for their lack of faith but also recognizing his father's own failures accordingly (see 50:1). The Torah in noting that Jacob expires, not dies, confirms that Am Yisroel lives on as Jacob (Israel) (see 35:10, 49:31), and that due to Jacob's failing in recognizing his sins and repenting therefor, the need to repent to God moves to the Jewish people.

God, in delivering the Ten Commandments and Torah, and cleansing the Jewish

it does not say Jacob said to Joseph but Israel said to Joseph, "Now I can die, after my having seen your face, because you are still alive." This is an insult to God again, having no faith all throughout his twenty two years, and, now, after he is given the strongest suggestions (even being directly told) that it is Joseph who is viceroy of Egypt, Jacob, *to the last moment*, shows no faith, now only finding happiness in seeing Joseph *face to face* that his descendants will represent Israel per the covenant God made with his forefathers.

> 47:7: Then Joseph brought Jacob, his father, and presented him to Pharaoh, and **Jacob blessed Pharaoh**.
>
> 47:10: **Then Jacob blessed Pharaoh** and left Pharaoh's presence.

Without admitting to the truth of the missed messages, one cannot appreciate the true depth of the criticism lodged by Torah showing Jacob as one bowing to man over God. Whereas Joseph from the very first held God in true esteem to Pharaoh, Jacob blesses Pharaoh in coming to him and leaving him, never ascribing anything to God, as did Joseph.9[9] In case anyone today is as stubborn as Jacob was

---

people in the Sinai, before moving them into promised Eretz Yisroel, gives the Jewish people a clean slate, making them the holy nation consistent with the holiness previously seen in Joseph. However, in still failing to recognize Jacob's failings, and the need to have apologized therefor, Israel lives and stands blind as Jacob, foreshadowing the arrogance that resulted in the destruction of the Holy temple and the expulsion of the Jewish people from the Promised Land. This dynamic is no better exemplified than by the Sanhedrin sitting on their hands with tape over their mouths when Solomon violated a direct decree of Torah which platformed the introduction of idolatry into Israel.

9[9] Otherwise, one could argue that the first blessing to Pharaoh was in his honoring Joseph and keeping him safe in order to save Jacob's family (and Egypt) and the second blessing to encompass the beneficence Jacob and his family were receiving and to receive in Egypt from this Pharaoh. However, there is no doubt that the Torah's pointing to two blessings without any mention of

yesterday, the Torah has Jacob, confirming the reality to be adduced from Torah, by telling Pharaoh that "Few and bad have been the years of my life," 10[10] showing that Jacob knows it yet never takes the time to stop and wonder why. Not one of the potent messages God gave him shocked him into a proper recognition of his sins and his need to repent therefor! 11[11]

God is to convey to Israel in the future that repentance is long due and owing for the obstinate sin of their father Jacob, and absent such recognition the reality would be that Israel would continue to turn its back on God, fail to make Him central to the lives of the Jewish people, and defer to the Pharaohs of other times for man-based solutions for Israel, over showing faith in God, and be under the cloud of perpetual persecutions and threat of losing Israel, after God restored it to the Jewish people as promised by His Torah.

10[10] Jacob has been shown to repeatedly falter in carrying faith for God, and the first egregious expression of it was in his participation in stealing Esau's blessings. Jacob's conduct in obtaining the birthright was one thing, where Esau was shown to think little to nothing of it. However, Esau thought greatly of his blessings, Jacob in stealing them, didn't give a second thought of the reality that Esau might be left with none at all. Moreover, and more significantly, he deployed fraud and deceit in the presence of God, and used God's Name directly in casting forth a lie in moving Isaac to give him Esau's blessings. Such egregious sins could not be dismissed, nor could he fail to recognize them from the many signs God offered to him to do so, so that like Rachel, he might repent for his sins, causing pain and suffering not only to him, but also to Am Yisroel, which thereby received the blessings through Judah, not Joseph. Jacob, in bowing twice to Pharaoh, shows himself to carry the very flaws seen today by the Jewish leadership in Israel which look to outside powers, not God, for solutions to Israel's problems. This dynamic also accounts for Am Yisroel's enduring a history that mimicked Jacob's statement to Pharaoh.

11[11] Why didn't Jacob recognize his sins before God and a need to apologize therefor? Why did Jacob say "Your God" not "our God?" Why did the Sanhedrin permit Solomon to take 1000 wives contravening a direct decree of Torah? Does the evil inclination of man platform a force within men to oppose God, reflecting an unrelenting need, want and desire to stand independent and/or equal to God? History shows us that man is very willing to curtail and control the evil inclination when man needs God to intervene in dark times. This being the case, then, without question, man should then do the very same during good times, it, the good times, being the result of God's intervention, letting light prevail over darkness, in the first place.

***When Jacob bought Esau's birthright for a bowel of lentil soup, he rightfully obtained for Am Yisroel the continuing potential to become a holy nation to God; to multiply, to be a fruitful people, to continue to carry the insignia of being God's wards. Jacob thus passed this birthright to Joseph. However, in receiving the blessings through deceit and manipulation, *in the known presence of God, using God's very Name to perpetrate the fraud and deceit upon his holy father, to blemish God's holy design in Torah*, the leadership of Israel went to Judah, and absent remorse and repentance by Am Yisroel to God, in the name of Jacob, the potential of this blessing has been undermined to allow religious, political and secular leaderships that have perpetrated fraud and deceit upon Am Yisroel via the self-serving deeds uncovered, in part, here, precluding Torah from being properly taught, sanctioning leaders such as Shimon Peres and Ehud Barak, who will continually bring the Jewish people to a state of odious resentment to the peoples of the world, where the Jewish people face death, destruction, perpetual persecution, and loss of the Holy Land. If you have read through the entire contents of this paper, there should be little doubt of the truth, which has been secreted from the Jewish people, the predicate for its being hidden, and the need for Am Yisroel *to obtain the blessings in addition to the birthright.* The blessings remains in a tarnished state, and to free them from their taint, *to get leaderships in the spirit of Joseph not Judah*, we need to apologize to God for the mistakes of our forefather Jacob, his stubbornness in admitting to them, his failure to apologize to God for the egregious sins committed against God, amongst others, including his father and his blood brother, Esau. Then Am Yisroel will recognize their own victimization and bring forth a leadership deserving of Israel's birthright *and* blessings.

JANUARY 6, 2002

~~~

The fifth inclusion in the Appendix is the full-blown analysis featured in Clarity. You can see how the author's discernment of the Moabite design extant since the time of Ruth in Israel, allowed him to deduce the common denominator to the Moabite scheme: double crossing both sides.

THE BUSH DOUBLE DOUBLE CROSS

JOSEPH EHRLICH

11-3-2002

(FOUR MONTHS PRIOR TO BUSH'S WAR AND FOUR YEARS PRIOR TO
OLMERT'S WAR)

THIS IS GOING TO BE A VERY DEEP AND SCARY ANALYSIS AND
INTERPRETATION ON TOP OF THE ONES WE HAVE ALREADY ISSUED
CONCERNING PRESIDENT BUSH AND HIS ADMINISTRATION. THOSE
WITH A NEXUS TO THE PUTATIVE AMORAL CREATION OF REQUISITE
MORAL OUTRAGE FOR THE WAR AGAINST TERRORISM REALLY MAY
HAVE EXCEEDED ALL BOUNDS OF DECENCY IN PLANNING OUT NEW
WORLD ORDER WORLD DOMINATION AND CONTROL.

LET'S GO BACK TO THE SAUDI INITIATIVE IN LATE MARCH 2002. IN
ACCORDANCE WITH OUR INTERPRETATION, THE ARAB LEAGUE IN
BEIRUT WAS UNIFIED ACROSS THE BOARD IN THE SAUDI INITIATIVE.
THIS ONLY SUGGESTED TO US THAT ISRAEL AND THE US HAD
ALREADY AGREED TO IT. NOTABLY, WITHIN 24 HOURS, SHARON
INITIATED THE CLAIMED "CRIMINAL" INCURSION INTO THE WEST
BANK, WITHOUT ANYONE, ANYONE AT ALL, BOLTING FROM THE
BEIRUT UNIFIED POSITION OR THREATENING TO. THIS IMMEDIATELY
RATIFIED OUR INTERPRETATION THAT ARAFAT WAS THE SAFEST MAN
IN THE MIDDLE EAST AND OUR TRULY INCREDIBLE BUT SADLY TRUE
INTERPRETATION THAT WHAT WAS PLAYING OUT WAS STAGED AND
ORCHESTRATED.

WHAT IS CRITICAL TO SEE AT THIS JUNCTURE IS WHAT WAS THE ARAB
LEAGUE AND ISRAEL TOLD BY THE BUSH ADMINISTRATION TO
PERSUADE THEM TO UNDERTAKE THE STAGING AND ORCHESTRATION?
WERE BOTH PARTIES TOLD THE SAME THING TO MANIFESTLY FURTHER
THE SAUDI INITIATIVE OR WAS EACH PARTY TOLD SOMETHING HIGHLY
BENEFICIAL TO IT AT THE EXPENSE OF THE OTHER?

ISRAEL NO DOUBT IMMEDIATELY RECOGNIZED WHAT WE OURSELVES
CONCLUDED: SIMPLE SERIOUS ACTS OF TERRORISM WOULD
UNDERMINE THE ENTIRE SAUDI INITIATIVE. THUS THE BUSH
ADMINISTRATION IN OUR RESPECTFUL OPINION SOLD THE ISRAELI
GOVERNMENT ON THE ABSOLUTE NEED TO ELIMINATE ALL
ARAB/ISLAMIC REGIMES THAT WOULD ULTIMATELY UNDERMINE OR
UPROOT THE PLANNED PEACE TO WIT: IRAQ, SYRIA AND IRAN. SHARON
WAS TOLD TO GO INTO THE WEST BANK AND GAZA AND ELIMINATE
EVERY KNOWN TERRORIST (AFTER THE PLATFORM WAS CREATED WITH

THE LIVES OF INNOCENTS INCLUDING CHILDREN), AND ONCE DOING SO THAT THE UNITED STATES WOULD THEN PROCEED AGAINST IRAQ AS A PRELUDE FOR THE US AND ISRAEL TO EFFECTUATE REGIME CHANGE IN SYRIA AND IRAN.

IT ALL LOOKED GOOD TO ISRAEL. THE UNITED STATES WOULD BE IN CONTROL OF ALL ENEMY STATES AND ISRAEL COULD ONLY BE A MAJOR BENEFICIARY OF THE US AGENDA.

WHAT ISRAEL NEVER SAW WAS THAT IT FELL INTO THE CHINESE TRAP AND DESIGN WHEN IT WENT INTO THE WEST BANK TO REOCCUPY IT IN PUNISHMENT FOR THE TERRORISM (AS A MASK TO UNDERTAKE ELIMINATION OF ALL TERRORIST CELLS). WHAT ISRAEL COULD NOT ITSELF SEE EVEN WITH ALL ITS INTELLIGENCE AND ANALYTIC BRILLIANCE WAS THAT THE US STRATEGIC DESIGN OF HAVING ISRAEL SUFFER FROM PALESTINIAN TERRORISM TO PREDICATE ITS INCURSION INTO THE WEST BANK AND GAZA TO ELIMINATE LOCAL TERRORISTS CELLS, PUT THEM INTO A REALITY OF ECONOMIC MALAISE APPROACHING ECONOMIC COLLAPSE (FORESEEN BY CHINESE INTELLIGENCE WORKING IN PARALLEL WITH THE ARAB/ISLAMIC NATIONS, THE CHINESE URGING THE ARAB/ISLAMIC NATIONS NOT TO TRUST THE US WHEN IT CAME TO ISRAEL).

ISRAEL LOST ITS VITAL TOURISM INDUSTRY AND COMPOUNDED THE FINANCIAL IMPLOSION BY PULLING OUT RESERVISTS FROM THE ALREADY DAMAGED AND SINKING ECONOMY. SHARON VERY SOON THEREAFTER REALIZED THE TRAP HE FELL INTO AND ADJUSTED THE DEPTH OF THE PLANNED REOCCUPATION OF THE WEST BANK. HE WENT TO PRESIDENT BUSH SEEKING ADDITIONAL FINANCIAL ASSISTANCE TO ESCAPE THE CHINESE DESIGN…. PRESIDENT BUSH HAS PUT SHARON INTO A QUAGMIRE TELLING HIM THAT HE IS COMPELLED TO CLOSE THE DOLLAR WINDOW FOR POLITICAL REASONS AT THIS TIME FOR BOTH ISRAEL AND THE PALESTINIANS (BUSH TELLING SHARON NOT TO WORRY --SHARON WORRIED HAS SUBMITTED A PLEA FOR $10 BILLION IN US AID TO COMPENSATE FOR THE STAGED AND ORCHESTRATED TERRORISM AND ITS UNFORESEEN CONSEQUENCES).

MOREOVER, WHAT ISRAEL NEVER EXPECTED, ONCE COMMITTING TO THE BUSH PLAN, WAS THAT ON JUNE 24, 2002, BUSH WOULD ESCALATE THE CONFLICT BETWEEN ISRAEL AND THE PALESTINIANS TO ONE BETWEEN ISLAM AND THE WEST (THE US). PRESIDENT BUSH CAME OUT AND RATIFIED WHAT WE HAD BEEN SAYING ALL ALONG: THAT THE US WANTED TO MOLD THE ARAB/ISLAMIC NATIONS INTO THE IMAGE OF THE NEW WORLD ORDER AGENDA TO WIT: REMOVE ALLAH FROM HIS CENTRAL ROLE FOR THE ARAB/ISLAMIC PEOPLE.

ISRAEL ALREADY IN THE ABYSS HAD TO ENDURE THE REALITY OF THE NATIONAL SECURITY STRATEGY, WHICH ANNOUNCED THAT

PRESIDENT BUSH AND HIS ADMINISTRATION WAS OUT FOR WORLD DOMINATION AND CONTROL. WHAT MUST HAVE PETRIFIED THE ISRAELI GOVERNMENT WAS WHAT WE IMMEDIATELY CONCLUDED: PRESIDENT BUSH DELIBERATELY WENT OUT TO UNIFY THE ARAB/ISLAMIC WORLD AND CHINA AGAINST NOT ONLY THE UNITED STATES, BUT ISRAEL AS WELL. WHY WAS PRESIDENT BUSH SO OPENLY BRAZEN ABOUT IT?

THE ONLY REASON WE COULD SEE FOR HIM DOING SO IS THAT IT COMMITTED THE UNITED STATES TO THE ATTACK AGAINST IRAQ. IT WAS LONG APPARENT TO US THAT SADDAM HUSSEIN DESPITE HIS BEING THE PERSONIFICATION OF EVIL WAS NEVER THE TARGET OF US POLICY BUT THE BOGEYMAN FOR ITS TRUE PURSUIT: ISLAMIC OIL. WHEN PRESIDENT BUSH POST 9-11 WENT INTO AFGHANISTAN, WE IMMEDIATELY NOTED HIS GLOBAL LANGUAGE PRAISING THE SAUDIS AND PAKISTANIS FOR THEIR SUPPORT OF THE US MILITARY EFFORT AND INCURSION.

THE SAUDIS AND PAKISTANIS LEADERSHIPS NO DOUBT CALLED PRESIDENT BUSH AND TOLD HIM THANKS BUT NO THANKS: NO NEED TO PRAISE THEIR COOPERATION WITH THE US AGENDA. {THE AUTHOR} PROFFERED TO THE HOUSE AND SENATE INTELLIGENCE COMMITTEES THAT PRESIDENT BUSH'S TRUE AGENDA WAS TO INITIATE REBELLION AGAINST BOTH GOVERNMENTS SO THAT HE COULD INTERVENE TO SEIZE AND CONTROL ISLAMIC NUCLEAR AND OIL.

REBELLION DID NOT MATERIALIZE. WHAT DID MATERIALIZE WAS THE SAUDI INITIATIVE, SUICIDE BOMBINGS AGAINST ISRAEL, SHARON'S INCURSION INTO THE WEST BANK TO ELIMINATE TERRORIST CELLS, TO LAY THE GROUNDWORK FOR THE US DESIGN TO NOW ATTACK IRAQ ON THE BASIS OF UNDERTAKING REGIME CHANGE OF ALL COUNTRIES SUPPORTING TERRORISM AND OPERATING AGAINST OSLO OR THE SAUDI INITIATIVE.

HOWEVER, TWO NEW DEVELOPMENTS. FIRST, SHARON WHEN HE REALIZED THE TRAP HE FELL INTO, DECIDED TO TURN THE TABLES AND PUT THE WEST BANK AND GAZA INTO A SIMILAR DYNAMIC, SO TO HIS MIND IF ANYONE WAS TRYING TO ENGENDER THE COLLAPSE OF THE JEWISH STATE, HE WAS RESPONDING BY ENCOURAGING THE PALESTINIAN PEOPLE TO ABANDON THE WEST BANK AND GAZA BY MAKING THEIR LIVES EQUALLY UNPALATABLE.

ISRAEL WAS CONSUMED WITH OFFSETTING THE ECONOMIC PHASE OF THE ATTACK UPON IT, AND REGRETTING HOW IT FELL INTO THE TRAP, NOW HAVING TO BEG FOR BILLIONS FROM THE US ON THE BASIS THAT IT SHOULD NOT SUFFER IN THIS MANNER FROM FOLLOWING THE US GUIDELINES "FOR PEACE." IT COULD NOT SEE THE FOREST AGAIN FROM THE TREES.

WE THEN OFFERED OUR EXTREME INTERPRETATION THAT ISRAEL WAS AT THE MERCY OF THE BUSH ADMINISTRATION, POINTING OUT THAT ISRAEL WAS OVERLOOKING THE TRAGIC OBVIOUS: HOW COULD THE US JUSTIFY ITS DESIGN FOR ARAB/ISLAMIC OIL BRINGING ALONG ISRAEL BEFORE THE WORLD AS A CO-BENEFICIARY OF ITS DESIGN AND ULTIMATE EFFORT?

THIS WAS A PRETTY GOOD POINT WE WERE MAKING. WE POINTED OUT THAT THE US DESIGN, EVEN BEFORE THE NSS AND THE ROSE GARDEN REMARKS, WAS FOR OIL. NOW, SINCE THE ROSE GARDEN REMARKS, IT BECAME VERY CLEAR THAT PRESIDENT BUSH AND HIS ADMINISTRATION WERE OUT FOR ALL THE OIL, ANY LINGERING DOUBT REMOVED WITH THE NATIONAL SECURITY STRATEGY. THUS, WHEN THE US ATTACKED, THE GAME PLAN AS UNDERSTOOD BY SHARON, WAS FOR ISRAEL TO ENGAGE SYRIA (HELPED ALONG BY THE FACT THAT THE CONGRESS NOW ONLY ALLOWS BUSH TO ATTACK IRAQ), TO REMOVE HUSSEIN AND ASSAD IN ONE MAJOR SWOOP. ISRAEL'S PROBLEMS WOULD BE ESSENTIALLY OVER. BUT WOULD THEY BE OVER? OR WOULD THE REALITY BE NO ISRAEL OR AN ISRAEL BARELY CLINGING TO LIFE?

WHEN SHARON RECENTLY WENT TO WASHINGTON FOR FINAL CONSULTATIONS WITH PRESIDENT BUSH PRIOR TO THE PLANNED US ATTACK ON IRAQ, HE WITHOUT DOUBT POSITED THIS DISTURBING DYNAMIC: HOW WAS THE US GOING TO FACE THE CONSEQUENCES OF A VICTORIOUS ISRAEL WHEN THE US WAS GOING TO UNDERTAKE AN OCCUPATION OF IRAQ AND CAPTURE AND SEIZE ALL ITS OIL?

WERE THERE THOSE IN HIS ADMINISTRATION WHO WERE TOUTING TO THE PRESIDENT THE MATERIAL BENEFITS OF A FAILED ISRAEL? WOULD MASSIVE DEATHS IN ISRAEL PROVIDE THE US WITH THE REQUISITE MORAL OUTRAGE TO CONTROL IF NOT SEIZE ALL MIDDLE EAST OIL? WOULD SUCH RESULTS GIVE THE US WHAT IT WANTED AND NEEDED: OIL AND REMOVAL OF THE CHINESE PRESENCE AND DESIGN IN THE MIDDLE EAST? IT BECAME INCREASINGLY APPARENT TO ISRAEL THAT IF ISRAEL WAS VICTORIOUS IN THE US OCCUPATION AND CAMPAIGN THAT IT WOULD CAUSE THE US MANY LONG TERM PROBLEMS AND THAT WITH A FAILED ISRAEL IT WOULD SOLVE THE REMAINDER OF THE US'S PROBLEMS.

WE NOW INTERPRET THAT SHARON WHO JUST THE OTHER DAY PROCLAIMED TO THE WORLD THAT ISRAEL NEVER HAD A BETTER FRIEND IN THE WHITE HOUSE THAN BUSH 43, NOW CARRIES SERIOUS CONCERNS ABOUT WHAT ANSWERS HE RECEIVED FROM PRESIDENT BUSH.

IT IS MULTI DIMENSIONAL AND DEEP BUT THIS IS ALL HISTORICALLY IMPORTANT. WE WERE CONCERNED A SHORT TIME AGO THAT SHARON WAS A POSSIBLE TARGET FOR ASSASSINATION. WE INTERPRETED THAT WITH AN IMMINENT ATTACK AGAINST IRAQ, THE NWO WAS NOT HAPPY IN HAVING A SUPREME MILITARY MAN LIKE SHARON IN CONTROL OF ISRAEL. HE MAY LAUNCH COUNTER ATTACKS OUT OF PRESET BOUNDARIES; SHARON LIKE RABIN WAS COMMITTED TO THE BEST INTERESTS OF THE JEWISH STATE WHEN UNDER ATTACK. SIMILAR TO THE TIMES OF RABIN, IF SOMETHING HAPPENED TO SHARON, SHIMON PERES WOULD ASSUME THE PRIME MINISTER POST AND THE MINISTER OF DEFENSE WAS ALREADY ANOTHER NWO PAWN AND POODLE.

HOWEVER, WHAT HAPPENED SINCE THAT PUTATIVE ASSASSINATION ASSESSMENT IS THAT PRESIDENT BUSH GOT SLAMMED BIG TIME AT THE UN BY ALL THE OTHER COUNTRIES FULLY KNOWING HIS AGENDA AGAINST IRAQ AND THE REST OF THE REGION AND TAKING THE US TO TASK FOR IT.

WHILE IT WAS ALWAYS CRYSTAL CLEAR TO US, IT SEEMS THAT SINCE THE NSS DOCUMENT IT HAS BECOME MORE CLEAR TO THE REST OF THE WORLD, WHO WAS NOW INTENT TO TELL THE PRESIDENT THAT HIS POLICIES OF UNILATERALISM WERE GOING TO BE REJECTED AND THAT HIS ATTEMPT TO OBTAIN A CLOAK OF APPROVAL WAS NOT GOING TO SUCCEED.

SO NOW, WE HAVE SHARON GOING BACK TO ISRAEL AFTER GETTING HIS FINAL MARCHING INSTRUCTIONS REGARDING THE US ATTACK ON IRAQ, AND ISRAEL'S OVERT AND COVERT ROLES, AND WE ARE SHOCKED TO SEE THAT PERES AND BEN-ELIEZER, THE NWO FOREIGN MINISTER AND DEFENSE MINISTER RESIGN ON THE FLIMSIEST OF PRETEXTS.

THE ORIGINAL NEWS REPORTS ARE FOCUSED ON BEN-ELIEZER, THAT HE UNDERTOOK THE STRATEGY TO SERVE HIMSELF IN HIS ATTEMPT TO REST CONTROL OF THE LABOR PARTY. HOWEVER, THESE CLAIMED POLITICAL MACHINATIONS ARE MINIMIZED BY THE OVERLOOKED FACT THAT SHIMON PERES AGREED TO RESIGN AND HE CONTROLS BEN-ELIEZER NOT VICE VERSA.

THIS TELLS US THAT BUSH WILL NOT NOW INITIATE THE ATTACK ON IRAQ BUT THAT HE PLANS ON FORCING ISRAEL TO INITIATE A REGIONAL WAR WHERE BUSH WILL INTERCEDE ON BEHALF OF ISRAEL AGAINST SYRIA AND IRAQ.

TO UNDERSTAND THIS NEW PERCEIVED PATH, WE HAVE TO NOW LOOK OVER THE DYNAMICS FROM THE ARAB/ISLAMIC SIDE OF THE EQUATION. FIRST, WHY WOULD THE ENTIRE ARAB LEAGUE IN BEIRUT SUPPORT THE SAUDI INITIATIVE? SECOND, WHY WHEN SHARON WITHIN 24 HOURS WENT INTO THE WEST BANK WOULD NOT A SINGLE STATE INCLUDING SYRIA AND LIBYA NOT BOLT FROM THE ACCORD REACHED JUST HOURS BEFORE IN BEIRUT?

ONE HAS TO TODAY CONCLUDE THAT WHILE THE BUSH ADMINISTRATION WAS SELLING SHARON ON THE ULTIMATE END OF UNDERMINING ARAB/ISLAMIC REGIMES, THAT THE ARAB/ISLAMIC STATES WERE BEING SOLD BY THE BUSH ADMINISTRATION THAT THERE WOULD BE NO ISRAEL OR A DRASTICALLY REDUCED ISRAEL AND THAT THE HOLY CITY WOULD BE THEIRS TO SHARE AS THEY PLEASED.

IT WASN'T JUST THAT THE 67 PORTION OF ISRAEL WAS GOING TO REVERT TO THE ARAB WORLD, BUT EVERYTHING. THIS IS THE ONLY INCENTIVE THAT COULD MAKE SENSE TO THE ENTIRE ARAB LEAGUE PLAYING ALONG WITH A STRATEGY, WHICH REQUIRED SHARON TO MAKE AN INCURSION INTO THE WEST BANK WITHOUT ANYONE BOLTING FROM THE ARAB LEAGUE ACCORD IN BEIRUT.

THE US SPECIFIED ITS INTERESTS IN TERMS OF ELIMINATING THE THREAT OF TERRORISM, ESPECIALLY SUICIDE BOMBERS, HITTING THE SHORES OF THE US, WITH THE ARAB LEAGUE, WE SURMISE, NOT UNDERSTANDING THAT ONCE ISRAEL REVERTED IN FULL TO THE ARAB WORLD THAT THERE WOULD BE NO NEED TO ELIMINATE TERRORISTS.

THUS, THIS SUGGESTED THAT THE NEED TO ELIMINATE TERRORISM HAD TO DO WITH WHAT THE ARAB LEAGUE THEREAFTER SAW WAS THAT THE TRUE GOAL OF THE US WAS NOT THE MASK OF WMD OR SUICIDE BOMBERS, BUT ITS CRITICAL ASSET OIL (PREVIOUSLY SEEING IT AS A PRETEXT TO SET UP ISRAEL FOR THE INEVITABLE UNDER THE BUSH NWO AGENDA). NOT ONLY IRAQI OIL AND OIL RESERVES BUT CONTROL OF ALL OTHER REGIONAL OIL, ESPECIALLY SAUDI OIL. THIS WAS NOT SUPPOSED TO BE SO OBVIOUS AND CLEAR TO THE ARAB LEAGUE BUT WE BELOW CITE THE DATES AND LANGUAGE OF SOME OF OUR ANALYSES MAKING IT CLEAR THAT WE CONCLUDED WE COULD NOT AGREE WITH US POLICIES WHICH PREEMPTIVELY WENT OUT NOT TO PROTECT OUR NATION BUT TO ILLEGALLY SEIZE AND CONTROL MIDDLE EASTERN OIL BECAUSE THE GOVERNMENT DIDN'T LIKE THE REALITY THAT CHINA WENT OUT DURING THE CLINTON TERM AND CAPTURED THE MIDDLE EAST AND NOW THE NWO OIL CARTEL WAS NOT GOING TO LOSE ITS RELATIONSHIP WITH MIDDLE EAST OIL POWERS AND INDIRECT HISTORICAL CONTROL OF MIDDLE EAST OIL.

WE MUST INTERJECT THAT IF THERE WAS ANY CHANCE OF SAVING IT, PRESIDENT BUSH IRREVOCABLY LOST IT AND PLAYED INTO CHINA'S HAND BY RELEASING THE NATIONAL SECURITY STRATEGY, THE DUMBEST MOVE FOR US INTERESTS ONE COULD EVER IMAGINE.

THE BUSH ADMINISTRATION IS PROBABLY ON SERIOUS MEDICATION HAVING TO PLAY THIS DEEPLY DANGEROUS GAME OF TELLING ISRAEL THAT IT IS ITS BEST FRIEND, AND STILL HAVING THE NERVE TO TELL THE ARAB LEAGUE THAT THE US IS SIMPLY DOING ALL THESE CONVOLUTED MANEUVERS TO SET UP THE ENVIRONMENT SO THAT THEY CAN HAVE BACK THE HOLY CITY AND THAT ISRAEL WILL NO LONGER BE AN ISSUE IN A FUTURE RELATIONSHIP BETWEEN THE US AND THE ARAB WORLD (SAYING THAT THEY HAVE REASON TO ALIGN FOR THE FUTURE WITH THE US RATHER THAN CHINA, WHO THE US TELLS THE ARAB WORLD, ESPECIALLY SAUDI ARABIA, CANNOT BE TRUSTED).

CONCLUSIONS: THE REALITY IS THAT NOW BOTH ISRAEL AND THE ARAB WORLD DO NOT TRUST THE BUSH ADMINISTRATION, AND QUITE FRANKLY, NO DOUBT AMERICANS WILL NO LONGER AS WELL AS THE BUSH ADMINISTRATION'S AMORAL NEXUS TO 9-11 AND OTHER DESIGNS UNRAVELS. HOWEVER, THE POINT IS THAT SHARON CAME BACK TO ISRAEL, KNOWING THAT HIS LIFE WAS AT RISK, AND ALSO NOW KNOWING THAT THE US MAY VERY WELL BE SETTING UP ISRAEL TO TAKE A FALL FOR THE REASONS ARTICULATED. HE CANNOT TAKE THE CHANCE THAT IT MAY BE THE CASE. THUS, HE WILL NOT GO BY THE BUSH GAME PLAN, ALLOWING ISRAEL TO SUCCUMB WHILE HE IS AT THE HELM.

THUS, PERES REPORTING ABOUT SHARON'S CONCERNS, WAS NO DOUBT DIRECTED TO LEAVE THE SHARON GOVERNMENT. THE QUESTION IS FOR WHAT PURPOSE? THE US (NWO) NO DOUBT HAS REACHED THE NEW CONCLUSION OFFERED ABOVE THAT ITS INTERESTS ARE NOW BETTER SERVED BY HAVING ISRAEL INITIATE THE ATTACK AND THEN HAVING THE US INTERCEDE FOR IT.

YOU HAVE TO UNDERSTAND THE DEPTH OF THIS NEW DESIGN. IN EACH STEP, DEPENDING ON THE RESULTS, THE BUSH ADMINISTRATION IS SITUATED TO PLAY EITHER SCENARIO, OR THE ONE WE BELIEVE IS NOW IN PLAY: THE BUSH DOUBLE DOUBLE CROSS, WHERE BOTH ISRAEL IS LOST AND THE ARAB REGIMES UNDERMINED PER US ENDS.

WITH THE ARAB WORLD UNDER US CONTROL (IN PUNISHMENT FOR THE DEVASTATION TO ISRAEL), THOSE WHO ARE LIVID OVER THE LOSS OF ISRAEL ARE ASSUAGED, WHILE WITH ISRAEL LOST, A NEW PLATFORM FOR A RENEWED US RELATIONSHIP WITH THE ARAB WORLD IS CREATED OVER TIME, GIVING THEM THE HOLY CITY AS A PRIZE FOR LOSING THE OIL AND THEIR SOVEREIGNTY. THIS LEAVES THE BUSH

ADMINISTRATION ONLY WITH CHINA TO DEAL WITH, NOW HAVING
EFFECTIVELY REMOVED IT FROM THE MIDDLE EAST.

NOW, ASSUMING THAT CHINA, ISRAEL AND THE ARAB LEAGUE
UNDERSTAND WHAT WE PROFFER, WHAT CAN WE EXPECT TO SEE TO
OFFSET THIS DESIGN?

(THE AUTHOR} HOPES YOU UNDERSTAND THAT ALL THE ABOVE
REPRESENTS OUR CONTENTION THAT ALL ROADS LEAD TO THE SAME
RESULT UNLESS ISRAEL PRIMARILY IN HERE UNDERTAKES THE
RELIGIOUS RESOLUTION WITH THE ARAB/ISLAMIC WORLD.

WHAT YOU HAVE JUST READ REPRESENTS MUTUALITY OF INTERESTS
BETWEEN THEM, BECAUSE THEY ARE BOTH BEING SET UP FOR THE
BUSH DOUBLE DOUBLE CROSS. THUS, WE ARE HERE TO PROMOTE THE
RELIGIOUS RESOLUTION BETWEEN ISRAEL AND THE ARAB/ISLAMIC
WORLD FOR THIS WILL PERMIT AS WE ARGUED LONG AGO THE US TO
CLEAN SHOP FROM THE NWO INFLUENCES WHO TAKE US ON THE
ROAD TO OUR OWN DESTRUCTION HERE AT HOME, AND THAT IS
WHERE CHINA COMES INTO THE PICTURE.

SUCCINCTLY PUT, WE BELIEVE THAT CHINA HAS GIVEN SYRIA FOR ITS
STEADFASTNESS, IN NOT CAVING IN TO US PRESSURES, PROTECTION
AGAINST US DESIGN TO OVERTHROW ITS REGIME, AND WE BELIEVE IT
HAS GIVEN THE SAME ASSURANCES TO IRAN, AND THUS YOU CAN SEE
HOW CLOSE WE ARE TO NOT ONLY REGIONAL BUT GLOBAL WAR, AND
THE REASONS THEREFOR.

HOWEVER, IN THIS PAPER, WE ARE DETAILING THE PERCEIVED
DOUBLE DOUBLE CROSS STRATEGY OF THE BUSH ADMINISTRATION,
MADE EVEN MORE EVIDENT TO US WITH THE FORCED COLLAPSE OF
THE SHARON GOVERNMENT. SHARON'S NEW DEFENSE MINISTER IS A
HAWK, AND THE US NO DOUBT, WILL ENCOURAGE ISRAEL TO DEFEND
ITSELF, AND THERE WILL NO DOUBT BE ENOUGH TERRORISM FOR
ISRAEL TO INITIATE A REGIONAL CONFLICT IN ITS LEGITIMATE
DEFENSE, WHERE THE US WILL ENTER TO "SAVE THE REGION AND
THE WORLD."

WHILE WE CAN ENVISION STRATEGIES ISRAEL AND THE ARAB WORLD
CAN OR MAY INDEPENDENTLY DEPLOY TO OFFSET BUSH'S DOUBLE
DOUBLE CROSS, THEY WILL BE TO NO AVAIL, FOR AGAIN, BUT FOR THE
RELIGIOUS RESOLUTION, ALL ROADS LEAD TO DISASTER.

LOOK AT SOME OF THE THINGS BELOW {THE AUTHOR} WROTE IN
EARLY 2002 AND SEE HOW TRUE THEY HAVE BECOME. THE US HAD
TURNED ITS BACK NOT ONLY ON GOD, BUT ON ITS OWN
CONSTITUTION, AND FOR THE STOCK MARKET WEALTH GIVEN UNDER
CLINTON, THEY LOOKED ASIDE AS CORRUPTION AND GREED BECAME

INSTITUTIONALIZED IN THE AMERICAN INFRASTRUCTURE. PAYMENT FOR THAT ERROR IS NOW BEING EXTRACTED.

WITH PERES GONE FROM THE GOVERNMENT OF ISRAEL, THE GATEWAY HAS OPENED FOR SHARON TO PURSUE A TRUE PEACE.

WE RESPECTFULLY SUBMIT THAT YOU DO EVERYTHING POSSIBLE TO CONVINCE THE PRIME MINISTER THAT ANY COURSE OTHER THAN THE RELIGIOUS RESOLUTION WILL LEAD TO THE DEVASTATION OF THE STATE OF ISRAEL.

THE ARAB NATIONS ARE NOT ISRAEL'S ENEMIES. BY FAILING TO RECOGNIZE THE CORRECT COURSE, ISRAEL AND THE ARAB/ISLAMIC WORLD WILL SUCCUMB, EACH IN THEIR OWN WAY, AND OPEN THE GATEWAY TO THE ULTIMATE CONFLICT AND CONTEST BETWEEN THE US AND CHINA, WHERE THE US WILL PAY FOR ITS GRIEVOUS ERRORS AND SINS {AS SURROGATE FOR THE MOABITES IN AN AGENDA THAT SEEKS TO DEFAME AND DIMINISH GOD}.

THUS, THE US, ISRAEL AND ARAB/ISLAMIC WORLD SHOULD ALL RECOGNIZE THAT THE ONLY COURSE TO SERVE THEIR OWN FUTURES IS THE RELIGIOUS RESOLUTION. ABANDON GOD AND THE FUTURE CAN ONLY BE DARK AND DIRE WITHOUT HIS INTERVENTION.

{EXCERPTS BELOW FROM AUTHOR'S ANALYSES ON DATES SHOWN}

KEY DATES:

JUNE 24, 2002, PRESIDENT BUSH'S ROSE GARDEN REMARKS

SEPTEMBER 20, 2002, NATIONAL SECURITY STRATEGY

MARCH 30, 2002: CHINA IS TELLING ARAB NATIONS THAT ISRAEL IS DYING ECONOMICALLY FROM THE TERRORIST ATTACKS.

APRIL 11, 2002: CHINA DRIVES PRESIDENT BUSH'S DECISIONS AND CONCERNS.

APRIL 12, 2002: THE US IS NOW COMMITTED TO A COURSE WHERE IT MUST UNDERMINE ALL REGIMES ALIGNED WITH CHINA (UNDER THE BANNER OF SUPPORTING TERRORISM).

MAY 5, 2002: US TELLS ISRAEL THAT IT ACCEPTS RESPONSIBILITY TO NEUTRALIZE IRAQ, IRAN, SYRIA, WHICH RESPONSIBILITY IT DOES NOT ASSUME WITH GREAT RELUCTANCE.

MAY 5, 2002: UPSETTING THE SAUDI PEACE INITIATIVE IS A DOABLE PROJECT FOR CHINA.

JUNE 17, 2002 (DAYS BEFORE THE PRESIDENT'S ROSE GARDEN REMARKS!): ... REPLACING REGIMES WILL SECULARIZE THE SUBJECT COUNTRIES DILUTING ISLAM. THIS IS AN INTENDED OR UNINTENDED END WHICH THE QUR'AN PROSCRIBES AND DEMANDS UNBRIDLED RESISTANCE. HOWEVER, FROM US STATEMENTS SINCE 9-11, IT HAS BECOME CLEAR THAT PART OF THE US AGENDA IS TO MOLD THE ISLAMIC WORLD TO ITS PERCEPTION OF ITS PLACE IN THE NEW WORLD ORDER. PRESIDENT BUSH SAYS THIS SEVEN DAYS LATER.

JUNE 21, 2002 (STILL DAYS BEFORE THE ROSE GARDEN REMARKS): SHARON MOVING IN TROOPS, WILLINGLY CALLING UP RESERVES, WILL PUT ISRAEL INTO A SERIOUS FINANCIAL BIND.

JUNE 21, 2002: US'S BEST COURSE MAY BE TO SEE ISRAEL FACE A SLOW DEATH, INEVITABLE FROM A COLLAPSED TOURIST INDUSTRY AND DEPLOYMENT OF PERSONNEL TO A REOCCUPATION OF THE WEST BANK.

JUNE 21, 2002: MANY OF THE EU'S AND US'S PROBLEMS ARE RESOLVED BY ISRAEL FAILING AS A SOVEREIGN STATE AND COUNTRY.

JUNE 21, 2002: IF PRESIDENT BUSH PULLS AWAY FROM A PREEMPTIVE STRIKE AGAINST IRAQ, AND ISRAEL FACES CONTINUAL TERRORIST ATTACKS (WHILE THE EU AND US DO NOT), ISRAEL HAS AN IMMINENT SURVIVAL CRISIS....IF THE STATE OF ISRAEL WANTS TO ACT AS THOUGH IT IS DEVOID OF ANY MAJOR NEXUS TO GOD, THEN GOD WILL NOT BE WITH ISRAEL IN RESOLVING THE CRISIS. THIS NOW FORESHADOWS THE POINT WE ARE MAKING ABOVE.

JUNE 21, 2002: WE TELL YOU RIGHT NOW THAT THE MIDDLE EAST WILL NOT RETURN TO ITS HISTORIC RELATIONSHIP WITH THE U.S.....MAKING IT VERY CLEAR TO THE ARAB/ISLAMIC NATIONS THAT THE US WAS INTENT ON UPROOTING ITS NEXUS TO ALLAH. THIS WILL

PROVE TO BE AN IRREPARABLE BREACH FOR THE FORESEEABLE FUTURE.

ROSE GARDEN REMARKS

JULY 4, 2002: THE US NEEDS GLOBAL MORAL OUTRAGE TO TAKE OUT STATES THAT SPONSOR TERRORISM. OF COURSE THE COLLATERAL BENEFIT IS THE TARGETED KEY BENEFIT: THE ABILITY TO RECAPTURE THE MIDDLE EAST FROM CHINA.

JULY 4, 2002: THE US KNEW MAJOR TERRORISM WOULD DERAIL THE SAUDI PEACE PLAN --ONLY CONCLUSION IS THAT THE US KNEW IT WAS EASY TO UPROOT, EXPECTED IT TO BE UPROOTED, AND WANTED IT TO BE UPROOTED.

JULY 20, 2002: SIMPLY SAID, THESE MEN CONCLUDED THAT THE AMERICAN FORM OF GOVERNMENT WAS TO BE ULTIMATELY RENDERED ANTIQUATED.

JULY 20, 2002: DESPITE THE MISINFORMATION TO THE CONTRARY, THE ISSUE IS OIL.

JULY 26, 2002: (RELIGIOUS RESOLUTION WILL) FREE THE CONGRESS FROM THE COERCIVE POWER OF THE POWER ELITE BEHIND THE ONE WORLD GOVERNMENT AGENDA. THIS MONTHS BEFORE THE CONGRESS GIVES BUSH THE GREEN LIGHT TO WAGE WAR AGAINST IRAQ.

JULY 29, 2002: THE WAR AGAINST TERRORISM HAS ALL ALONG BEEN THE WAR AGAINST CHINA.

JULY 29, 2002: POWELL SAYS US TROOPS WILL STAY IN ASIA "TO GUARD AGAINST NATIONS THAT MIGHT HAVE AGGRESSIVE INTENT."

JULY 31, 2002: THE US KNOWS THAT CHINA HAS PREVAILED AND IT IS ESSENTIALLY GOING OUT AND SAYING WE ARE TAKING IT BACK LIKE IT OR NOT AND IF YOU DON'T LIKE IT WE ARE READY TO SEE WHAT

YOU ARE GOING TO DO ABOUT IT. THIS REPRESENTS NOTHING HIGHER THAN ADOLESCENT LOGIC AND THINKING.

JULY 31, 2002: {THE AUTHOR} BELIEVES THAT SAYING THAT WE ARE GOING TO TAKE OVER THE OIL FIELDS AND PUT IN A CARETAKER GOVERNMENT IS UNDERTAKING A COURSE OF INSANITY....THE LEADERSHIP IS ACTING AS THOUGH IT IS DESPERATE. THIS IS USUALLY THE NEXUS TO MAKING A MISTAKE.

AUGUST 1, 2002: ISSUE NOT WMD BUT TO OBVIATE REALITY THAT MIDDLE EAST HAS BEEN LOST...TRANSLATES INTO A COMPROMISE OF OIL SUPPLIES FOR NOT ONLY THE US *BUT THE EU.*

AUGUST 4, 2002: IS IT IRAQ OR SAUDI ARABIA THAT IS THE FIRST TARGET? {THE AUTHOR} BELIEVES THAT PRESIDENT BUSH HAS ORDERED AN AFFIRMATIVE EFFORT TO REPLACE THE SAUDI LEADERSHIP. THIS IS ONE OF THE BEST KEPT SECRETS IN WASHINGTON (ASSUMING WE ARE CORRECT). CONFIRMED BY THE WASHINGTON POST ON AUGUST 6TH AFTER OUR APPEARANCE ON THE POINT ON THE JEFF RENSE SHOW ON AUGUST 5TH.

AUGUST 9, 2002: ISRAEL ADMITS THAT IT UNDERESTIMATED THE SIGNIFICANCE OF SUICIDE BOMBINGS.

AUGUST 9, 2002: ASSAD GIVEN FULL ASSURANCES BY CHINA THAT IT WILL PROTECT SYRIA FROM US/ISRAEL MACHINATIONS.

AUGUST 12, 2002: AMERICA DOESN'T SUBSCRIBE TO A GOVERNMENT THAT TELLS ITS CITIZENS WE ARE GOING TO WAR WITH ANYONE WHO WE DON'T LIKE WHO COULD POSSIBLY POSE A THREAT TO US. IF WE SUBSCRIBE TO SUCH A TENET OR CLAIM, THEN WHAT STOPS CHINA FROM PROFFERING TO ITS PEOPLE THE VERY SAME TENET OR CLAIM? IF THEY DID IT FIRST, THE UPROAR FROM WASHINGTON WOULD BE DEAFENING. THIS IS WRITTEN MORE THAN A MONTH BEFORE THE RELEASE OF THE NSS.

AUGUST 13, 2002: WHY SHARON AND WHY NOW? SHARON NOT INCLINED TO FOLLOW US MILITARY DIRECTIVES WHEN ISRAEL UNDER ATTACK.... PM SHARON'S DEATH = MORAL OUTRAGE = ATTACK ON SYRIA.

ALL OF THE ABOVE WAS WRITTEN OVER A MONTH BEFORE THE NSS AND THE CONGRESS GIVING BUSH THE GREEN LIGHT TO ATTACK IRAQ. PRESIDENT BUSH NOW AWAITS THE ELECTION, THE CHINESE CONGRESS, AND THE UN RESOLUTION, BUT WE HAVE INTERPRETED THAT IT WANTS ISRAEL TO ATTACK OR FACE THE SPECTER OF ECONOMIC COLLAPSE. IF ISRAEL FACES FURTHER TERRORISM, WHAT OPTIONS DOES SHARON REALLY HAVE IF HE REFUSES TO UNDERTAKE A RELIGIOUS RESOLUTION? REMEMBER, ALL ROADS ABSENT A RELIGIOUS RESOLUTION LEAD TO ACROSS THE BOARD DEATH AND DEVASTATION FOR ALL THOSE UNDER THE PALE OF MONOTHEISM.

IF ISRAEL WAS FOLLOWING THE CORRECT COURSE WOULD IT BE IN THE RUT IT IS IN? IF THE UNITED STATES WAS FOLLOWING THE CORRECT COURSE WOULD IT BE IN THE RUT IT IS IN? ***

THE UNITED STATES AND ISRAEL MUST MOVE AGAIN BACK TO THEIR RELIGIOUS TENETS. ISRAEL MUST ASSESS WHAT PURPOSE TORAH, ITS BIBLE, AND ITS BELIEFS, IF THE STATE OF ISRAEL LOSSES IT HISTORICAL AND INTENDED NEXUS TO GOD?

THE ANSWER IS OBVIOUS AND THUS IS BOTH THE SOLUTION AND THE CONSEQUENCE.

http://www.rense.com/general31/thebushdoubledouble.htm

The author sent the following as E-mail to influential people known to him on or about October 11, 2001, after bringing the focal element highlighted below, that President Bush was pursuing preplanned paths to invade Arab/Islamic nations, to the attention of the House and Senate Intelligence Committees. Note the emphasis on the interpretation that China would be the net victor in that the paradigm of power would shift to the East.

Deep Cover

Before the dust settled on the World Trade Center building collapse, President Bush *nearly immediately announced* an American military response **that would be implemented over an extended time period**, and would require great sacrifice from the Nation. This showed us that the government agenda was on **autopilot,** *having been planned some time before.* Otherwise, the President's remarks in such regard could only be accepted as impulsive, reflecting the emotion of the day. That they proved accurate and true *attests to the advance nature of his words*.

Moreover, the President exhibited some obtuse behavior for a politician and President in the period preceding the collapse of the World Trade Center buildings. He took the entire month of August off from Washington and the White House. No President had ever matched this time away from the Nation's Capital. Moreover, on his return just prior to Labor Day, he was off and away to various states, despite all the criticism lodged against him. When the World Trade Center buildings collapsed, days after Labor Day, one of the busiest times for the Nation, President Bush had just completed visiting an elementary school in Jacksonville, Florida on September 10th and was at another elementary school in Sarasota, Florida on September 11th.

Thus, fair comment from the above would include that the U.S. was expecting an attack and knew that its focus would include Washington, D.C. to wit: the White House, and kept its President constantly away from it, or otherwise, on the other side of the spectrum, *it was prepared for it, not in terms of stopping it, but in terms of implementing a strategy and agenda that had important people endorsing it.* Similar to the Japanese attack on Pearl Harbor, the attack on the World Trade Center towers spurred the people of the United States into a mindset supporting the intrusions since then, looking at anyone questioning them with jaundice eye. **The stage was set for military action, without a need for justification for what might unravel.**

Now, some weeks thereafter, we see the United States blasting Afghanistan to a degree where it will look as though it were hit with a series of atomic weapons. The amount of firepower far exceeds any identifiable political need or result. Thus in the search for meaning among the smoke, and the U.S. baiting the Islamic world with talk of seeking terrorists in other sovereign lands, **we perceive an intent by the government to fuel a response in the Islamic world.**

Michael Boyce, chief of the British defense staff, told a news conference today, "We must expect at least to go through the winter into the next summer at the very least." A U.S. defense official said,

"We dropped a lot of bombs. We have said this will be relentless, and it will." An Afghan witness to the bombings said, "It was like an inferno. The explosions were so huge and so massive, that it felt like an earthquake, as if an atomic bomb had been dropped on Kabul."

The reaction to such U.S. military action is predictable. The AP report states, "Muslims outraged at the raid on Afghanistan staged protests in countries including Bangladesh, Jordan, South Africa, India, Iran, Pakistan and Indonesia." **Thus couple the bait of entering more countries, with the intensity of the attack, and the commitment to an enduring presence and what does this all translate into?** Here is what we wrote to the Senate and House members on the U.S. intelligence committees yesterday:

"Has anyone outside the ambit of the administration assessed the consequences of a putative overthrow of the current regimes in Pakistan (Islamic nuclear) and Saudi Arabia (Islamic oil)? Would not these be likely and doable projects encouraged by the American presence and activity in the area and thus worsen rather than improve things for America long term, unless the U.S. intends to then invade and occupy these two countries to in fact remedy the situation it itself encouraged? Could such a plan be implemented without your review and vote?"

Conclusion: This tactic is very high risk and for the reasons expressed in Peres Personified is destined to lead to a massive conflict where the result will be other than what the U.S. anticipates. **It is exactly during this time that serious oversight must rest over secret government plans, especially when they do not seem to add up or otherwise make sense.** However, instead of the people or the media encouraging oversight, they allow the President to tell the country that he is going to withhold intelligence from the Congress and just offer it to eight or so Congressional representatives. While he immediately thereafter said that he was just relaying a message to those with loose lips, the message from our perspective is other than what is initially apparent, to wit: that everything **that will soon unravel will be by the will of the few** over the wishes of the country, if they of course knew the truth, not to say had a choice or say in it.

With Israel, it was our position that all Clinton's efforts would fail because no peace could be supported that lead Israel away from (the new world order agenda) rather than to God (the only true course for peace). No matter what signs the Israeli people and government receive or have put before them, they refuse to accept the correction. Now, the World Trade Center buildings, as most subliminally perceive, is a final sign: that the paradigm of world control under the monotheistic religions will collapse. **In our opinion, the emerging new power is China.**

314

President Bush, his dad, and their cohorts are betting Texas style, that China will not intervene into these events. For the reasons expressed and explained in Peres Personified, it is highly likely that China will ultimately intervene. In its attempt to wrestle the next step of world control and domination, <u>again under the deep cover of world peace, the new world order group will take us beyond the precipice</u> and into a Holocaust where the living will envy the dead._Thus, we continue to hold by the proposition that the only safety valve to escape a destiny which has now been signaled, is to do whatever is possible to have a leadership in Israel that understands the historical lessons in Peres Personified. After many years, what seemed far-fetched now seems close, for many, too close. The real demarcation line is when it is irreversible.

The U.S. will now call in its markers and demand Israel to turn over the West Bank and the Holy City. Thereafter the line will be crossed and the historical reality of Peres Personified will be carved in stone. Start learning Chinese as the world turns into the dust and ash seen around the World Trade Center Towers after their collapse, a reality which would have been seen fifty years ago had God not intervened to assure victory for the U.S. and its allies, when the U.S. adhered to religious tenets which allowed the U.S. to grow and prosper. **Now, with a management worshipping the domination elixir of the new world order, under a pretense and façade of peace, where it sacrifices its children, allowing drugs, sex and violence to dominate, it will be no surprise to find that a reckless and dangerous strategy turns false,** as did Clinton's when he strong-armed Israel into accepting the U.S. peace plan. Now, President Bush's success in the created environment in foisting such a result only proves that the biblical warnings of the trilogy of religions under monotheism are about to take an irreversible hold and status. Thus, the clock really has just about run out.

JOSEPH EHRLICH
SENDER, BERL & SONS INC.
OCTOBER 11, 2001

PS. One of the most often heard questions is why the U.S. did not oppose Syria's admission into the U.N. Security Council? We have routinely addressed China's behind the scenes presence in Syria. The U.S. thus provided ying to offset China's yang. The U.S. knows that Syria is a key player, particularly with China behind it. The U.S. is desperate to neutralize China. Thus, we can expect that after the Palestinian State and the return of the Holy City that Israel will say good-bye to the Golan, if not whatever more Syria asks, now that it is an esteemed member of the select U.N. Security Council community

This very short article is one of the author's favorite vehicles for summarily putting forth key issues regarding the Moabite intertwinement against the USA, Israel and the Judeo Christian ethic. It is vitally important for people to realize that the true goal of the Moabites was never simply regime change, but culture change for all nations under the Judeo-Christian (and also the Islamic) ethic. These are the nations that are derivative to Abraham. These are the nations God favored and thus the nations the Moabites detest.

Regime and Culture Change Unmasked

The criticized American policy and agenda embodied in President Bush's National Security Strategy is one aimed at not only regime change but also culture change in the Middle East, which little-emphasized dynamic answers those scratching their heads in Washington why many throughout the world are opposed to the U.S.'s "war against terrorism."

What is also overlooked is that President Bush's attitude toward regime and culture change was in place as a matter of covert U.S. policy since the presidential term of his father, George H.W. Bush ("Bush 41"). It was witnessed when the United States stood back when a coup in Russia uprooted Mikhail Gorbachev, Time Magazine's Man of the Century, from office. While Mr. Gorbachev was instrumental during the Reagan years in the dissolution of the Soviet Union and removing the former Soviet Empire as a global threat, he was seen by the Bush 41 administration as soft on eviscerating all remaining threatening elements of Communism, having his own political roots therein, and a more compliant Boris Yeltsin replaced him in the manner recorded by history.

The current President Bush ("Bush 43") deployed a similar modus operandi in the spring of 2002 when a coup took place in Venezuela to uproot Hugo Chávez from power. Industrial and oil powers within Venezuela, with ties to U.S. interests, initiated a military coup, which not only failed but also resulted in the type of criticism applicable to President Bush's drive to bring democracy to the Middle East. The wide criticism spewed forth by the entire spectrum of Latin and South American leaders put a black eye onto Bush administration tactics and hypocrisy. When the Bush administration's preferred oil industry aligned replacement, Pedro Carmona, immediately dissolved Venezuela's National Assembly and Supreme Court, thereby assuming dictatorial powers, these actions were opposed across the board by Latin American democracies. When 48 hours later Chávez regained power, Bush National Security Advisor Condoleezza Rice publicly warned Chávez to "...respect constitutional processes," further undermining U.S. credibility in the entire region. Since the invasion of Iraq, it has become crystal clear to the world that democracy and open and free elections are part of the Bush administration's noble agenda and goals in Venezuela, Iraq and soon elsewhere (according to Bush 43 rhetoric against Syria, Iran, Saudi Arabia and Egypt), as long as the candidates, and certainly the winning candidate, meet its approval.

Israelis should consider whether they have been subject to regime and culture change under policies that arose under the Bush 41 administration, post the success in seeing Gorbachev replaced by Yeltsin. Ariel Sharon ultimately was elected to reflect Israeli dissatisfaction with the policies of Shimon Peres and Ehud Barak. Within hours of his election, Ariel Sharon offered Barak the position of Minister of Defense and Shimon Peres the position of Foreign Minister. This all reflected US foreign policy first carved for the Bush 41 agenda by Jim Baker, preemptively intervening in foreign states and promoting democratic principles as long as election results allow the continuation of covert approved policies for that foreign state and nation.

Now, the State of Israel, as a natural result of Bush 41 preemptive policies put into place, finds itself supporting Bush 43 policies that have effectuated culture change within the U.S. itself, allowing the U.S. to put aside, under the cover of 9-11, its own Constitution to promote the Patriot Act and a continuing string of laws abrogating basic freedoms and protections, allowing a foreign policy where anyone can be assassinated or invaded under an executive level perception that a person or foreign state represents a current or future threat to U.S. interests; changes in culture that openly promote and allow corruption and cronyism, thus lending support to a de facto attitude of benign authoritarianism. Has Israel allowed itself to become a willing victim of Bush policy of both regime and culture change, thereby serving, as an invaluable needed ally to legitimize globally recognized wrongs and wrongdoings in the Middle East?

The Arab/Islamic nations want to be free from U.S. intervention as to what serves the best interests of their own populations, and preclude regime and culture change promoted under the banner of bringing both technological advancement and democracy to those nations. The Arab/Islamic nations have the right to honor, protect and live under their own heritage and culture without outside intervention. Israel has to understand the consequences of culture change for it, especially in terms of how it views and acts toward its Arab/Islamic neighbors.

The biblical and religious heritage of Israel attests that Israel never had enemies when the Jewish people occupied the holy land. Those that did historically arise, the Assyrians, Babylonians and the Romans, were all the creation of the reality that the Jewish people accepted a change to its culture. The Jewish people remember their mistake in accepting inappropriate culture change through memorializing it through a day of mourning each year ("Tish'aB'Av"). The Jewish people thus should understand that accepting culture change, one arguably with a strong nexus to Bush 41's covert policy for regime and culture change for Israel, precludes their continuation in Israel, when submission to it, especially under the current Bush administration's painted picture for the new Middle East, would operate to defile God's gift and name. Thus, the Jewish people recognize that biblical and religious history attests that they were cast out of Israel not because of enemies but because enemies arose to effectuate the required consequence of their own failings in accepting culture change.

Similarly, it is important for the U.S., founded on Judeo-Christian precepts and principles, to recognize that it is accepting culture change, reflected best when a mainstream media outlet, America-on-Line, posits, on its opening page, whether Americans any longer find God and religion relevant. The implications of this culture change are onerous when one sees Tommy Franks, former chief of the Central Command, who led the war against Iraq, who like the President grew up in Midland, Texas and attended high school with Laura Bush, stating that in the event of a WMD attack, "our form of government would go out the window. The Western world, the free world, loses what it cherishes most, and that is freedom and liberty we've seen for a couple of hundred years in this grand experiment that we call democracy. (Emphasis added)"

"Many Ask Is Religion Relevant?"

This type of talk is massaging the public to expect the installation of a military government and control in the United States (especially under unabated Cheney rhetoric that one has been imminent since 9-11) and compels the American people to think long and hard whether current policies of this presidential administration were in place way before the Project for the New American Century and even far before Bush 41 assumed the presidency in 1988 or before he nearly assumed the presidency in 1981: for the Bush family was aligned with one world government a long time ago, as noted by the Dallas Morning News, many years back, when it connected Senator Prescott Bush to H. Neil Mallon and the Dallas Council on World Affairs. The Dallas Morning News wrote:

> "In fact, the one-world views of Mr. Mallon, close friend of U.S. Sen. Prescott

Bush of Connecticut and financial patron
of Mr. Bush's son George's entry into the
Midland oil industry, even became suspect
as Dresser's sales leaped the Iron Curtain
and the McCarthy era found fertile soil in
Big D."

There were very good reasons the founding fathers created
documents finding policies in pursuit of regime and culture
change anathema to what this country represented. It is
time to protect and find the Constitution of the United
States of America again relevant, to unmask policies of
regime and culture change as treacherous to the
fundamental defining principles and ideals of this nation.

Joseph B. Ehrlich
Hewlett Harbor, New York
December 9, 2003

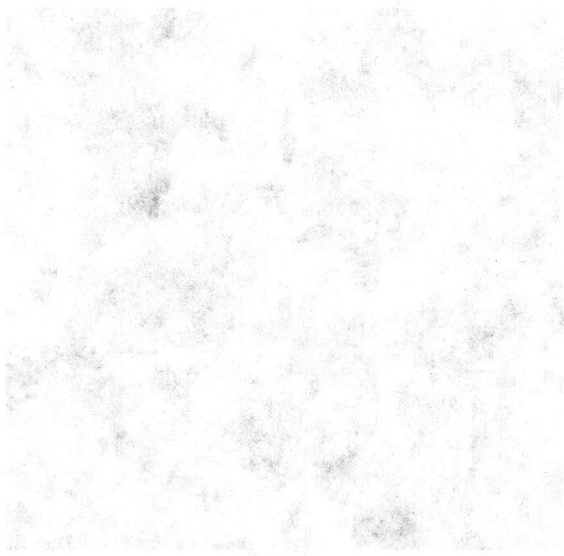

www.ingramcontent.com/pod-product-compliance
Lightning Source LLC
Chambersburg PA
CBHW061002280326
41935CB00009B/796